Drumbeats, Masks, and Metaphor

Drumbeats Masks and Metaphor

CONTEMPORARY AFRO-AMERICAN THEATRE

Geneviève Fabre

Translated by Melvin Dixon

Harvard University Press
Cambridge, Massachusetts
and London, England
1983

Drumbeats, Masks, and Metaphor is a translation and abridgement of *Le Théâtre noir aux Etats-Unis*, published by the Centre National de la Recherche Scientifique, Paris, in 1982.

This book is printed on acid-free paper, and its binding materials have been chosen for strength and durability.

Library of Congress Cataloging in Publication Data

Fabre, Geneviève.
   Drumbeats, masks, and metaphor.

   Translation of: Le Théâtre noir aux Etats-Unis.
   Bibliography: p.
   Includes index.
   1. Afro-American theatre. I. Title.
PN2270.A35F3213 1983   792'.08996073   83-4344
ISBN 0-674-21678-4

Acknowledgments

I WISH TO THANK the black theatres and artists in California, New Orleans, Washington, and especially New York who gave me the opportunity to see their work and to interview them, and the writers and friends who put me in touch with artists of their community who made documents, manuscripts, and other material available for study: Marvin X, John O'Neal, Tom Dent, Glenda Dickerson, Eleanor Traylor, Sonia Sanchez, Archie Shepp, Gil Moses, Woodie King, Vinie Burrows, Novella Nelson, Ishmael Reed, and many others.

I also thank the library at the International Theatre Institute, the New York Public Library's Lincoln Center theatre collection and Schomburg Library, and the libraries of the following universities: NYU, Yale, Harvard, Iowa, and Howard. I am grateful to Robert Corrigan and Charles Davis, who helped me at the start of my research; to James Hatch, who gave me access to material in the Hatch-Billops Collection, and to Henry Winslow and Roy Hodges, who sent me useful documents. The American Council of Learned Societies provided grants that allowed me to conduct research during several visits to the United States.

Special thanks to Marie-Claude Peugeot, Bernadette Beauvais, Odile Redon, Robert Delort, Marie-Hélène Gold, friends who read and criticized my manuscript; and particularly to Suzanne Simon, Nicole Boyer, and my husband, Michel Fabre, all of whom had the patience to read the entire manuscript. Special thanks also to Ed and Claire Margolies, who have given me so much help during my stays in New York; to Werner Sollors, who provided useful suggestions; and to Melvin Dixon, who encouraged me to pursue this endeavor.

Contents

Illustrations

Drumbeats, Masks, and Metaphor

Introduction

IN AMERICAN THEATRE today hardly a season goes by without one or more black productions appearing on the legitimate stage. By now some companies have become famous, and their works are followed by interested critics and the general public. For most people, however, the term "black theatre" means little more than the names of artists or the titles of shows. It can suggest either theatre *about* blacks or theatre written, acted, and directed *by* blacks. Yet theatre production by Afro-Americans has a long and distinguished history, and any analysis must take into consideration the work of individual playwrights, actors, and directors in such varied genres as political theatre, agitprop, musical comedy, naturalist drama, and religious ritual.

The emergence of black theatre is above all a sociocultural phenomenon and must be examined as such. The term is taken here to mean theatrical production by blacks that serves as a tool for research into ethnic identity and the most appropriate means to express it artistically, for analysis of the situation of blacks in North America, for symbolic expression of the black world view and experience. As an ethnic theatre it is born out of historical conflict. At the heart of its beginnings is the quest for identity.

Afro-American identity derives from both the biological fact of race and the historical experience of slavery and domination. It also stems from an awareness of political subordination and of color prejudice that has made blacks pariahs and victims. No emancipation has yet erased these stigmas; one holds firmly in the collective memory, the other is a reality that Afro-Americans confront daily.

Regarding Europe as the mother country, as the infallible source of civilization, America ensured its unity as a young nation by assimilating those newcomers who best conformed to established norms. For two centuries the cultural politics of the United States was based on the need to create a homogeneous nation and to assure the hegemony of Anglo-Saxon culture, whose values were deemed universal. Whites never stopped opposing other cultures. Black culture was denied, ridiculed, and falsified. The rejection of blacks included a lack of appreciation of their artistic ability, particularly in the realm of theatre where talent has often been considered innate.

Only by rejecting the images that white America has offered them can black Americans define their ethnic identity. They must recover their voice and a form of power. The movement to reclaim cultural identity rejects both the systematic exclusion from white society and reductive assimilation. It has at times assumed a violent and radical turn, merging

1

with nationalist or pan-African political and messianic forms and with the concept of negritude. In its exact meaning, negritude is the essential reality of being black that raises up an alternate truth and new possibilities. It goes beyond folklore and exoticism, beyond mere particularity or originality. Black culture is perceived as a body of knowledge, a symbolic universe, a language and matrix that articulate ethnic identity. It cannot be considered a subculture or a counterculture, for that would define it too simplistically as a reaction to a dominant culture.

The problem of ties with Africa pervades the black American's quest for identity. Two images converge: that of a mythic land belonging to a distant past, revived only by nostalgia or collective memory, and that of a real continent of nations struggling for liberation, with which solidarity must be established. The actual relation of black Americans to Africa is more symbol than fact.

If theatre is seen as both the manifestation and the formulation of culture, then an analysis of black drama will suggest several answers to the problem of Afro-American identity. Theatre is a unique form in this regard, for it offers the enactment of group conflicts, the displaying of masks worn and games played. It is also the best forum to express the social roles around which images of the new identity will form (roles meted out authoritatively, accepted or rejected, held consciously or unconsciously, inverted, subverted, or imagined). The Afro-American calls upon his own truth rather than the truths of others. He substitutes his own language for words borrowed from others. Thus Caliban frees his speech in order to grasp a different view of the world. Theatre brings into discourse his first person, the "I." As a place for critical inquiry and creative action, the theatre creates the experience of freedom and, by affirming its dual apollonian and dionysian vocation, it communicates wisdom in an exuberant atmosphere. Theatre can transform blacks from "spectators crushed with their inessentiality" into "privileged actors seized by the grandiose glare of history's floodlights upon them."[1] The stages of this metamorphosis can be seen in the specific elements of performance.

Theatricalization merges the real with the imaginary, combines dream, reflection, and action. Black theatre could qualify as a "utopia" that "feeds upon man's involvement and future in the world."[2] It tries to free itself from the authority of white authorship and seeks to create a rupture; it mobilizes members of the community for a common action and summons the imaginary to invent a past and a future.

The impetus for black militant theatre is the movement toward rejection, revolt, and negation. Injustice, violence, and death are denounced as the barbarism of whites. The desperate longing for justice turns protagonists into judges, theatres into courtrooms. The score must be settled. The drama will attempt to redefine the debt incurred by whites for crimes perpetrated against blacks. Sentence is to be rendered without chance for appeal. A utopian advance unleashes a plan for action. The new "actors" will rise up in a great moment of revolt.

Black drama did not come directly to this extreme point of insurrection. Conciliatory at first, it engaged whites in a dialogue to convince and implore them about injustice. When its pleas went unheard, its language changed to invective and imprecation; whites were cursed, their irrevocable destruction vowed. Black accomplices of whites were accused of allowing themselves to be misled. The drama called upon them to change their ways. Masks and metamorphoses assumed their fullest meaning. When the "white masks" were torn off, "black skins" suddenly appeared. At first a shout of anger and challenge, the militant theatre then became an inspired, almost visionary word. It prophesies the advent of a black nation, the coming of an era when blacks will be creative and free.

In contrast to the didactic speech of the militant theatre which demonstrates and prescribes action, a "theatre of experience" develops out of a dialogue in the language of blacks about their own experiences. This theatre is both collective and individual. It embraces the rituals of daily life, deriving its major models from three areas: the liturgy of the black church, religious and secular music, and the oral tradition. New relations between art and life are established. Rather than advocating change in the condition of blacks, this theatre proclaims the existence of a black culture that continually invents itself outside the codes of the dominant society.

Militant theatre and the theatre of experience thus reveal the same hope for liberation. The former strains the lines of domination to the breaking point and frees the mind from oppression; the latter reveals other restrictions that have paralyzed sensibility, creativity, and imagination. Renewing ties with lived experience, this drama suggests new paths on the way from bondage to freedom.

The Historical
Precedent

 AFRO-AMERICAN THEATRE is too often viewed as a product of the black movement of the sixties and considered, like a passing protest demonstration, to have offered little more than propaganda. New movements in the theatre usually do appear during times of change and rupture in society, times that inspire creativity. However, contemporary Afro-American theatre maintains firm ties with tradition, and the outburst of activity since World War II cannot be viewed as an isolated phenomenon.

Black theatre was born out of practices older than the presence of Africans on American soil. From the time they boarded ships for the passage to the New World, slaves provided shows for the entertainment of whites. On plantations, masters continued to request these performances. The slave was cast in a double role as laborer and entertainer.

From their very first appearances, these shows took on a subversive character. Similar in form to African ceremonies or festivals, they were clearly occasions to perpetuate certain customs and to preserve the cultural heritage. Not only in the United States but throughout the New World, these shows conveyed their virulent message. Mimed songs that had all the appearance of praising whites actually satirized them. Slaves were thus able to express their dissatisfaction and unhappiness without risking punishment for their insolence.

Such performances are an interesting example of the ways typically African institutions survived in the New World. Satire was commonly used in many African societies to express grievances against a relative, friend, or superior while avoiding violent confrontation. The criticism was cast in the form of public entertainment. It became a powerful means of social control when used to call attention to transgressions or to neglected duties; it provoked laughter, but it also invited the audience to render immediate judgment. Satire was frequently used in colonial times to denounce the injustices and reveal the foibles of the white colonizers.

In the American slave community, at wakes and on certain holidays, improvisations were presented that gave free reign to sarcasm and joking. The great virtuosity of the "libelists" was so well noticed by visitors and travelers that the talent became a sort of cultural stereotype.[1] Their rhyming form and accompanying melodies made the lampoons easy to remember, and they passed easily into popular wisdom. Dance and mime also played important roles; using precise gestures and a minimum of direction, the performances took on the appearance of a show.

Other occasions that strongly influenced the development of contemporary black drama were the celebrations that were held on election days from the eighteenth century on, especially in the North. At the start of official ceremonies reserved for white citizens, slaves were allowed to elect their own leader or governor. It was an occasion for costumed parades to the accompaniment of drums.[2] The forms these pageants took in the New World, together with the use of chants and music and the importance of the drum (usually forbidden in the South), created an African atmosphere.

Another type of theatricalized ceremony was the religious gatherings that blacks organized secretly in the woods at night or in their cabins after returning from church services with whites. Participants would gather in a secluded place.[3] The blankets, quilts, and pots used to smother the sound of their voices also served as scenery; the service that followed unfolded like a well-written script. Slaves dramatized episodes from the Gospels and staged their own interpretation of Creation. The devil, that great manipulator, was a major character in these "mysteries." His traits were borrowed from the Old Testament and from African dieties who played with the destiny of man and who, in both tragic and comic roles, appeared frequently in black folklore. In this manner, he resembles Anansi, spider of the Caribbean, Eshu of Brazil, and Legba of Haitian Vodun. Historians have often pointed to the role this secret church played in the organization of slave revolts. The theatrical character of the religious services, however, has not been sufficiently examined. All the elements of the future dramaturgy are there.

These various dramatizations, official or secret, in the presence of whites or without them, on secular or religious holidays, provided opportunities for black collective expression and a means of reflection about communal life. They granted liberties that were usually forbidden. Spoken language became bolder, gestures grew more emphatic, and emotions could be released without fear. The actors poked fun at themselves and improvised the duties of director or playwright. These productions are the precursors of contemporary Afro-American theatre in the way they dramatize life and arouse audience reactions through the use of call and response patterns. The slave theatricals also gave birth to the minstrel show, a genre that would be popular on the American stage for decades.[4]

The blackface minstrel gradually set the pattern of relations between blacks and whites that would dominate the world of theatre. Material drawn from the first entertainments given by slaves was appropriated and vulgarized, and the theatre was stripped of its satirical effect and of its symbolic language. The black audience was systematically excluded, and when blacks were finally admitted to the troupes they had to submit to the will of white producers and to the conventions of a genre that perpetuated negative racial stereotypes. But at the same time, black minstrel actors, recognized as artists, probably opened the door for the prominent black actors of the twentieth century. American theatre had discovered a profitable commodity.

For blacks, however, the national stage excluded important elements: a black audience, a black dramatist, a black producer. The one attempt made at the start of the nineteenth century to bring author, actor, and audience together was the short-lived African Grove Theatre.[5] Kept out of theatres owned by whites, blacks had to look elsewhere for entertainment. As for the black dramatist, his plays were never produced on the legitimate stage. Plays by the abolitionist William Wells Brown, for example, were known primarily through the author's public readings and what small distribution his works had from London.[6]

At the end of the nineteenth century several black artists tried to bring an end to the white monopoly in show business. Following the lead of Bob Cole—dramatist, composer, and actor—blacks entered the theatre professions, notably at the Worth Museum in New York.[7] Musicians, singers, and other theatre artists were able to collaborate.[8] Bob Cole teamed up with songwriter Billy Kersands and later with J. Rosamond Johnson. Other celebrated teams included Sissle and Blake, Miller and Lyles, Williams and Walker. Their shows, however, catered to the tastes and prejudices of white audiences. It was not until *Shuffle Along* in 1921 that musical comedy broke away from earlier styles.[9]

For nearly two decades black artists managed to build a production network that assured them at least minimal artistic control. This ended in 1910, however, when a wave of xenophobia overtook the United States and hit blacks before it touched immigrants. Discrimination became institutionalized across the country and had grievous effects on theatre.

Black artists fell back upon the community. Black theatres began to open in Harlem. At first the Lincoln, the Lafayette, and the Alhambra theatres presented Broadway successes, but soon the public showed a preference for musical comedy.[10] This concentration of talent in the black community provoked a literary and artistic revival, a black Renaissance. The success of the Harlem Theatres inspired similar experiments throughout the country, including parts of the South. For example, the Lafayette Players, organized by Charles Gilpin in 1919, went on to create the Karamu Theatre in Cleveland.[11]

Some efforts were supported by whites as part of the "Little Theatre Movement." Black theater had its patrons like Mrs. Sherwood Anderson and Raymond O'Neil, who created the Colored Folk Theatre, soon renamed the Ethiopian Players. The NAACP organized a commission on drama, which was responsible for the production of several plays. Randolph Edmonds founded the Negro Inter-Collegiate Dramatic Association and the Southern Dramatic Association. Some theatrical agencies like TOBA (Theatre Owners Booking Association) tried without success to secure employment for black actors. To encourage the writing of plays, the periodicals *Crisis* and *Opportunity*, magazines of the NAACP and the Urban League respectively, organized annual contests. And for the first time Afro-American plays were collected in anthologies.[12]

Theatre and the Black Community

Surprisingly, the emerging black theatre gave little attention to the black community and to the development of a cultural politics on its behalf. If one defines black theatre as a theatre about blacks, written by blacks, and acted by blacks for a black audience, then only the first of these conditions was satisfied. Blacks were able to take a larger part in interpreting roles, but their participation in dramatic writing was barely recognized. The question of links between theatre and community seems to have been largely ignored.

Why did the project of organizing theatrical activity in black neighborhoods fail? Several answers can be found in Harlem, whose cultural history is of great significance and assumes a representative quality. As its population increased from 50,000 inhabitants in 1914 to 200,000 in 1930, the Black Mecca became an economic, political, and especially cultural capital.[13] The opening of theatres there raised the hope of freeing black theatre from the obstacles that had caused the failure of earlier attempts such as the African Grove. The presence of a large Afro-American audience and the kind of exchange that could take place between audience and stage provided previously unheard of possibilities for theatre. Afro-Americans were known for creating spontaneous shows by turning ordinary incidents into group demonstrations, and for participatory ritualized responses like "Amen" and "right on." Their traditions made theatrical expression familiar and rendered them more apt to decode an oral and visual message than a written one. All the conditions seemed to exist for strong links between artist—actor or dramatist—and the community.

When plays were presented in the new theatres of Harlem, black audiences reacted to them without inhibition, counter to conventions that tended to separate the audience from the stage. Yet, instead of recognizing the role such an audience could play, the promoters of theatre in Harlem adopted a scornful attitude. The behavior of black audiences appeared inconvenient and incongruous, a sign of lack of education. These "louts" had to be educated by a repertory that would elevate their tastes, and by theatrical models that conformed to those of the dominant society.

Thus at the moment when a black audience emerged, the cultural politics postulating that the black audience needed a theatre did not admit that the theatre was in desperate need of a black audience. The plays developed elsewhere for white audiences did not take blacks into consideration either as subjects or as spectators.

The different crises that occurred in Harlem's cultural life revealed the importance of a link between theatre and the community. Harlem as cultural capital of the black world chose to submerge itself within another capital, New York. The black elite satisfied its own interests before those of the community and offered no material support to black artists. It is not surprising then that white intellectuals like Carl Van Vechten and Emilie Hapgood would serve as their patrons. White cultural paternalism rapidly drove the Harlem movement to its demise.[14]

When circumstances were favorable for the appearance of ethnic theatre—in which dramatist, actor, and audience would participate—the cultural politics developed by whites and adopted by blacks led that theatre to failure. Ideological and economic conflicts obscured the real problems. The theatre did not know how to define its function in relation to the dominant society and to the black community, or to ensure its economic as well as artistic survival.

On the aesthetic level, one finds a middle-class rejection of popular forms of expression, the control of whites over artistic material and over black actors constrained to silence or to imitation, the isolation of black dramatists, and the near absence of a black audience. On the institutional level, the white monopoly prevailed, appropriating the profits, indeed, running the entire show. It must also be said that the Afro-American intelligentsia did little to stimulate the theatre revival and that the middle class shirked its responsibility to the community.

Social relations in the theatre resembled those in the larger society: for whites, domination, authority, and monopoly; for blacks, exclusion, lack of initiative, half-silence. No compromise was worked out between the strategies for integration, which valued the white world, and the separatist striving for artistic self-determination.

The Pitfalls of Integration

Efforts to create a black theatre reached an important stage with the founding of the Federal Theatre Project (FTP). Without examining all the activities of its "Negro units," one can make several points about the Federal Theatre and its cultural politics. The idea of the Negro Theatre Units was first suggested by black actress Rose McClendon as a program to develop theatre in various communities. By 1936 this division had established centers in nearly twenty-five cities and had hired more than a million blacks.[15]

The FTP's first concern was to fight discrimination at all levels in the theatre, and in the society at large.[16] It protested the persistent use of blackface, which excluded blacks from certain roles and left prominent actors such as Charles Gilpin or Rex Ingram unemployed. The National Board was concerned about the way some shows perpetuated black stereotypes, and it fought against the cultural prejudice that kept blacks out of professional training.[17]

While the FTP reproached other productions for being racist, the U. S. Congress found the FTP's shows to be subversive. In December 1938, the Federal Theatre was formally accused of subversion by the Martin Dies Committee on Un-American Activities. The committee alleged that the campaigns for racial equality were inspired by communist propaganda.[18] The program was abolished, but not before the FTP had developed a body of work aimed at creating political theatre in the United States. Its agitprop style would serve as a model for many productions to come.

In measuring the influence of progressive ideas of the thirties and the consequences of the Federal Theatre's initiatives for Afro-American theatre, one realizes how minimal these changes were. Certainly there was a revival of theatre activity. The cultural activities sponsored in black communities from the end of 1935 contributed much to restore a kind of order after the disruption caused by the Depression. Unemployment of artists was practically ended, and an effort was made to raise political consciousness. In the drama, however, the character became most important: blacks and workers, jobless or on strike, were presented as victims of a crisis born out of the contradictions of capitalist development. Plays were both generous and unrealistic in depicting black and white workers struggling together and denouncing racial and social injustice.

Although many plays were still written by whites, several black dramatists were being read and produced, thanks to the Federal Theatre. The ideology reflected in their works nevertheless had to conform to "proletarian" theatre. The first play produced by the FTP in New York was Frank Wilson's *Walk Together Children*. The director of the FTP's New York center, John Houseman, chose this play not for its subject—the riots that came in the wake of black migration to the North—nor for its dramatic qualities, but because Wilson had been the original Porgy in the play by DuBose Heyward and was very popular with black audiences. The production was a sure success. In March 1936 Joseph Losey directed *The Conjure Man Dies* by Harlem physician Rudolph Fisher. Ironically, while the Federal Theatre searched for black authors, Langston Hughes was breaking all records for a black play on Broadway with *Mulatto*, which ran from October 1936 until December 1939.[19] In order to encourage more dramatists, a writers' workshop was organized in Harlem, the Negro Dramatists Laboratory. But it was in Chicago that the work of Theodore Ward, the most representative dramatist of the period, appeared. His play *Big White Fog*, which with rare dramatic power raised the issues of poverty, unemployment, discrimination, and rivalry between Garveyites and communists, was produced by the Federal Theatre in 1938.

One may wonder why so few plays were staged by the Federal Theatre, with its financial means and its large numbers of black writers and actors. Its national director hesitated to let blacks take charge as managers and artistic directors.[20] The blacks who became local directors felt uneasy simply following FTP's policies. Carlton Moss, who had high hopes for the Lafayette, openly expressed his disillusionment at seeing his theatre become a mere branch of the WPA and not a community theatre.

Basically, the situation of Afro-American theatre did not change much as a result of the FTP. Although less a tributary of Broadway, it was overshadowed by the other institution. The militant repertory of the FTP forced black characters and actors into new stereotypes and made them too vulnerable to communist influences and to the charge of engaging in "un-American activities." The closing of the FTP centers forced the artists to return to the commercial stage.

After the demise of the Federal Theatre in Harlem new community theatres arose that kept alive the dream of an authentic black theatre. In 1937 Langston Hughes and Hilary Phillips founded the Harlem Suitcase Theatre, which presented several plays by Hughes, notably *Jericho Jim Crow* and *Don't You Want to Be Free?* That same year Rose McClendon

started her own company, the Rose McClendon Players, which staged
Joy Exceeding Glory, a play about Father Divine by George Norford,
and *On Strivers Row*, a satire on the black bourgeoisie by Abraham Hill.
Members of the company were taught by Theodore Komisarjevsky. Mc-
Clendon's first goal was to create a professional theatre that would be independent of Broadway. In 1940 Abraham Hill and Frederick O'Neal,
the militant union leader who defended the rights of blacks before Actors Equity, founded the American Negro Theatre (ANT). In the same
year dramatists like Theodore Ward, Powell Lindsay, George Norford,
Theodore Brown, and Owen Dodson began the Negro Playwrights
Company (NPC). Their primary goal was to continue the work of the
Federal Theatre.[21] The NPC staged Ward's play *Big White Fog*, but the
company's career was all too brief. A new era was beginning that would
defer once again the dream of an ethnic theatre.

The spirit of commitment of the thirties gradually died out, although
certain writers tried to rekindle it, notably Theodore Ward with *Our
Lan'* and Paul Green and Richard Wright with their adaptation of
Native Son. The theatre was cut off from social reality. Black actors went
back to working under white directors and playing the same few roles.
The black dramatists were reduced to silence. During the McCarthy era,
even the expression of blackness that had continued in light entertainment became suspect. White liberals avoided the company of black artists, some of whom were blacklisted for their "subversive" activities and
forbidden to perform in the theatre. Paul Robeson was forced into exile;
others like Canada Lee were persistently harassed. At last the black
theatre community became alarmed. The Council of Harlem Theatres
was formed by the four remaining theatres: the Harlem Showcase, the
Committee for the Negro in the Arts, the Elks Community Theatre,
and the Penthouse Players. The Council's hope was to revive local
theatre and to produce plays that treated black culture fairly, such as
Alice Childress' adaptation of the short stories by Langston Hughes
from *Simple Speaks His Mind*.

In October 1951 the Council presented its first production, *A Medal
for Willie* by William Branch and directed by Elmwood Smith, at the
Club Baron. The show came to the attention of white producer Harry
W. Gribble, who had staged *Anna Lucasta*. Gribble then tried to use
the Club Baron to house a show that he could not stage in Greenwich
Village, *Riding the Right Bus*, and the performances of *A Medal* were
suspended, provoking a scandal. Blacks launched a campaign immediately to stop the eviction of a black author's play for the conve-
nience of a white producer.

By 1952 theatre life seemed to have returned to Harlem: the Negro Art Players, organized by actor and designer Roger Furman, presented a series of one-acts at the Elks Theatre; Loften Mitchell's *The Cellar* was performed in a small workshop; Ed Cambridge directed several productions at the Harlem YMCA; and Alice Childress staged *Gold Through the Trees* at the Club Baron. Yet many problems remained. Actors were paid less than they were off-Broadway. For this reason the play *Alice in Wonder*, created in Harlem in 1952 by Maxwell Glanville and Julian Mayfield, was able to continue its run only after it was taken over by Stanley Greene, who then produced it at the New Playwrights Theatre under the title *The Big Deal*.

More shows had to move to off-Broadway. During the fifties a campaign was started in Village theatres, notably the Greenwich Mews, to integrate black actors. A wave of indignation was unleashed. The effort was seen as a political act to take the actor out of his culture and community. When Ruby Dee was "integrated" into the cast of *The World of Sholom Aleichem* as the female lead, Jews accepted this more readily than blacks who were suspicious about how this innovation would actually help their theatre.

By this time, however, Harlem was no longer the center of black culture. The community had lost practically all its artists, and the middle class was moving to the suburbs. The competition between Harlem and the commercial theatre that began after the Second World War resulted in a clear-cut victory for the latter. Artists were lured away from Harlem. Theatres were inundated with mainstream productions, and the black community was left without resources.

Although the movement for integration left Harlem disaffected, it did encourage the black playwrights who brought theatre to its militant stance by dramatizing black aspirations and by protesting the conditions that kept those aspirations from being realized. In large measure the dramaturgy of the fifties adopted the civil rights ideology of liberal America. Now more than ever before the audience for black theatre was white; the dramatists spoke to the white audience directly, for a guilty conscience predisposed liberals to listen to the voice of the oppressed.

William Branch's next play, *In Splendid Error*, written while he was stationed in Germany, depicted the strained dialogue between John Brown and Frederick Douglass about the insurrection planned for Harper's Ferry. It was staged at the Greenwich Mews in 1954. Soon after, Branch adapted a South African novel, *A Wreath for Udomo* by Peter Abrahams, and established an implicit parallel between the consequences of decolonization and the struggle in the United States against discrimination. The play examined the avenues for African development by dramatizing the choice available to Kwame Nkrumah after Ghana's independence: compromise or the risk of unconditional autonomy. (In 1959, when the play was produced on Broadway, Philip Burton directed and his son Richard played the role of Udomo. Once again, black actors were left out. Branch soon abandoned theatre for television.)

While Branch tried to keep a distance from direct experience, Loften Mitchell did just the opposite. His play *A Land beyond the River*, showed New Yorkers what was happening in the South. Staged at the Greenwich Mews in 1957, the play drew upon current events which pitted racists of the White Citizens Council in Clarendon county, South Carolina, against advocates of desegregation. The play indicts southern violence as well as the inefficiency of northern leaders of the Civil Rights Movement.[22] Mitchell's play became the banner of the United Automobile Workers Union when it joined the struggle against segregation on the side of union leaders and politicians such as A. Philip Randolph, Roy Wilkins, and Adam Clayton Powell. The Greenwich Mews also presented a play by Alice Childress, whose work until then had been produced only in Harlem. Her *Trouble in Mind* evoked the period by using a theatrical situation, a rehearsal by a black troupe, thus commenting on white attitudes about blacks.

The most significant event of the decade for black theatre occurred in March 1959, when *A Raisin in the Sun* earned for Lorraine Hansberry both the Critics Circle Award and endless controversy. The play's title, from Langston Hughes's poem "Harlem" in *Montage of a Dream Deferred*,[23] effectively showed how the dream of integration was constantly thwarted. Given the general obscurity in which black dramatists had been held for so long, the attention Hansberry received could be considered a revolutionary event in itself. However, this recognition had a more ironic result: honoring the appearance of a black author, as if there had been none before, perpetuated the myth of the lack of black dramatists.

Written just before riots broke out in the ghettos, *Raisin* seemed to appease liberals who feared such a violent uprising. The play also proved that ghetto life did not necessarily lead to crime or disgrace. It showed blacks as having virtues which—according to the Protestant ethic that the play echoes—deserved the reward that integration would bring. Moreover, the play used the tradition of social realism to show an idealized image of the working class. Hansberry was acclaimed as the

Clifford Odets of the new generation that would strengthen the workers movement.[24]

Harold Cruse, among the most vehement of Hansberry's detractors, considers the play representative neither of blacks nor of the working class.[25] For Cruse, this saga of a family's search for the American Dream is a swan song of the integrationist tradition, having reached the goal set in the 1940s by the Committee for the Negro in the Arts. Ignoring the values in the black world, the play embraces the supposedly universal white ideal. In fact Hansberry's play was essentially written for whites; it did not question the situation of blacks or the destiny of black theatre. In an interview in 1964 Hansberry stated that *Raisin* was not a *black* play, but a play about an American family in conflict with a corrupt society.[26] The Younger family pays for its integration into the American middle class by losing its ethnicity. Black theatre will come to the same dead end, Cruse argues, if it follows Hansberry's path.

A controversy of a different nature began in 1961 when Jean Genet's *The Blacks* opened at St. Mark's Place in Greenwich Village. The European play about blacks dealt with violence, a subject that was now reality. The play's violence, purely verbal and directed away from the audience, was easily accepted by American critics, who found the hostility inoffensive because it came from a white author and from a European tradition they respected. Blacks, however, reacted more to the play's message than to its ritual form. They accused Genet of knowing nothing about them or their history. Genet's solution for black liberation, in their opinion, was strictly theatrical and had no basis in American reality. Paradoxically, although Genet's work was disparaged by blacks in 1961, it would have an important influence on the development of a new kind of black drama that in the late sixties would stage its own rituals of violence.

The period from 1960 to 1966 saw the debuts of many important new playwrights: James Baldwin, LeRoi Jones, Adrienne Kennedy, Ron Milner, and others. Greenwich Village and Broadway had usurped Harlem. And in spite of the attention given to black writers, the authority of white dramatists remained unquestioned, as proved by the success of *In White America* by Martin Duberman. Show business became a center for black theatre that was still defined as theatre *about* blacks. People also developed an interest in events outside the United States. Plays from South Africa were introduced: *Blood Knot* by Athol Fugard and *Sponomo* by Alan Paton and Krishna Shah at the Court

Theatre in April 1966. In 1965 Howard da Silva and Felix Leon staged an adaptation of a story by Dan Jacobson, *Zulu and the Zayda*. West Indians were represented by the production of *Moon on a Rainbow Shawl* by Errol John at the Guild Theatre in 1962. Ideologically, plays with moderate protest and much optimism were preferred. Directors and producers conformed to the climate of the Civil Rights Movement, and their works showed faith in interracial collaboration. This ideology dominated to such an extent that it was imposed on the actual message of some plays. Thus, for example, when Ketti Frings adapted Richard Wright's novel *The Long Dream* for the stage at the end of the fifties, she obscured the meaning of Tyree's sacrificial death, which paid for his challenge to the authority of white police.

On the artistic level, dramatists of the early sixties tried many experiments. Adrienne Kennedy explored the surrealistic side of the ethnic consciousness in her plays. In *The Amen Corner* and *Tambourines to Glory*, Baldwin and Hughes, respectively, examined the role of the church in the black community and the dramatic forms it offers to the theatre; Loften Mitchell and John O. Killens wrote a pageant called *Ballad of the Winter Soldiers*. To the extent that they supported these works, American critics insisted on the originality of each undertaking and isolated one from the other, thus failing to see the significance of a collective movement or the development of an ethnic theatre. Black theatre appeared to prosper in a relatively serene atmosphere, but it was right at the edge of a gathering political storm.

When riots broke out in a succession of "long hot summers," the government considered making use of the theatre to help curb civic disorders. One of the traditional functions of theatre was as a catalyst to maintain order in society. Allowing conflicts to be played out on stage could neutralize subversive activity. Thus the revival of black theatre from 1964 to 1966 was partly the result of government policy aimed at developing ethnic theatre as a tool for social "integration," in the Marcusian sense of the term. The entire movement in theatre from 1965 to 1975 must be understood in light of this contradiction: the dominant society helped to promote black theatre mainly out of a desire to control its development and its integration into existing social structures.

Once again black artists and intellectuals were under the patronage of whites and, in an ambiguous, somewhat risky predicament, were torn between the hope of realizing some of their dreams and the fear of betraying their ambition to create an autonomous black art. They would develop different strategies according to personal temperament and local conditions in response to the cultural politics of the larger society. Taking sides, they would invent bold new practices.

Creating a Community Theatre

At the time when racial problems dominated the American political scene and when different militant groups were mobilizing, black theatre surprisingly withdrew from the community. Earlier productions of plays in Greenwich Village rather than in Harlem had already diminished the possibility of contact with black popular audiences. The movement for integration had placed so much importance on whites that new plays were fashioned to appeal to that audience.

Two experiments offered a possible remedy to the situation. The Free Southern Theatre (FST) began in 1963 as part of a cultural renaissance in deprived areas of the South from Mississippi to New Orleans. In 1965 the Black Arts Repertory Theatre (BART) started in Harlem as one of several antipoverty programs aimed at bringing theatre to the black community of New York. Although BART was short-lived, its repercussions reached far and wide, not only because the organizer, LeRoi Jones, soon became the most influential theoretician and practitioner of the new theatre, but also because the failure of the program exposed the shocking extent of the cultural crisis. Although these two experiments happened in different sociopolitical contexts, they stemmed from the same need. During the next decade, the failure of BART and the contradictions at the core of the FST would take black theatre in radically new directions.

The FST is regarded as a model project because of the circumstances surrounding its creation and for its close ties to both the political movement and the community. Its struggle to remain ideologically and geographically apart from the commercial network as well as its development within the confines of the Mississippi Delta made it an original undertaking.[27]

The theatre took its name from the Freedom Summers, which were often marked by violence and riots. This "free southern theatre" embraced the ideas of those groups fighting for black political, intellectual, and cultural liberation. The word "free" also suggests free admission, nonrestrictive and nonpaying. Cabarets, community centers, the street, and especially churches, which held services and political meetings, had been the principal gathering places for black people. The FST added another: the theatre proper. Finally, the FST wanted to be free on the institutional level, independent of the constraints of show business and of dominance by New York. It was a theatre for poor people, a popular theatre, a theatre more decentralized than provincial, and an experimental theatre which strove to find a language and technique suitable to reinforcing ties with the community.

The founders of this theatre clearly defined its functions. They emphasized the social and educational aspects: theatre must raise the consciousness of the audience. Making up for the defects of the educational system, it must be a place for learning, reflection, and debate. As a committed and political theatre, it should play a role in the liberation of black people. It should also be integrated, offering whites and blacks the opportunity to work side by side. This was a bold initiative at a time and place when blacks, if they went to the theatre at all, entered by the back door. While aligning itself with movement politics, the FST never forgot that it was a theatre first. Its specific tasks were to train actors, playwrights, and technicians, and to build an audience.

In establishing contact with the community in a region unfamiliar with a theatre tradition, the FST turned to existing institutions: sporting events, public dances, national or school holidays, musical programs, and especially religious celebrations. The church, in effect, represented the real cultural home where performances unfold, combining ritual with improvisation. The FST found the church to be a reliable partner and a model for the development of a dramaturgy. Religious services suggested forms of theatricality and audience participation that the theatre could well use. The community often experienced the theatre like a church service, through the body and emotions. Dance and music played decisive roles. The FST in this way did not set out to bring cultural enrichment from afar, but sought to work in close association with the community.

These were the initial objectives of the FST, but the program and ideology it actually followed from 1964–1966 reveal a change in orientation. From the very start, the FST was faced with many contradictions. Although it set out to serve the southern rural masses, it was managed by northern white liberals and middle-class black students. In this it was no different from other young radical companies like the San Francisco Mime Troupe. Its contacts with the rural Delta populations were difficult. Some of the plays it presented had already been staged in New York by professionals; many were too long for rural audiences. The company also had trouble recruiting local actors and did not spend enough time rehearsing. On the road, the company ran into trouble:

racist violence increased; fires, police raids, bomb threats, arrests multiplied. A group of black militants, the Deacons, and local branches of the Movement had to protect the actors.

Relations with New York were strained and ambivalent. When the FST was invited to participate in a New York festival celebrating the anniversary of the Movement in February 1965, the troupe came grudgingly, against the wishes of some members who refused to perform on command and away from the South. The stay in New York went badly. To add to the misfortune, one of the company's principal directors, John O'Neal, was arrested by the FBI, which claimed that his status as a conscientious objector prohibited him from political activities. For several years, the company had to do without him.

In 1965, succumbing to financial problems, the FST accepted an invitation from Richard Schechner to move to New Orleans. The Movement was not as strong there as in Mississippi, and local people were less prepared for radical theatre. When the company set up in a Creole neighborhood, it was immediately unwelcome. The Creoles wanted neither a black theatre nor a political theatre; they expected refined entertainment. They supported neither separation nor integration and considered the interracial composition of the FST more of a nuisance than a political act.[28]

At the time when the ideas of Malcolm X and the black revolution were quickly replacing tactics of reform and nonviolence, the FST also changed, taking up Gil Moses' slogan, "the fire next time in Mississippi." As a southern theatre, it also became a theatre for all people of color and of the Third World. "Free" in this perspective now meant free from the hold of the white world. Leaving the Creole neighborhood, the theatre established itself in the ghetto named Desire and came closer to the community. Finally, the repertory itself changed to become entirely black.

Located in the heart of the most deprived black neighborhood of New Orleans and, while on tour, in the rural communities, the FST spoke to the people. It also tried to awaken the black middle class to shared problems. Determined to find a balance between political action and theatre craft and to maintain its autonomy, the FST sought to resolve the contradictions that emerged in the Movement between cultural and revolutionary nationalism. Though a product of the Civil Rights Movement, the FST did not fade as the Movement died down. As a popular theatre it strove to express what the people felt was vital and significant, and it defined black theatre more rigorously than most other groups: that is, a theatre about blacks, located in a black community, and run exclusively by blacks. These three conditions, however, did not suffice, for blacks had long been writing plays that were "white" in their form and ideololgy, and black actors, lured by the glitter of stardom or compelled by economic neccessity, had portrayed racist stereotypes. But the FST experiment made it clear that an authentic black theatre would have to maintain dialectical and creative relations with the community; it would have to be located in places other than those sanctioned by the dominant theatre institution and to use different dramatic structures and forms. It could exist only in opposition, and in this way it would be a political act.

The movement that brought black intellectuals back to their community during the sixties is best understood in light of the experiences of the postwar generation, the "uprooted" generation. The international climate of war left blacks without the solid, though restricted, influence of the community. They were drawn further away from ethnic concerns, cut off from the past and a knowledge of their history, and set adrift in a nationwide no-man's-land where their place was poorly defined or in a minority identity that continued to elude them.

In 1965 the younger generation was caught up in an outburst of violence that hit the black community harder than any of the wars in which its people had fought. Not since the Harlem riots of 1935 had such a crisis swept through northern urban ghettos. Faced with explosive discontent and the repression that followed, the young artist and intellectual was forced to reexamine the relation of his art to the community. To write as an individual without reference to the world around him whose problems he shared was scandalous.

This commitment led LeRoi Jones to leave Greenwich Village, where he had known general acclaim, and embark on a mission in Harlem. In May 1965 he opened the Black Arts Repertory Theatre (BART). He received a grant of $40,000 from the government, which had just started its antipoverty programs for ghetto youth, and he immediately recruited four hundred participants.

From the start, Jones wanted a theatre run exclusively by blacks for blacks. The idea appeared dangerously radical, and many people objected to Jones's plans. He held firm to his position: actors would perform only for black audiences, and if they had to play white parts they would use makeup. Jones's proposition brought about a symbolic reversal from "burnt-cork white minstrel" to "chalk-faced black minstrel." Jones did not come to this point by accident. His plays, produced off-Broadway in 1964, had already stirred the waters. In *Dutchman* and

The Slave violence had been suddenly thrust upon the stage. Jones's vehement attacks on whites, especially liberals whom he once had considered allies, led both whites and blacks to disown him and to dub his theatre a "theatre of hatred." The revolution Jones wanted to bring to the stage by using new dramatic modes could gain full meaning only when accompanied by new theatre practice. His experiment with BART thus began at the point the FST attained by 1966. Only by deliberately turning his back on white society could Jones succeed in his project.

It seems illogical that Jones would seek financial support from the government for such a theatre; it is even more surprising that the government would provide the money. Did the power structure consider the project inoffensive, or did it want to exert control over him? Jones's tactic, one commonly used by militants in the United States, succeeded in getting some of reparation for the cruelty inflicted upon his people. One is tempted to see in American society's tolerance of such a radical enterprise proof of its confidence in the power it wields and in its capacity to absorb dissent, a major feature in cultural politics. Jones, by accepting the government grants, ran the double risk of appearing to blacks to be ideologically bought off, even if only to reach a state of financial autonomy, and of losing all support if he remained completely faithful to the project.

During its seven months' existence, BART presented shows before a small but exclusively black audience. Jones wanted to avoid repeating the situation of the twenties when whites easily stormed Harlem. He raised the problem of the relation of theatre to the community in overtly nationalist terms. The text that defined his project constitutes one of the first documents of the new theatre and places art back in the service of the people. Theatre is a magic art which must move and entertain while making people aware of the forces that control the world.[29] During the summer of 1965, Jones organized five weeks of performances through the streets of Harlem, and down to the northern tip of Central Park. He used techniques of street theatre to express a revolutionary message calling for immediate action. This theatre without walls created a panic. Yet his off-Broadway plays had caused little worry. In fact the cultural establishment had honored him with the Obie Award for the 1963–1964 season. But it never admitted that the author had actually upset the institution of theatre by questioning its social function. The press, however, made an issue of the federal funds BART received and started a vicious defamation campaign. The Office of Economic Opportunity finally withdrew its money under the pretext that Jones was using it to corrupt minors by presenting plays that were racist and that contained "foul" language.[30]

Jones was unable to resolve the contradictions that came with his two areas of support: the nationalist ideology still inadequately defined, and the antipoverty programs set up by the government he so fiercely opposed. The separatism he proclaimed as guarantee of autonomy was compromised by the very means he used to gain it. Also, the power structure would not tolerate for long a program that accepted its money but refused to grant it any control over its activities. Jones's experiment failed because of rigid cultural politics on both sides. It did open the way, however, for a big break in 1966, and it stimulated a more rigorous reflection on the role of the artist and intellectual in the black community.[31]

That two theatre experiments as different as the Free Southern Theatre and the Black Arts Repertory Theatre came to the same organizational crisis and to the same political awareness was an important sign of the times. The problem of separatism affected them both. In New Orleans as in Harlem, black cultural survival was inextricably bound to the search for autonomy from the white world. Forced out of Harlem, Jones launched another more durable venture in Newark, where he founded a center called New Ark. As for the FST, which managed to exist in the South until 1979,[32] it inspired the creation of many troupes throughout the southern United States. The formation of a free southern theatre was no longer the responsibility of one group alone, but of many institutions still active today.[33]

Black Fire

The years 1964–1966 thus raised questions about the functions of black theatre. The ideal of integration had pushed theatre in a direction that might have become irreversible had it not been for those first attempts to return theatre to the people. The wave of revolt stemmed not from isolated individuals but from a collective need expressed under the rallying cries of "Home" and "Black Power."

The theatre revolution that occurred is a fact of history. Black America once again questioned the Civil Rights Movement and the ideology that had inspired it.[34] Blacks were no longer content with the hyphenated identity that white America bestows on its immigrants, and even less with the second-class citizenship blacks had gained with such difficulty. National assimilation no longer made any sense; the

American Dream was denounced and the idea of a pluralistic society appeared to be a decoy. Submissiveness and nonviolence had come to an end.

Without doubt, this historic movement was influenced by the message of Malcolm X. Other factors included the availability of Frantz Fanon's writings, the liberation movements in African countries, the Cuban revolution, the Civil Rights Movement, and the ghetto riots. The new nationalism laid down principles of cultural revolution that involved artists directly. Racial pride, a dawning of black consciousness, a search for identity based on knowledge of the ethnic past and the collective memory, an analysis of black history and culture, the creation of new myths and symbols, were all stages of a new awareness without which political and economic power would have little meaning. Any hope for liberation had to come through cultural action. On the level of language, the revolution was marked by a change in terminology; the search for different names signified a new baptism,[35] a rebirth, which — in a general subversion of linguistic structure — moved from passive to active modes of expression. Blacks rejected the names given to them by white America. The term "nigger," reminiscent of scorn and insult, and that of "Negro," which had lost the significance the Harlem Renaissance had given it and come to symbolize a half-life accepted for too long, were replaced by one word, "black." Family names, formerly given to slaves by their masters, were sometimes abandoned in favor of names of African origin, freely chosen: LeRoi Jones became Amiri Baraka, and Don L. Lee became Haki Madhubuti.

The idea of a black nation brought with it the possibility of a collective identity. Individual suffering took on new meaning in light of the history of a whole people. Africa and Islam provided a heritage, more mythic than real, and offered the new ideology a religious code, a cultural tradition, and an entire mythology. Nationalism also brought about solidarity, a sharing of common trials and battles. It addressed blacks from the North and the South, from country and city; it pointed out the white man as the common enemy and oppressor. This Manichean vision evoked the triumph of good over evil and restored strength and beauty to black people.

Nationalism in this way is as much a takeover of language as it is a takeover of power. The principles of building a black nation come through the word. The writers are endowed with a primordial role. They will forge words as weapons, shape a new language that can offer new truths. This new aesthetic is a form of power itself: taking power through language, merging speech and magical power with occult forces, using the power of words to reveal a different vision of the world. "We are black magicians, black art/s we make in black labs of the heart."[36]

The Theoretical Foundations of New Black Theatre

The years from 1964 to 1969 saw lectures, debates, and panel discussions organized by institutions that wanted to be part of the Movement. The topics covered the major themes of integration, acculturation, and the relations between blacks and American culture. Black and white intellectuals were invited to talk to each other, and for the first time in the history of American theatre black dramatists discussed their work with critics before a black audience.

LeRoi Jones's essay "The Revolutionary Theatre," still considered to be the most significant document of the new movement in theatre, was presented in April 1965 at a panel called "What Black Dramatists Are Saying," which brought together writers and critics such as Richard Gillman of *Newsweek* and Gordon Rogoff of the *Tulane Drama Review*. The violence expressed in Jones's text brought an abrupt end to the hope of reconciliation between black artists and representatives of the dominant culture. The great trial of white America was about to begin. The theatre became the battlefield where the two worlds confronted each other symbolically, where the destruction of the treacherous world and the birth of a regenerated world would happen.

As a work by a poet who claimed to be a prophet and a magician, "The Revolutionary Theatre" is less a theoretical essay than a kind of poem-scenario that would inspire many black dramatists for years to come. Jones describes a series of imaginary acts and shows how this "black magic" will affect spectators: "All their faces turned into the lights and you work on them black nigger magic, and cleanse them at having seen the ugliness. And if the beautiful see themselves, they will love themselves . . . White men will cower before this theatre because it hates them."[37] As a magical art, theatre must expose beauty and ugliness, preach courage and the strength to act, terrify those who have never been afraid, empower those who have been victims. Magic alone can transform former victims into heroes and reveal the wickedness of a technological civilization which the spirit will conquer.

The theatre becomes a court where whites are judged, where victims are exhorted to defend themselves, to accuse, attack, and exterminate: "It is a political theatre, a weapon to help in the slaughter of these dim-witted, fatbellied white guys who somehow believe that the rest of the world is here for them to slobber on."[38] As part of reality, this theatre can change the world and make dreams come true.

This text, which blends imprecation, rowdy slogans, and polemical declarations, suggests the stages of development of a revolutionary theatre. The first task should be the trial of white America and of its insane leaders—WASPs, MAD, or MAWP (Mad American White People).[39] The drama should develop around two groups of characters: the victims and their oppressors, "brothers" and enemies. The action is didactic and instructive as it shows how this distinction can be made. If the protagonist fails to recognize the enemy under his many disguises, the spectator certainly will not be so mistaken: "Our theatre will show victims so that their brothers in the audience will be better able to understand that they are the brothers of victims, and that they themselves are victims if they are blood brothers."[40]

Theatre also involves the writing of history. The black dramatist must reclaim the collective memory, express the emotional situation of the Western black,[41] and retell the fundamental stages of Afro-American experience: "Let black people understand that they are lovers and the sons of lovers, warriors and the sons of warriors, are poems and poets."[42] The advance of an entire nation will be shown. The theatre draws upon the community; it gives energy back to the very people who have given it life.

For the artist, a degree of self-restraint is required. He must forget himself, renounce excessive emotion. His role as witness and chronicler is to organize experience in the name of truth and justice. His art is moral, his aesthetics inseparable from ethics.[43] He brings back hope and restores the power of the imagination, a faculty that can escape the control of the oppressor. He encourages sensitivity, symbolic action, and proposes a new mythology. "Black is a country."[44] The artist must keep his vision of the world inviolate, free it from any deformity it has suffered. Theatre thus generates the impulse for deep collective fervor, a language and a space in which the creation of the world will be acted out. The artist becomes the decisive power: he is the Creator.[45]

Two actions converge. The artificial world, dispenser of injustice and violence, must be overthrown with equal violence. Various scenarios repeat the same basic action of the destruction of America. The act expresses hope not hopelessness. Then the theatre should celebrate and reveal truths that owe nothing to the oppressor. In contrast to what occurs in real life, the theatricalized action unfolds like a ritual, continuously performed. It demands changes that are absolute, that do not merely grant temporary satisfaction, and that affect all the heart and mind.

This theatre thus creates dialectical relationships between what it destroys and what it creates. On one side is the West, kingdom of rationality and technology. On the other is the spirit, called soul or blackness, which breaks away from reason in order to save the world. On one side domination and the restrictive law of the oppressor; on the other side liberation, freedom, and an enduring reconciliation among blacks. The theatre stages repeated confrontations between these two orders.

A dialectic also exists between two kinds of reality: what is, and what can be or what should be: the "is" and the "ought." Sociohistorical reality thus opposes the imaginary. Theatre begins with the former and proceeds to the latter. It no longer offers an image of existing reality; rather, it transcends everyday life, breaks away from history in order to situate itself in a mythic space and time.

The proposed solutions exist in the imaginary world and not in immediate practice as dictated by revolutionary ideology. The artist responds with his own weapons to problems around him. Paradoxically, this art affirms its autonomy from the real world while proclaiming a commitment to it. Jones vacillates between this commitment and the affirmation of a mythic reality, even an improbable one, where a remote possibility is projected. His objective is to change the world, but he will not carry out the transformation himself. Instead, he offers a symbolic representation. The revolutionary act is staged, "rehearsed" in a theatre that tears off masks and dismantles the mechanisms of domination and rationality in a world of oppression. From this point on the necessity for liberation is fundamentally clear. First there must be an absolute breaking away, then a radical change of values. The condemnation of society is an ethical one, indeed metaphysical, and not merely political. The society to be built emerges as truth; what must be destroyed is conceived as falsehood. Theatre thus transmits the vision of a free world, which is more utopian than real. The immediate goal of theatre is to reaffirm its right to exist as an art and as a means to influence the dominant ideology. Because art itself is possible only in a free society, theatre will search for the path to its own emancipation.

Therein lies the true meaning of "revolutionary" theatre. It advocates change and exhorts to action, but it also places itself on trial in a moment of revolt. It presents new characters and dramatic action, and it establishes new dialectical relations with its material and its audience.

At this stage it would be pointless to ask how effective this revolutionary theatre is in practice, but one can still inquire about the aesthetic relevance of such theory when it is put to work to generate new kinds of drama.

LeRoi Jones was not the only spokesman for the new theatre. Many people contributed ideas, which were disseminated by such journals as *Negro Digest*, *Freedomways*, and the *Liberator*.[46] It was Larry Neal who pulled together several concepts under the name of the Black Arts Movement, which translated into artistic terms the political and economic precepts formulated by advocates of Black Power.[47] This movement pointed out the need for reconciliation between the artist and his community; the artist had to respond to the spiritual needs of his people and go far beyond the protests of earlier generations. The development of an aesthetics of negritude was shown as an urgent task, for to accept white aesthetics was to endorse a society that denigrates black existence.[48] From now on the black dramatist would be accountable only to his people.

Clayton Riley also criticized the "Negro theatre" of those actors who had always aspired to perform in plays written by whites, and of directors of Harlem theatres who offered only an obsolete repertory of white plays.[49] Riley exhorted black theatre to break away from Broadway, that commercial "world of lies and corruption" and to achieve its autonomy away from criteria established by white dramatists. The black theatre envisaged would no longer have to please the audience, as indicated ironically by the title of Loften Mitchell's article, "I Work Here To Please You."[50] Its aim is to generate concern. Most interestingly, it expresses the attitudes of a character whose strategies and equivocations are legion in black popular culture, the "signifyer" who is by turns swindler and agitator, and who enjoys confusing his interlocutor and his audience.[51] The popular tradition becomes a source for theatrical innovations. The most eloquent model is found in music—alternately a debate and a celebration, a wail of despair and a song of hope. The blues singer becomes a prototypical creator.

The word "soul," used more and more frequently to define blackness, often means a quality unique to black experience, something no other culture has been able to create or to imitate. Theatre draws upon the styles of life that define and characterize a people, integrating its jokes and laughter, its cries of suffering and shouts of revolt, its manner of walking, dressing, speaking. It is not enough, however, that this theatre be made up of black figures alone. In his essay "The Myth of a Negro

Literature" Jones condemns the use of protagonists who are only white definitions of blackness. One cannot simply play chess with black pawns instead of white ones.[52] Nor can inspiration come only from black life; sociological truth does not suffice. One must touch the "soul" of a people by concrete manifestations of its life and must revitalize a culture that has been scorned.

The different advocates of the Black Arts Movement were careful to bring together three essential concepts — art, culture, and nation — in a multidimensional rather than a linear relationship. Fanon is often cited for emphasizing, as does Jones, the inseparability of the concepts of nation and culture ("To free the nation is to free the culture").[53] The poet Don L. Lee reminds us that what destroys the culture also destroys the people.[54] In this revolutionary era, when black people must be liberated and build a nation, the cultural heritage must be protected. Art should lay the foundations of ethnic identity and break the chains of ignorance.

The advocates also attack the concepts held by "philistines, puritans, and the proletarians" and equally reject the hedonistic idea of art by proclaiming the functional and moral character of creative activity. The essential postulate is an unbreakable tie to the community. The word "home" assumes its fullest meaning. Around it, Ron Milner based a program of black theatre that returns to ethnic sources on all levels: psychically, mentally, aesthetically, and physically.[55] The black community is not only a place where theatre finds its raw material and its audience; it is one of black theatre's principal *actors*. It participates in the creation of art, shapes it, directs it. The audience becomes part of the cast.

The reciprocity of ties between black theatre and its audience is at the core of the Black Arts Movement. The theatre exists only by restoring a dialectical relationship with the audience. This affirmation, which may seem emphatic, is much more than the reiteration of a cliché about the nature of all theatre: without an audience no theatre. In 1966 the black theatre did not think of any audience, but of a specific one. It eliminated first the whites, then the black bourgeoisie, that nonethnic element of the community which had internalized the values of the dominant society. The bourgeoisie at a later time could be reintegrated — but it must be ready to learn. This dramaturgy includes the dual ritual of condemning bourgeois complicity with white America and of celebrating its eventual redemption.

Art is thus dedicated to black people. It is also created by them. Each work produced by artists of the movement is conceived as a microcosm of the black nation whose vision of the world is set forth. Black people themselves become the proposed work of art, and the creation of art coincides with the building of a nation.

The Militant
Theatre

 SILENCED OR FORCED to prevaricate for too long, Afro-American theatre entered the second black renaissance of the sixties as an act of free speech. From author to author and from play to play the message of rehabilitating black people drew upon the traditions of the fifties and twenties. But this time the black dramatists took the floor and wiped the slate clean of the exotic images left by white writers.

At first, theatre simply presented the facts and showed what was wrong in the world. History was its witness. The promises of Emancipation and Reconstruction had not been kept. The theatre patiently examined interracial relations and their effect on black life. It made its case primarily to a white audience that was directly involved. The theatre tried to make America aware of its national responsibility by presenting its message with humor and moderation so as to avoid alienating the audience it needed in order to survive.

The theatre artists were temperate in their militancy. They tried to improve race relations and took care not to question white supremacy. They chose dialogue rather than battle. They no longer railed against the system of theatre production or its traditions in America. They might play the part of agitators, but only agitators in favor of the kind of integration that was already in practice. Although they hesitated between conciliation and denunciation, they offered the rough outlines of a process that would become more and more violent. Just as the Civil Rights Movement organized people into "civil righters," black theatre started its own campaign for the integration of blacks into show business and national culture as "civil writers."

The failures of the Civil Rights Movement and the disillusion that followed brought an abrupt end to this conciliatory protest. Whites no longer deserved any consideration, nor were they asked for any recognition. Little by little the theatre changed into a courtroom where rage and hate erupted—and where whites were summoned to hear themselves condemned—or into a battlefield where the rites of a bloody revolution took place. Warnings gave way to rhetoric and curses, damning whites and their black accomplices.

The force of language, like the acts of vengeance it prescribes, provokes questions about the function of theatre as conceived thus far. It brings into the new drama self-criticism and debate about the practices and the ideology of a young revolutionary theatre. Once its mission as denouncer and purger is accomplished, the theatre becomes an instrument for the building of a black nation. It gives up its violent language and destructive acts in order to celebrate the regeneration of black people. Productions are held in the black community, to address it exclusively. The black audience finds a place in the theatre as spectator-participants. The theatre gives black people the final say, something they have been denied for so long. Like music, the theatre becomes the voice through which the blues people can express and become themselves.

In "militant" theatre this goal is accomplished in a didactic manner. When the dialogue becomes stripped of rhetoric, ideology, and cant, drama becomes a theatre of experience, more concerned with the artistic quality of black life than with leading struggles. New forms of drama are created, and the theatre, freed from political and revolutionary language, immerses itself in experiments with reality and the imaginary.

This brief account may give the false impression of a linear progression in the development of black theatre. Any discussion of theatre will certainly follow the evolution of the ideological debates of the past decades, which moved from the tentative dialogue with whites in the hope of integration to the passionate affirmation of black power and nationalist militancy. Yet the relation between drama and ideology is at best complex and ambiguous, for ideas and creative work do not follow the same paths. If the diachronic approach reveals certain directional lines, one must not make the mistake of following them: even today some plays use the language of the early sixties, and conversely, certain early plays presented new dramatic forms. Not all dramatists discovered the same freedom of speech at the same time: their accents differ, and conflicts and divergences often appear. The drama that today may seem strongest as a body of work may have been prefigured by individual works that were not so well noticed in their own time. Finally, the debate between separatism and integration is not over, and some works refuse to take sides. While some argue for the universality of their perspectives, others emphasize the particularity of their points of view.

In the analysis that follows I seek to trace the development of the new theatre by considering each play as a link in a chain of possible meanings, taking into account the fits and starts that led the theatre from one form of drama to another and the often contradictory fluctuations that characterized its progress.

Several ambiguities must be emphasized, including that of creating conflict out of dialogue, and the ambiguity of language itself. Black drama reclaims the unquestionable right to express a life that no white person can experience and that no outsider can properly convey. It seeks freedom from the established conventions of theatre and the images of blacks therein. But it also wants to be heard and to enjoy a large audience. It demands free access to all levels of the theatre institution and to the means of production and distribution. This legitimate desire for integration runs counter to the objective of freedom. Aimed at gaining recognition, theatre is tempted to respect the customs and conventions it rebels against. Afro-American drama continues to fluctuate between the poles of integration and autonomy.

The precursors of the militant theatre of the fifties and sixties go as far back as the nineteenth century, when playwrights presented images of resistance and liberation. One of the directors of the African Grove Theatre, a Mr. Brown, was reputed to be the author of *King Shotoway*, which in 1820 depicted a slave revolt on the island of St. Vincent. Another dramatist was William Wells Brown, who used theatre in his work as an abolitionist. His play *Escape; or A Leap for Freedom* (1858) depicted a double liberation: slaves escaping to freedom and black characters refusing to follow conventions established by whites. During the first half of the twentieth century, black authors continued to protest both the social injustices inflicted upon blacks[1] (from *Rachel* by Angelina Grimke to *Flight of the Natives* by Willis Richardson, from *Natural Man* by Theodore Brown to *Our Lan'* by Theodore Ward)[2] and the treatment of black characters in mainstream drama which either caricatured them for entertainment or exhibited their excesses in a "Negro" theatre written by whites. In this wave of protest, *Natural Man* occupies an important symbolic place. Brown removes the term "natural" from its exotic connotations and emphasizes John Henry's message of freedom and solidarity; his hero who proclaims himself "free as the mountains and the rivers" could serve as a model for the new theatre.[3]

Bolstered by campaigns for equality during the fifties, Afro-American theatre became progressively more militant, but its spirit was different from the militancy that was growing on the political scene. It provided a dialogue with history where an ideological debate could be established, and it paid homage to those who struggled.

The dialogue with history began with William Branch's *In Splendid Error* in 1954.[4] This historical play depicts the possible collaboration between Frederick Douglass and John Brown on the raid at Harper's Ferry. Although Branch took up the debate about the links between insurrection and madness, he especially wanted to reveal the little-known role played by Frederick Douglass. The theatre, Branch argued, must not be content merely to create idealized heroes, but must resuscitate real heroic figures who have been ignored in the history written by whites. Branch's perspective on the past encouraged his contemporaries to look to history for models for current action.

Branch's *A Medal for Willie* (1951)[5] portrays a mother's challenge to those who try to interpret for her the meaning of her son's death. A small southern town, with the symbolic name of Midway, prepares to commemorate the death of a young black soldier killed in action. Discrimination ceases for the duration of the ceremony. The town thus expresses its recognition of the black population and encourages it to support the national effort. *A Medal* denounces the hypocrisy of a society that pays posthumous tribute to those it neglects in life. The educational system that fails to meet the needs of black children, job discrimination, and unemployment are attacked, as is the ability of whites to prolong their education and thus avoid the draft. Branch accuses society of making false promises and encouraging blacks to fight its murderous wars when it declares blacks heroic only after death. Before going off to war in other countries, he insists, blacks should fight for freedom at home.

In attacking the representation of blacks as heroes willing to die for their country or as grieving but grateful parents, the play also indicts a certain form of theatre. In this skillfully constructed ceremony-play the roles and dialogue are dictated in advance — such as the speech showing the importance of her son's death that the mother is supposed to read. Instead of delivering the prescribed speech, Willie's mother improvises another that exposes her suffering, indignation, and anger. She refuses the medal and in so doing rejects the paternalistic approval of white society. This refusal, interpreted by the citizens of Midway as a sign of misguided grief, serves as Branch's metaphor for a manifesto on theatre. The mother represents the agent of change between the tradition to be rejected and the one to be created. The play is also interesting for the important role it gives to a female character and for the speech whose rhetoric and tone reverse the listener's expectations. The action, however, lapses into melodrama, and *A Medal*'s message is weakened by a contrived moralistic epilogue.

Earth and Stars,[6] written by Randolph Edwards in 1945 and revised in 1961 to set the action in the midst of the Civil Rights Movement, stages another kind of militancy: that of a pastor and his revolutionary son who wants to involve the church in a nonviolent struggle for black equality. Both father and son die in the repression that follows.

Similarly, a pastor is the hero of Loften Mitchell's *A Land Beyond the River*, in which the courage of the militants confronts an implacable repression.[7]

Black theatre thus takes on the mission of guarding against the American Dream and debunking the hope of integration. This theatre of disenchantment often uses adolescent protagonists. *Take a Giant Step* (1955) by Louis Peterson presents without exaggeration or melodrama the frustrations of a black youth new to a white neighborhood who struggles against undisguised hostility or an embarrassing kindness.[8] His resentment of his family for uprooting him brings discord. Only Christie, the family maid and an admirable female figure, can free him from black self-hatred. The play criticizes integration for causing new traumas. The ambitions and dreams of the black middle class are denounced by one character, the grandmother, whose diatribes become more and more harsh. It is not white society that is so severely attacked, but the black family — not those who keep the dream from being realized, but those who persist in dreaming. Developed through several dramatic episodes, the criticism collapses in the ending when the rebel son returns to his family. The suggested break is not completed. Although the title *Take a Giant Step* echoes *Escape; or A Leap for Freedom*, the "step" toward black liberation is not yet taken. Does Peterson's retreat signal a concession to audience tastes and to the ideology of the period? One can measure the distance that separates this play from the more militant theatre of the sixties. Peterson's hero does not want to be reminded that he is black. Uneasy in the white world, he prefers to accommodate to it following his juvenile attempt at revolt rather than to return to the ghetto. An identical situation would be taken up again a few years later, but as we shall see it would lead to an opposite resolution. In 1953 the return to the ghetto, or "going home," was still considered a regression.

A Raisin in the Sun accentuates the retreat begun with *Giant Step*. The subject is the same — the integration of a black family into a white neighborhood — but instead of showing the consequences of such a "leap," Hansberry depicts the efforts that precede the realization of the dream. Here only a son's greed is questioned. These descendants of slaves who came north for better opportunity have found only destitution in the Chicago ghetto. However, an insurance payment received on the death of the father provides a way out of poverty. Each member of the family pursues an individual goal: the son, Walter, wants to buy a liquor store; the mother wants to buy a house where "there ain't no colored people." Hansberry is less concerned about the causes of the family's poverty than about the moral conflict between family members over what to do with the money. In spite of obstacles and temptations, the dream house becomes a reality in a happy ending where perseverence and integrity triumph.

The image Hansberry gives of the black community is deliberately selective. She avoids lowlife and mobsters; her representation of the ghetto includes only those who merit leaving it. The ghetto is a place to leave, and the most worthy can escape it. *Raisin* fuels a certain ambiguity, for without the insurance money, the Younger family would have to remain in the ghetto despite the heroic virtues of the mother. The analysis of the economic situation is thus diverted to moral considerations.[9] Hansberry turns her attention to people who are not embittered or alienated by their life. This choice is as much aesthetic as moral: debauchery is too ugly to be shown on stage. And Broadway audiences preferred to consider *Raisin* not a black play but an "American" play.[10] The ambiguity of Hansberry's attitude and the paradox of its success are objects of an eternal controversy that reflects the conflicts and problems of Afro-American theatre. With *Raisin*, black theatre had reintegrated into the Great White Way, and the swing of the pendulum took another direction.

Militancy is asserted in a friendly, humorous way in *Purlie Victorious* by Ossie Davis.[11] Led by the intrepid Purlie, a group of blacks confront the white oligarchy of a small southern town by taking over a building to turn it into a church. The powerful Cap'n Charlie Cotchipee opposes their project, but with wily craft and imagination Purlie triumphs over the obstacles. The situation is a familiar one: a confrontation of unequals in which the weaker contestant wins. This pattern is frequent in black folktales and serves as a parable about the relations between masters and slaves; the weaker (Brer Rabbit, the trickster, or Signifying Monkey) triumphs over the stronger, usually by a ruse. Purlie, like the Signifying Monkey, resorts to flattery of his opponent. After numerous adventures, blacks regain ownership of the land when the tyrant dies; they pay tribute to him by burying him in the position in which he died—standing up. The Cap'n's son gives the building to Purlie, not as a gift, but as restitution. In his new role as pastor, Purlie delivers a long sermon on racial pride and the joys of a rediscovered pastoral life. This idyllic vision of black life on the plantation, presented by a character who is something of a braggart, is both a parody and an act of faith in the beauty of black people. The battle Purlie leads in the white world occurs through too many screwball episodes to be really threatening. One may wonder if these entertaining mishaps, through which the hero also mocks himself, are designed to attenuate the "revolutionary" message expressed by the inveterate rebel that Purlie is. Although directed mostly against whites, the satire and parody mock blacks as well. The flux of race relations in the South — hierarchical relations between black servants and the white aristocracy, blood ties between masters and slaves — gives rise to many comic moments. In this imaginary world, the most surprising facts are credible: if a tyrant can die standing up, then blacks like Purlie can triumph over whites. [12]

The theatre of James Baldwin offers a more pessimistic view of black-white relations. Baldwin evokes interracial conflicts in the mode of the blues; he gives voice to the sorrow and pain of a people who shed tears, sing about suffering, or proclaim revolt. The title of *Blues for Mister Charlie* [13] is significant, for the play shows the causes of black pain and anger. Its audience is the white man who is responsible for the discontent and whom Baldwin both implores and abuses. This theatre of "understanding" tries to show compassion for a people who are *victims* of the blindness and violence of whites. The drama was inspired by a real event: the 1955 murder of Emmett Till in Mississippi.

The plot is relatively simple. Richard, an unemployed black youth who returns to his home town when he is unable to continue his study of music in the North, is killed after an argument with a white man. Lyle, the murderer, is aquitted by the jury, although he is also suspected of having killed Old Bel, the husband of his black mistress. The action occurs in three places: the church, the courtroom, and the streets, each of which is divided into two worlds, the black and the white. Everything suggests polarization, a total segregation. The encounters take on the character of open defiance; attempts at conciliation led by Parnell, the town liberal who calls himself a friend of blacks, are in vain, for these tensions exclude every kind of mediation. In this world, blacks do not die a "natural death." Contradictions abound: the white shopowner, Lyle, fights blacks with his scorn and beats them at the slightest provocation, yet he depends on their business, and he has a black mistress. The black man avenges himself by abusing whites in the North, but the slightest suspicion of such an attitude in the South can bring about his death.

Through the character of the Reverend Meridian, Richard's father, the play retraces the movements that led blacks to revolt. According to Meridian, the black man became a Christian in order to find the dignity that had been denied him. The death of Meridian's wife and son forces him to see differently, and he indicts the church for teaching submission. He starts to doubt the wisdom of black people who see their children massacred without wincing. When the liberal Parnell comes to ask his mercy, Meridian explains that friendship and trust are impossible between the two communities. As in *The Fire Next Time*, Baldwin wields terror and persuasion, inciting both revolt and reconciliation. The town plays the role of the spectator, and the guilt it refuses to attribute to Lyle will be revealed by the theatre, which is set up as a criminal court to criticize the course of "justice" that obscures the truth.

The play is structured around two falls: that of an anonymous corpse toppled over into the void, and the more metaphorical fall when Richard's death is reenacted in court. The play's chronology must be reconstructed between these two scenes in order to reveal the continuity of events to certain characters and to the spectators. Parallel and often antithetical scenes present each world separately: while one is celebrating Lyle's wedding anniversary, the other is preparing for Richard's funeral. Parnell is a link and messenger between the two, but his role is ambiguous. Is he a moderator, a sincere friend, or a spy and deliberate traitor? Since he never denies that Richard might have committed rape, his testimony helps to acquit Lyle, who also has a lawyer in Baldwin himself who (as he says in the preface to the play) wants to conduct an autopsy of the murder. Lyle is portrayed as a poor, frustrated white man who turns against those weaker than himself. It appears that Baldwin wanted to break free of the stereotypical character of a racist used so often in militant theatre. His defense plea is two-fold: he defends blacks and denounces racism, and he shows the poor whites to be victims of an economic situation in which blacks are scapegoats. At certain moments the play urges taking sides so that justice will be done; at other timed it prefers to suspend judgment.

In spite of Baldwin's good intentions, which avoid the excesses of reverse racism, his argument remains ambiguous. The core of the ambiguity lies in his preface, where he seems to be speaking for all Americans when he uses the pronoun "we" in deploring the evil men inflict upon one another. The "we" joins the speaker with white America. Several years later, speaking for blacks, the theatre would substitute for the artificial unity contained in a single pronoun the opposition between "them" and "us," between two distinct and irreconcilable worlds. White America in 1964 did not embrace the vision *Blues for Mister Charlie* proposed for race relations. The play failed on Broadway where *Raisin* enjoyed a great success. Baldwin's play too clearly denounced the status quo and defied certain ideas cherished in theatre as well as in American culture at large.

LeRoi Jones / Amiri Baraka: An Iconoclastic Theatre

Unlike his predecessors, LeRoi Jones makes no concession to American theatre tradition or to the tastes of white audiences. He argues aggressively for the liberation that others had timidly asked for. He disposes of Hansberry's conciliatory dialogue, Baldwin's calls for compassion and understanding, and Davis's entertaining excursions. Proceeding to judge white society, Jones transforms the theatre into a courtroom. Summoned to trial will be all the representatives of the white world and their black accomplices who for four hundred years have helped to destroy black life.[14]

The white world is sentenced to annihilation. Black theatre thus becomes the symbolic place where rites of expiation, vengeance, murder, and sacrifice unfold and where the liberation of black people will find its righteous path. A purified world will be reborn from the ashes.

Jones's titles suggest this movement: the path leads from the middle passage (*Slave Ship*) through an underground world where the black man goes astray seeking retribution (*Dutchman*), to serving the revolution (*The Slave*); from wallowing in filth (*The Toilet*) to purification (*Baptism*); from police brutality (*Police*) and the sacrifice of a black victim (*The Death of Malcolm X*) to bloody rituals (*Madheart*, *Bloodrights*) which destroy the monsters alive since the beginning of time (*Black Mass*) and which bring a new world into being (*Ressurection in Life*).

The parable of *Dutchman* [15] invites several readings. The plot is quite bare. In the ghostly world of the New York subway, an alluring white woman, Lula, meets a young black man, Clay. She sets out to seduce him, talking about how well she knows blacks and claiming that Clay is merely posing as an intellectual. Taken aback by Lula's verbal and sexual games, Clay suddenly rebels and reveals in a flash all the anger and hatred of which even the most "submissive" blacks are capable. Lula fatally stabs Clay, who has become dangerous. With the silent complicity of other passengers, she gets rid of the body and prepares to begin the same ritual with the next young black man who enters the subway car.

The title of the play is doubly significant. Historically, it recalls the slave ships of the Dutch East India Company, which hoisted the "Flying Dutchman" flag. Metaphorically, it evokes the legendary phantom ship condemned to wander in pursuit of an inacessible victim. But if love could assure the redemption of the cursed ship, as in Heine's story and Wagner's opera,[16] there is no such redemption possible for Jones's vessel. This double allusion indicates the dimensions of the play: the historical condition of blacks in America (capture, revolt) and the metaphorical representation of America as slave ship/subway. Aboard this vessel blacks are held captive, condemned to wander in an underground world, and exposed to the provocations and violence of those who want to be their masters.

The dialogue between Clay and Lula and the various characters Clay is called upon to portray reveal the history whites want to control for themselves and their posterity. Shaping and manipulating the maleable mass indicated by the name Clay, Lula is a kind of god who dispenses life and kills when the creation threatens to turn upon its creator. This image of creation, as well as the successive characters Clay embodies, brings to mind the metaphor of theatre: Clay is under the control of an expert director who feeds him his lines and who won't tolerate his breaking out of the assigned roles. Here whites attempt to define blacks, as American theatre has always tried to do. Reclaiming the power of speech, denouncing the roles that imprison him, and revealing what whites have appropriated, Clay becomes a symbol for Afro-American theatre in a struggle for liberation.

In this play within a play each historical character of blacks—from slave to Uncle Tom, from assimilated intellectual to potential rebel—is a disguise, and each change a step toward total transformation. Clay's manner of dress, language, and behavior immediately identify him as an emasculated product of colonization, a "house nigger," one of the pillars of the system he faithfully serves. With the books and eyeglasses of a studious intellectual, he is the innocent victim of Lula's provocations. He takes her insults in stride and, joining the game, delivers the lines that set him up as a worthy opponent. But he wants no trouble, and to that end he sacrifices his pride.

Lula, whose role is not without ambiguity, embodies the temptations America uses to seduce blacks: the apple she is eating makes her an Eve offering herself to Adam. She also represents the paternalism and perverse cruelty of racist America. She assumes the right to determine how Clay will live and when he will die; she dictates his conduct and even the paths his revolt should take. Like her namesakes, Lilith, daughter of Satan, and Lulu of Wedekind, she is primarily a seductress. Using the stereotypical images whites have of black sexuality, her games reveal the stratagems America uses to entrap blacks: flattery, seduction, degrading provocation, castration. In his essay "American Sexual Reference," Jones examined this sexual metaphor long before Eldridge Cleaver used the same idea in *Soul on Ice*. Jones sees castration culminating in the ritual of lynching when the black man chokes on his own genitals stuffed in his mouth.[17] *Dutchman* attests to the close ties between power and sexuality and invites the spectator to watch the castration of Clay, whose virility is worked up only to be better smothered. Clay's death repeats the numerous lynchings for which the white woman was historically responsible. The perpetrator of rape is the woman herself; the stereotype of black sexual aggression is reversed ("I am Lena the hyena"). Lula is the devouring beast and Clay her victim (p. 14). Perhaps here one can see a reference to the Lil' Abner comic strip where a certain Lena is the ugliest contestant in a beauty pageant. America is represented by a character whose blonde beauty is vulgar and aggressive, hardly the delicate features of the heroine of southern romance. Lula, the greedy and treacherous hyena, offers herself to Clay to prove that in the sexual games she is always the winner (p. 31). Witty, knowledgeable, heir to the liberal tradition that prides itself in knowing blacks, she engages Clay in a differrent dialogue. Clay discovers too late the deception in the attraction white women have for blacks and in the liberal pretense of knowing what blacks feel.

The confrontation between Lula and Clay is verbal, and it shows the impossibility of communication. Language serves as a tool for domination. The rapid cues exchanged between the two adversaries indicate one of the meanings of the title: "I am a Dutchman if . . ." Insults fly back and forth. If Lula's games are reminiscent of the "dozens"—where each interlocutor counters insults with stronger ones—Clay does not play by the rules. He endures her insults without retort, perhaps because his bourgeois respectability keeps him from playing such a vulgar game. Otherwise, his silence is a weapon; he challenges his opponent by his studied calm.

Lula is given an exceptional function in this play, namely, to denounce the "white Negro": "You middle-class black bastard . . . you liver-lipped white man . . . so full of white man's words . . . there is Uncle Tom. I mean, Uncle Thomas Wooly Head" (pp. 31–32). Like a sphinx, she poses riddles, but paradoxically, it is she who reveals Clay to himself, makes him discover virtues he has ignored and the compromises or concessions he has made in order to survive. She takes the role of provocator/revelator that the theatre itself assumes for the black community. Having raised Clay's consciousness ("You're an escaped nigger"), she also has the power to stop its flow. She can as easily incite him to revolt as suppress him totally, let him speak or reduce him to a dead silence. Clay's awakening, when he discovers the truth about his adversary and himself, is brutal. Jones is defining at once theatre's func- tion to warn—the shout of alarm and war it must sound—and its very limits. But he also announces the beginning of a new revolutionary era that will come after the music and the show have ended: turning against whites the very lessons learned from them, blacks will kill:

> And then maybe one day, you'll find they actually do understand exactly what you're talking about, all these fantasy people. All these blues people. And on that day sure as shit, when you really believe you can "accept" them into your fold, as half-white trusties late of the subject peoples . . . and not a watermelon in sight . . . and with eyes for clean hard useful lives, sober, pious and sane and they'll murder you. (P. 36)

Clay's awakening comes too late (he has accepted for too long his dependency in history, like his duel with Lula) for his liberation. Or, on the contrary, this awakening happens too soon: individual revolt leads to defeat, and a purely verbal assault remains ineffectual. Blacks may not be ready for a revolution, which requires concrete planning and organization. In his critique of Clay, who prefers rhetoric to action, Jones is beginning to question the black intellectual who is alienated from the masses ("My people don't need me to claim them") and con- demned to isolation.

The white audience to whom *Dutchman* is addressed can mistake the resolution, which seems to contradict Clay's message: when Clay an- nounces the destruction of America, it is he who is killed. Clay's death thus appears to reestablish order and restore harmony to a threatened system. Yet Clay's death must be seen not as a concession to the white audience but as a dramatic necessity dictated by a faithfulness to history and theme. The ritual murder perpetuates the infernal cycle of repres- sion, and Clay is only one of many victims.

The targets of Jones's drama are precisely those objectives that Lor- raine Hansberry presented as desirable: integration, access to the middle class, dialogue with liberals. Through Clay's experience, intended as that of the black bourgeoisie, Jones reminds us that mobility into white society is a lure, that the black man remains a second-class citizen: Jones cautions against the conquest of the white woman and the illusion that vengeance comes through fighting her.

Clay's point-by-point attack on Lula for her assaults initiates the trial of the liberals, which will follow that of the "white Negroes." Clay's monologue serves a rhetorical and militant function. It is an act of denunciation, of a faith in regaining independence. Clay reclaims the right of the black man's heart to beat its own rhythm, the "good Negro's" right to be the "nigger" when he feels like it. He affirms his belief in the strength of the blues people and challenges whites to understand the message transmitted through the music:

> that Bessie Smith is saying, "Kiss my ass, kiss my black unruly ass." Before love, suffering, desire, anything you can explain, she's saying, and very plainly "Kiss my black ass" . . . And I'm the great would-be poet. Yes, that's right: Poet. Some kind of bastard literature . . . All you need is a simple knife thrust. Just let me bleed you, you loud whore, and one poem vanished. (Pp. 34–35)

In rejecting the white woman—"You great liberated whore"—Clay demystifies the attraction black men feel for her and denounces her seductive pretensions. He foretells the apocalyptic doom of the entire white race: "We'll cut your throats, and drag you out to the edge of your cities so the flesh can fall away from your bones, in sanitary isolation" (p. 36).

For the black artist every creative act is a burst of violence. "If Bessie Smith had killed some white prople she wouldn't have needed that music." This essential phrase comments both on Clay's speech, whose effect is questioned again, and on black theatre which in spite of its verbal violence remains powerless. Clay must die not only because there is no place for him in fossilized America (as Jones saw it upon his return from Cuba) but also because the destiny of a knowledgeable and consenting bourgeoisie equals a half-death. More than Clay's death, the play dramatizes the death of a country that no longer offers anything but destruction. The other travelers on the subway are accomplices, eyewitnesses who intervene only to set the stage for another encounter and another death. Lula, as captain of the cursed ship and a crew of living dead condemned to an eternal voyage on the ghostly train, records each murder as a death-stop. As for Clay, he is less dead when Lula stabs him than he was in first yielding to her seductions. As victim, he dies regenerated and his death represents a necessary sacrifice.[18]

If Clay embodies the prerevolutionary hero, an adamic figure who holds onto a certain innocence, then the protagonist of *The Slave*[19] makes a double leap in history. The play goes back to the past of the impenetrable, shuffling slave who hides under many masks. It projects into the future to a new phrase of revolutionary struggle that Clay had prophesied. In the character Walker Vessels, two personalities merge: the renegade slave eager to break his chains and the revolutionist already in the struggle. Walker touches upon the slave's potential without ever eliminating the vestiges of servility. Like a ghost of history the slave haunts the fires of the revolution.

The plot of *The Slave* harks back to Clay's speech in *Dutchman*. Racial war has been declared and blacks have risen in battle against their oppressors. Jones, however, is not interested in the military action. The gunshots and explosions serve only as a backdrop to the confrontation that happens on stage. Walker Vessels has left the battle for a brief return to the white world where he used to live. He visits his former wife, Grace, and her liberal intellectual husband, Easley, to claim custody of his two daughters before they become cultural mulattoes. While the battle rages outside, words fly like bullets among the three characters. Walker judges white America in the persons of Grace and Easley, who in turn denounce the black revolution. The verbal violence becomes physical. Walker kills Easley, and Grace is crushed by a tumbling wall at the moment when she worries about her children's safety.

Walker, like Clay, vilifies the system that dictates his identity; he rejects pity and opts for violence. Also like Clay, he knows that the language he speaks is not his own, but at least his ability to express himself is a weapon that can be used against his enemies. Words fall like fists to the face; it is a time for action.

Grace and Easley, in response, denounce the excesses of the new revolution in the name of a humanism they all used to share. The world Walker seeks to create is thus confronted by the one he left behind and is about to destroy. According to Easley's cultural criteria, Walker is a "dirty nigger," dangerous and racist. Taking his enemies literally, Walker is about to assume the role of sexual aggressor (he will attack his former wife) and killer. If Easley insists on casting him as Othello, Easley's own role as Iago will be no more enviable ("If a white man is Iago when you see him, chances are he's eviler when you don't").

In *The Slave* as in *Dutchman* the white protagonists criticize blacks. Lula's insults, which judge the black middle class, are echoed in Grace and Easley's liberal critique of the revolution — it is suicidal. Other plays of the sixties will repeat their objections: "Is the whole world yours . . . to deal with or destroy? You're right! You feel! You have the only real vision of the world? . . . You're crazy now. This stupid, ugly killing you've started will never do anything for anybody. And you and all your people will be wiped out, you know that" (p. 820). Grace denounces the immaturity of the black leaders and the horror of a war that kills so indiscriminately. Easley contests the revolutionary process because it does no more than reverse the roles: "What do you hope to change? Do you think Negroes are better than whites and that they can govern a society *better* than whites . . . so the have-not peoples become the haves? Even so, will that change the essential function of the world? Will there be more love and beauty in the world?" (p. 821).

The reversal of roles is exactly what blacks anticipate. And it is also the foundation of the new drama. *Dutchman* makes Clay into a victim, and *The Slave* takes revenge by making Walker a killer. The black revolution has reached the stage where it cannot accept the arguments of an obsolete morality and a decadent aesthetics that condemn murder as an assault on love and beauty. Walker recalls the prejudice brought against blacks who supported the American left in the thirties. The time is past for the political neutrality advocated by an elite frightened by violence.

Walker accepts neither judgment nor advice from whites. The point of his struggle is not to understand white consciousness or the rationalism that leads to Easley's death. Jones proposes a resolution that goes beyond logic. When Easley pounces on Walker he is killed in self-defense. "Easley was in his right mind, that's the reason he died." Grace's death from an explosion is a dramatic necessity. When Walker tells her that the children she wants him to save are already dead, she dies asking the same question as the spectators: "How do you know they're dead?" Walker's affirmation is contradicted by the crying of a child, and the ending is unresolved.

Despite the vehemence of the revolutionary message, the play remains ambivalent. On the one hand, the appearance of a black actor in arms on stage has a manifest significance. The weapon is more than a symbol: it affirms that blacks have given up defending themselves with words learned from whites. In this sense *The Slave* prefigures the advent of the Black Panthers. In the history of Afro-American theatre, Easley's death marks a symbolic turning point between words and acts. After so much dialogue and verbal jousting, Jones's theatre will eliminate all intellectualization and will emphasize stage directions and action. Ritual gestures will take over from verbal displays.

On the other hand, Walker's entrance in the play's prologue underscores the duality of his character by giving him historical dimensions. The prologue represents both the hero's origin and his return after revolutionary awareness. The slave is a potential revolutionary, but the revolutionary can still be a slave. One critic, Henry Hewes, sees the death of the revolution prefigured in the character of the old slave: the vanquished revolutionary has become an old man who wanders like a ghost reminding America of its inexplicable injustice to blacks.[20] Having the dual function of prologue and epilogue, Walker-the-slave's monologue frames the action and transforms it into an intermediary episode; it also comments on the events that follow:

> Whatever the core of our lives. Whatever the deceit. We live where we are and seek nothing but ourselves. We are liars, and we are murderers. We invent death for others . . . But figure, still, ideas are still in the world. They need judging . . . just because they're *right* . . . doesn't mean a thing. The very rightness stinks a lotta the time . . . Time's a dead thing really . . . and keeps nobody whole. (P. 813)

The slave becomes the image of "an old man full of filed rhythms . . . and great ideas." He is perhaps only an idea that "might set you crawling like a thirsty dog, for the meanest of drying streams. The meanest of ideas."

Walker, like Clay, is an unfulfilled man. Jones acknowledges Walker's weakness,[21] which shows him to be more preoccupied with the past than with revolution. One cannot help drawing a parallel between the character and the author who has accounts to settle with the Greenwich Village intellectuals around whom his own poetic vocation had developed and with the white woman he first married. The autobiographical temptation is not unimportant: Walker is still a slave to the white world to which he returns in order to justify himself. He has not shed the past represented by the old man in the prologue, whose elliptical phrasing embodies both the submission of a slave and his future metamorphosis. However, Jones does not complete a personal destiny; he projects it metaphorically as the fate of black theatre. Like Walker, the theatre must free itself from the desire to explain itself to whites and to offer reasons for its revolution.

Arm Yrself or Harm Yrself, the formula title of another play by Jones, indicates the choice blacks must make and the path the new drama will follow: a celebration of armed struggle, a denunciation of evil perpetuated by the acceptance of the rules or language of the enemy. Precise rituals and new images will create a mythology of destruction and regeneration outside the modes of white theatre.

Dutchman and *The Slave* represent decisive steps. Clay's revolt and the implacable war led by Walker against the white world open the way for a theatre that, far from seeking reconciliation, lays bare an irreconcilable antagonism. Beyond the moralist realism of Hansberry, Jones aspires to the realm of myth from a firm basis in history.

The Toilet, presented for the first time at the Actors Studio in 1962, is another play about settling accounts.[22] Ray (alias Foots), a sensitive and intelligent youth, is another version of Clay; like Clay, Ray is marginal and ambivalent. The action, as in *Dutchman*, takes place in a subterranean world, this time in a gloomy and nauseating school lavatory, which serves as a metaphor for America.

Ray receives a love letter from a white boy named Karolis and is forced by his black friends to meet Karolis in the bathroom for a smoke. Verbal jousts among the adolescents lead to a fistfight. Karolis at first has the advantage, and he reveals that Ray has responded to his advances. The attraction is reciprocal, but the code of the gang disavows any love between blacks and whites as a threat to group solidarity. Having betrayed his friends, Ray must publicly deny his attachment to Karolis. Inflicting violence on Karolis is a ritual through which Ray restores his shaken authority. Having atoned for his fault, and left alone with his "enemy," Ray extends a gesture of love by cradling wounded Karolis in his arms.[23] Thus the love between blacks and whites is not totally condemned: it can overcome the rules imposed by both groups. Ray's liaison is doubly perverse since it involves another boy and one who is white. It is this homosexuality that is condemned in a world which values virility. Theodore Hudson suggests that sexuality is initially brought into question by setting the action in the urinals, for urine is a symbol of sterility.[24] Yet, that does not keep a contradiction from surfacing between the denounced perversion and the tenderness of Ray's last gesture.

The homosexual attraction between Ray and Karolis appears as an aesthetic challenge to the social order. It is disavowed by the gang in the name of a code of ethics that sees it as a betrayal. Ray's friends think his love for Karolis is a way of being accepted in the white world. Karolis is identified with white power that threatens black virility. Metaphorically, homosexuality appears as suicidal and reminds us of Cleaver's analysis in *Soul on Ice* of the "racial death-wish": homosexuality as a sign of degeneration and misused creative energy is an escape from reality.

Langston Hughes once recommended a double cast for *The Toilet*, suggesting that the action take place in a white school where a black boy would be beaten up. This suggestion would obscure the point of the play, which is not to denounce racial inequality but to eliminate obstacles to awareness. Hughes's interpretation would all but obliterate the new level reached by black theatre.

The play's main interest is not homosexuality or the assimilated in-tellectual. Rather, for the first time, Jones plunges to the core of black life to find dramatic structures. He studies the world of ghetto youth, a world governed by a highly theatricalized code that expresses anguish, hate, and frustration. In this realm every speaker is a rival who must be conquered, and aggression is verbal before it becomes physical; the play follows the same pattern as *Dutchman* and *The Slave* in attempting to become less intellectual. In a more general way, these verbal assaults in Jones's early plays may remind us of the cruel games in Albee's theatre (*Who's Afraid of Virginia Woolf* shared a bill with *Dutchman*); but they are more specifically modeled upon the dozens, verbal contests played by ghetto youths.

The insults exchanged in the dozens are often the same as the stereotypes whites attribute to blacks, particularly concerning physical features or sexuality. The obscene language defies the taboos and puritan norms of American culture. A youth may endure the insult without flinching and respond with humor and detachment; at other times he may take it to be an aggression. But he must always improve upon the insult and turn it back against his opponents. In theatre, these affronts take on a ritualized form. Each line is delivered not to con-tradict the other but to go one better: the retort is both an attack and a new insult. Tone and tension mount until one of the two players gives up or loses his temper. The winner is the one who literally has the last word. The game is always played before a listener who serves as a jury and a chorus; he taunts the players, comments on their achievements, and sees that the rules are followed.

These verbal games usually are accompanied by the athletic movements of basketball or boxing, which bring to the performances a whole set of gestures full of dramatic possibilities: teammates pass around an imaginary ball, imitating the moves of professional players; each player has a nickname according to his skill, Big Shot, Foots, and so on. Musical effects are sometimes added: fingers drumming on a table, feet tapping, or heads bobbing to an imaginary rhythm. Anyone watching the dozens becomes an active spectator, contributing hand-clapping, shouts, whistles, or boos to encourage the adversaries. It is not difficult to see how the inclusion of these ritual bouts can enrich the new theatre. Through them black culture discovers its own theatricality.

The central ritual of *The Toilet*—the expiation for betrayal which happens through ridicule in a sordid sanctuary, where someone's bleeding head can be pushed into a toilet bowl—is modulated by numerous games, gestures, and exchanges charged with the same

metaphorical functions for violence and cruelty as are modes of performance. The dramatic form thus borrows from black culture and
not from the dominant culture, which is alluded to only through
parody.

Jones's *The Baptism*, first performed at the Writers Stage in 1964,[25]
sets up a confrontation between the church and the message of love it
pretends to preach. The title is ironic, for the play rejects baptism as an
immersion in a hypocritical religion. A tearful black youth takes refuge
in a church, declares himself a sinner, and asks the pastor to pray for
him. The pastor discusses with a homosexual his ideas on love and fails
to save the youth who is seduced by the homosexual. An elderly black
woman accuses the boy of masturbating during prayers; she assumes the
role of confessor and asks the pastor not to intervene on the sinner's
behalf. The homosexual denounces the hypocrisy of the church and its
fascination with spirits, and asks the youth to dance for freedom. A
chorus of virgins offers him a new temptation. Sensing his return to sin,
the boy asks for baptism. The women think he is Jesus. Aroused by him,
they try to repress their attraction and to punish the cause and object of
their desire: Christ must be crucified. A messenger arrives, sent by the
Father (father of the boy? Father of Christ?), and despite the boy's protests, puts a stop to the ritual of sacrifice.

Jones is writing his own version of Christianity. God, the Father,
understands his error and destroys his creation; he calls his son back
before he can be crucified once again. Caught up in a world in ruins, the
Savior is nothing more than a naive creature. Far from redeeming the
world, he comes instead to plead for his own salvation. He knocks at the
wrong door, for the church is impotent, and his childlike innocence cannot save him from evil. Adhering to the judgment of the church, the
boy confesses, but he is led astray. The real baptism lies elsewhere; the
world needs not love or mercy but one big grenade to blow it up. In the
last scene, the homosexual, the only wise figure in the play, stands alone
among the corpses piled on the floor.

The church is tried without pity. The pastor who heads it is vile,
greedy, hypocritical. The old women have given their lives to religion
out of spite; it becomes a territory they can control and an outlet for
their emotions. Jones here denounces the role the church plays for
women and the role they play in the church, transforming it into a
matriarchal institution to emasculate the black man who is branded as a
sinner and a lost sheep. The homosexual is the denouncer whose morals
are no more perverse than those of the women obsessed with the "omnipotent" god. The church, moreover, is condemned for its pharisaism;

its compromise with power has done irreparable harm to the black psyche. The Christ child renounces his redemptive mission and takes up arms, for there will be no second crucifixion.

Baptism is more important for the theatrical use of religious ritual than for its message. Religion is not only an institution that is blamed but also a dramatic mode that sets up a dialogue between the individual and the group; it is a whole complex of emotions expressing the frustrations and fantasies of waiting for a messiah. The actual baptism is an immersion in weapons and blood. The great Christian rituals—confession, baptism, crucifixion—are evoked only for parody. This blasphemous irreverence is expressed through the sexual metaphor that describes both divine action and the dealings of the pastor. The juxtaposition of sexual and religious words in the willfully sacrilegious language exposes the obscenity of the church in which sexual perversion is a metaphor for all other perversions. The humor in the play relies upon this incongruity. The sacred church is shown to be more sordid than the urinals of *The Toilet*; it is not childish masturbation that profanes the sanctuary, but the hysteria of the repressed virgins and the corruption of the pastor.

Turning to the chapter "Heretics" in Jones's novel *The System of Dante's Hell* (1965) we can see how iconoclastic acts should help recover the full meaning of rituals in a different religion: a black man estranged from and frightened by his blackness is invited by a woman to immerse himself in black life in order to establish contact with his brothers, far from the control of whites. By rejecting the traditional rituals, *Baptism* announces this same rite of regeneration for the black man; the burlesque mode turns it into a kind of farce, but the allegorical intention also makes it a morality play.

Jones/Baraka: A Revolutionary Theatre

Following *Baptism*, a whole series of Jones's plays present different rituals that try to identify and eliminate the forces of evil. One among them, *A Black Mass*, first staged in Newark in 1965, holds a special place.[26] Whereas *Baptism* used a Christian setting, *A Black Mass* returns to the time of creation when evil came into the world and was first opposed.

Jacoub, one of three magicians in a laboratory, pursues his research to create a new, autonomous organism. He invents a white beast. His friends entreat him to get rid of the evil creature, and he gives in only when the monster turns against him. He decides to exile it in the North, but it is too late. The beast attacks and kills the magicians before going on a rampage throughout the world.

Jones's interpretation of the myth of Yacoub differs slightly from the creation myth of the Black Muslims. According to them the first men, who were black, discovered they could change pigmentation; Yacoub was a genuis of the black nation who created the first white man. For this diabolical invention, he was banished by his peers from the earthly paradise. In creating the demons, however, Yacoub was obeying the will of Allah, who wanted to put the black nation to a test for six thousand years. The blue-eyed devils proved their wickedness, and the time has come for their reign to end.[27]

In *A Black Mass* the dramatization of the modified myth works on two levels: as a theoretical debate that sets Jacoub against his colleagues and as a visual action when the hideous beast is set loose in the world, devouring everything in its path. The play also raises several issues about the power and limits of science, time, madness, and logic. Man is his own creation; his weakness and his blind faith in his powers give birth to the unclean beast. In another version of the myth, Yacoub simply falls asleep after locking up the beast in a cave. The beast escapes and roams the earth; generations later, blacks wake up, reclaim their former power, and recover their true place in the universe.

This argument continues the trial of Western culture sketched out in *Dutchman* and *The Slave* where Jones denounces intellect devoid of feeling. His criticism is taken from the myth and from the cosmological vision of creative forces in struggle. Yacoub's curiosity is scientific and aesthetic (here a sign of decadence) while the other magicians are concerned about the ethical order. Evil is disorder, a tipping of the scale in favor of demonic forces. In the infinite space where the scientists live, time is the enemy because it alters the rhythm of the universe, turning it into frenetic pursuit. The evil caused by the beast is translated into cosmic terms. Human beings are affected, women first. Space contracts, and harmonious relations among men are destroyed. Life itself is threatened.

Here the didactic function of the theatre consists not only of ideological debate but also of symbolic representation of the myth through images. Forces come into conflict before our very eyes: one good, the other evil; on one side blackness, a soothing music, rhythmic and harmonious dance; on the other side whiteness, violent outbursts and howling, and unrestrained license.

White culture and the Judeo-Christian myth of creation are symbolically inverted. Whiteness connotes corruption and evil. The magician's perplexity before the strange animals responds to the perplexity of Western scientists discussing the complexion of the continent they seek to conquer. Just as blackness is only a construction on the part of whites, the white monster is created entirely by blacks. The magicians' discussion about this diabolical creature — symbolically represented by a lizard — too closely resembles European attitudes toward Africans not to be taken as a parody. Just as to white explorers' ears blacks emitted only grotesque sounds, the monster in *A Black Mass* expresses itself by grunts and groans, offering the burlesque image of its ability: "You. I me. White . . . (stroking its own chest, slobbering smile crosses his face) Me. Me. White. Me. Me" (p. 32).

Black theatre now responds to white theatre, whose minstrels presented a bestial image of slaves for so long. Here, the beast is seen as a vampire that cannot procreate but that like the plague reproduces by contact. Incapable of giving life, it absorbs it. Whiteness is the symbol of an anemic absence of color, as revealed in the description of the beast's first victim: "Her face draining of color . . . She laughs and weeps in deadly cross between white and black. Her words have turned to grunts" (p. 33).

The black woman, now a colorless robot, returns to the mineral world. The didactic force of this metamorphosis goes beyond the reprimands of magician Nasafi who points out Jacoub's error. The debate among the scientists trying to rid themselves of the plague parodies the talk of whites worrying about "the black problem." Jacoub, an idealist, wants to save the beast, just as liberal and paternalistic America once tried to domesticate and assimilate blacks. Jacoub agrees that the beast cannot be educated (a favorite argument of slaveholders) and would be better off sequestered (that is, segregated) in the fields of the North (an image of the ghetto). The monsters are believed to be incapable of love or compassion. And when Jacoub tries to show he can instill love in his creature, it attacks him; it turns upon the magicians with obscene growls and kills them. The last scene has a dual meaning. It shows the destructive madness of the white cultural ethos: after corrupting the black woman, the beast devastates the world. And it evokes the sudden awakening of black power: the beast breaks free from those who try to control it.

Here Jones uses myths and legends for parody. The character of Jacoub recalls other sorcerers and magicians, notably Faust and Frankenstein. *A Black Mass* offers a burlesque modification of Western legends. By the semantic changes that give it racial implications (the black scientists versus the white creatures), the conventional dramatic pattern is altered. The play abounds with mocking references to the biological laws that brought so much credit to white scientists. Jacoub embodies the romantic delirium, the Western hubris of scientific knowledge—he is Faust, Frankenstein, and all the racist theoreticians combined. Bringing in religious myth, popular legend, and pseudo-scientific theory, Jones shows the power black theatre holds to rewrite the myths. He is encouraging black audiences to revive former beliefs and to prepare a "black mass" in order to correct the errors of the past.

The epilogue, spoken by a narrator through a loudspeaker, turns spectators into witnesses of the drama that has occurred: "And so Brothers and Sisters, these beasts are still loose in the world. Still they spit their hideous cries . . . Let us find them and slay them. Let us declare Holy War. The Jihad" (p. 39).[28] This epilogue attests to the heuristic function of the theatre: an action involves the dramatis personae, who in spite of their wisdom and intelligence do not grasp its full meaning. The theatre must show their error and the unforeseeable consequences of their acts. The spectator is warned; he should see to it that these events do not happen again. But the epilogue, addressing the black spectator, brings out Jones's major innovation: whereas white spectators were attacked in Jones's first plays, A Black Mass alludes to whites only secondarily, in reference to the images of blacks in the white mind. Resolutely didactic, this theatre educates blacks by presenting images drawn from myths that provide a broad and coherent explication of their situation. This vision of the world is Manichean; it dictates an unequivocal line of action: good and evil must be differentiated as clearly as black and white. Only then will blacks be able to restore harmony to the world. If the black man fails in this mission, he will not deserve to live.

Two other works in the collection Four Black Revolutionary Plays present the fate of those who do not deserve to live. The episode of the black woman contaminated at the end of A Black Mass is continued: in spite of herself she becomes an accomplice of corrupt powers. The theatre pursues a symbolic pattern: having denounced the evil that whites propagate in the world, it also threatens blacks who deliberately or unknowingly collaborate with whites. This act of purification, of ridding the black nation of all contamination and restoring its unity, begins with Experimental Death Unit # 1.[29] In this play two white men want to have sex with a black woman, from whom they hope to recover the feeling of real vitality. As they compete for her attention, she becomes eager to give in to their advances. But black militants arrive and kill the two men and the woman before departing for other battles.

By attacking the white men the militants avenge the insult their racial sister has suffered. But they kill the woman to punish her for complying with whites in a degrading relationship. The murders serve a double punishment. The woman, however, dies without understanding her crime; it is up to the spectator to realize the intent and meaning of the punishment. The death of the prostitute, here taken literally, elsewhere symbolically, should set an example. Just as the adolescent in *Baptism* fails to reedeem a rotten world, the black woman cannot save whites from the decadence that condemns them; contact with them only corrupts her. But while the adolescent escapes the catastrophe, the black woman must perish so that the community can be purified. Jones explores the image of the black as an object for the caprice of whites. At the same time he inverts the myth of black hypersexuality by showing the obsession that drives whites to their deaths. Although the theatre had often denounced the black woman's complicity, it had never before sentenced her to death. The militants show no hesitation or regret about their act. A line from one of them—"That bitch looks just like your mother"—borrows from the dozens and is just as irreverent: woman is whore and mother. Herein lies another warning: family ties will not stand in the way of purification. Significantly, too, the indictment of the white woman (*Dutchman, The Slave*) is here extended to her black sister.

Experimental Death Unit implicitly alludes to Beckett's theatre. Duff and Loco, the crazy and comical whites, closely resemble Gogo and Didi, Pozzo and Lucky, of *Waiting for Godot*. This reference to the play that best represents Western decadence actually mocks the theatre of the absurd. It also reclaims black theatre's ability to rid itself of stooges like Duff and Loco in order to accomplish more constructive goals.

In the allegory *Madheart*[30] Jones unveils another kind of prostitution to the white world. Two women, Mother and Sister, unwittingly devote themselves to death. A black man and woman try to save these victims from the clutches of a white Devil Lady, a kind of vampire who thinks she is immune to death. As her wounded body jerks in spasms and refuses to die, Mother and Sister express their loyalty to the world of "white magic" by performing a pantomime of sterile roles: science fiction "niggers," salesmen hawking the charms of available black women, prostitutes defending their territory, blacks becoming "white" by embracing the ethics of America. Finally exhausted and barely breathing in the contaminated air, the women are about to dress up in fake mink coats to follow the funeral of frozen roaches. The Black Man tries in vain to bring them back to their senses, but they prefer a white man "just as sof' and sweet as a pimple." When the black man again raises his sword against the Devil Lady, Sister doubles over as if she were the one stabbed. The Black Woman becomes angry seeing her companion pity these creatures already sold to the devil, for she alone merits his attention: "I am the black woman . . . The one who runs through your dreams with your life and your seed. I am the black woman. The one you need . . . Now you must discover a way to get me back, Black Man. You and you alone must get me. Or you'll never . . . Lord . . . be a man" (p. 81). She pleads for the wholeness of a life without illusions. But instead of advice, the man wants her submission and love. Only then will man and woman be reunited. In a last resort, the Black Man vows the annihilation of Devil Lady and her culture. As for Mother and Sister, they will have to choose between living black or dying white. The man sprays them with a firehose; this baptism brings about their rebirth.

The punishment here is less extreme than in *Death Unit*. Once the object of corruption is suppressed, the two women can perhaps be saved. They must be helped, not destroyed. For the first time, the elimination of a fellow black poses a problem: may one's own flesh and blood be killed? In contrasting the scrupulous Black Man with his lucid but severe companion, Jones stages the dilemma of the young revolutionary. *Madheart* proposes a message of compassion even if love is first manifested by a slap that reduces the woman's pride and by a violent bath that destroys and purifies the body. Two groups, the assimilated ones and the revolutionaries, are brought together as one family, which must be preserved.

This play is important for understanding the significance of the black woman in Jones's work and the fundamental ambiguity of her situation. The ideal black woman (as opposed to the corrupted and alienated one) is held up as an object of veneration and a powerful force in the community and at the same time is made submissive to the black man, the leader of the nation. Her submission to the man is considered essential; it is as crucial to the building of a black nation as is the bringing together and the redemption of all its members.

The subtitle of *Madheart* as a "morality play," a miracle or allegory, shows it to be a parable of the cultural problems that collide with black nationalism. The sexual metaphor of *Dutchman* comes up again in a new exploration of the fundamental relationship between the black man and the white woman. As much coveted as she is protected, the white woman continues to be an object of desire: conquering her is a way of triumphing over taboos. But this passion and conquest divert the black man from his true mission and compromise the success of his revolution. *Madheart* thus achieves the exorcism that Clay and Walker never attain. Devil Lady is stripped of the sexual allure that Jones attributed to Grace and especially to Lula. The devil woman is a dream; killing her, the black man purges himself of a degrading desire.

By suggesting a fascination that the white woman exerts on black women, *Madheart* takes the metaphor of enslavement a step further. The Mother is condemned for encouraging this dependence and perpetuating the emasculation begun by whites. This condemnation leads one to think that Jones is arguing against the tradition that, in *Raisin*, makes the black mother a heroine of integrationist theatre. In revolutionary drama, the black woman frees her companion from the mother who chains him to white society. Infusing him with strength and a lost creativity, she embodies a new consciousness. The militant man, for his part, will keep her from making the mistakes of Mother and Sister. The former gods—the desired white woman, the respected mother—are discarded by the iconoclastic theatre that proposes new models for drama.

Madheart's symbolic structure is organized around a scenic space that is polarized between the horizontal ground crawling with despicable creatures and the vertical strength of those who dominate them. The polarity permeates all movement in this space: contortions, stabbings, falls, tumbles into immobility, quick leaps, slow awakenings. This pantomime, a free dance of life and death, is carefully staged; it is accompanied by background music and sounds (shouts, moans, laughs) that register the range of human emotions. The color symbolism remains what it was in *A Black Mass*: "Blood. Snow. Dark cold cave. Illusion. Promise. Hatred and Death. Snow. Death. Cold waves. Night. Drab. White. Sunless. Moonless" (p. 71). Cold is death; a total liberation is necessary before either the sun or the moon will rise, illuminating virility and femininity, and lighting the march of the black nation to its destiny.[31]

Through an entirely different ritual and the modes of irony and the burlesque, *Great Goodness of Life* dissects the same disease: the blind error of the Negro who wants to be white.[32] The protagonist is the "fattening insurance nigger graying around the temples" discussed in *Madheart*. The exact opposite of the Black Man as "the soul force of our day-to-day happening universe," he acts like the "coon" who made the minstrels so famous.

The play is dedicated to the author's father, as *Dutchman* and *The Slave* were dedicated to his grandparents. Jones pays homage to each generation of victims ignorant of the evil that overtook them. At the same time, he judges the black middle class. Child of a postal employee and a social worker, and sent to Howard University "where Negroes are taught to be white," Jones discovered early the symptoms of "Negro sickness"; he uses his own background in the play—his character Court Royal is a civil servant—and creates a world where the imagination can reclaim its due.

A voice accuses Court Royal of harboring a criminal. Shocked, Court pleads innocence, reeling off the titles of his bourgeois status in a litany recalling the service he has given his country. The thunderous voice reiterates the accusation. Summoned to present his attorney, who turns out to be the court-appointed one, Court is astonished not to recognize his friend Breck in the strange creature who appears: a bald, grinning "house slave" crawling about mechanically with electric wires attached to his back and a large key protuding from his temples. This grimacing robot spews forth discordant sounds and a programmed message. His repeated phrase "Plead guilty" parodies Court's own language. And his body, manipulated by very visible tools, offers Court a mocking image of himself. A second voice, young and strong, accuses Court of being no more than a half-white coward. Although the voice seems familiar, he doesn't recognize it. The attorney is dismissed. Angry that he is left without defense, Court tries to catch up with his friend in a desperate escape, but the sirens sound, machine guns go off, search lights shine on his tracks. The Voice stops him with a formidable laugh that gives way to rattling chains and moans. Terrified, Court declares his submission to the Voice and dances about grotesquely. Men in white hoods enter and exit. A screen projects pictures of martyrs of the black revolution. When commanded to identify the "terrorists" Court admits to knowing them. "Oh son! . . . son . . .dear God, my flesh." He has also admitted to loving the good life, and the Voice offers to spare him. But Court has to participate in a ceremony of "final instruction" and prove his loyalty by executing a terrorist. He is told that it is only a ritual, that the shadow, not the person, will be killed. The shadow, says the Voice, must return to wander in a cold space (the same place the magician in *A Black Mass* wanted to send the white beast). Court Royal agrees to complete the rite in order to return to the good life with his soul washed white as snow. The moment the shadow collapses crying "Papa," Court is returned to the life of a robot. Around this flabbergasted character, a whole pageant has been mobilized to restore history to black people who have been chained, manipulated, massacred, terrified, lost.

Through this protagonist *Great Goodness* also offers a parable about the relations between actor, show, and audience. Before this "coon show" Court allows himself to be manipulated like a bewildered spectator, incapable of emotional involvement or critical distance. He is the "coon" of the theatre, which nevertheless represents the real tragedy of black people; his presence makes comical what should fill us with horror. Grinning even in his sorrow, a stupid and often pathetic puppet, he embodies the comic figure of the *alazon*, not the *pharmakoi* of tragedy that such a situation would claim. As both actor and spectator he is ineffectual, for he fails to see how he is being used on stage or the meaning of the images shown him. The ambiguity of the words he hears eludes him totally. He is anonymous in this world of change and incapable of giving face and reality to the voices that assail him. Accused by both the white power that organizes the repression and the revolutionary tribunal that charges him with betraying his people, Court reacts only to fear and blackmail. He is a victim of the hold of the white world like the woman in *Madheart*, and in the eyes of the black nation his weakness and ignorance are criminal.

Here *Great Goodness* seems to be responding to Genet's *The Blacks* in the same way that *Death Unit* responded to *Waiting for Godot*. Jones borrows several dramatic situations from Genet, only to invert them. He questions and rejects the concepts of the theatre of the absurd.

In *The Blacks* Genet plays on the gap between illusion and reality on many levels. The first level is the ritual "masque" that black actors perform for a white audience. The theatrical game brings Genet's black characters to life. Their victory over whites is acted out in the imaginary world of the *stage;* it is a spectacle. But "this imaginary world draws upon revolt, hatred, and fascination," and "in contrast to the caricature of whites, it is the only real life."[33] When the black actors restage the ritual murder of the white woman and mime the trial of her murderer, Village, the scene is performed before a white court attending the funeral. But there is no body in the coffin, and the action remains purely symbolic. Offstage, however, a real trial is being held, without masks: a black court judges a traitor who must be executed for having abandoned the struggle against white tyranny. The blacks, finally, are capable of destroying only one of their own. The fictive character of the ritual onstage seems to contaminate the real action in the wings. It is only onstage that the play ends with an apocalypse as Village and Virtue become aware of themselves and renounce the imitation of whites. It is thus on the level of the imaginary that victory is glimpsed.

Like Genet, Jones explores the relations between the dominator and the dominated through the mix of hate and fascination that the latter exerts on the former. He dissociates the two feelings, attributing fascination to Uncle Tom and hate to the revolutionary. Moreover, he inverts Genet's scenic pattern: the tribunal of masked black actors in *The Blacks* is concentrated in Court Royal who becomes, paradoxically, the accused. It is petty bourgeois blacks, not whites, who are caricatured. Genet's actors consciously play the role of a court; while Court Royal, persuaded to take real action, does so unconsciously. Never doubting the reality of the disembodied Voice, he follows orders without question. The Voice becomes that of an individual stage director whom Court—a parody of the historical black actor—obeys without fail. The "coon" is both a black bourgeois, who in real life imitates instead of lives, and a traditional black actor onstage who imititates and fails to create. The image of a blind and enslaved life that this character projects connects both to the world of entertainment and to historical reality, each a metaphor of the other. For Jones, the ritual murder happens in the wings. Onstage Court commits the fictive murder in what he thinks is a ritual of purification: "This act was done by you a million years ago. This is only the memory of it. This is only a rite. You cannot kill a shadow, a fleeting bit of light and memory. This is only a rite to show that you would be guilty but for the cleansing rite" (pp. 61–62). By accepting this role, Court becomes an accomplice to white repression and a counterpart to the traitor who, in Genet, is executed offstage. For Jones, judgment takes place not in the background but onstage.

The major difference between the two plays is that Jones is accusing not whites but their black collaborators. In contrast to Genet's blacks, Jones's characters are not aware of being dominated. In a flash of insight on learning of his son's death, Court pleads guilty; he agrees to kill the shadow, the spirit of his son, without understanding the symbolic scope of this act: whoever destroys the spirit of a man is far more guilty than he who harms the body. In this play, subtitled "A Coon Show," Jones presents his character without ambiguity as an antihero, a counter-revolutionary. Breaking with the minstrel tradition that *Great Goodness* parodies, Jones's theatre strives to identify the "coons" more than to punish whites.

In *J.E.L.L.O.* [34] Jones presents the inverse of a "coon show." This time the character refuses his role and takes the initiative to deliver a different message without altering the form of the show. A parody of the popular television comedy "The Jack Benny Show," the play uses the traditional master-servant relationship to show what happens when the black chauffeur, Rochester, refuses to do his employer's bidding. The revolt occurs in the mode of farce: to each order or reprimand from Jack

Benny, Rochester answers with a witty remark that reverses the roles.[35] The servant easily takes the lead, for he knows his employer's weaknesses. When the other stars of the show, Mary and the credulous Dennis, arrive they think at first it is a new script. The expression on Benny's face tells them otherwise. After stealing from the house, Rochester attempts to rape Mary, but he is less interested in sex than in the money hidden under her skirt. The white woman takes pleasure in the idea of rape and faints with vexation when it does not happen. Rochester then kills them one by one, including the show's announcer who comes on to read the commercial: "The Benny Show has been brought to you by Jello, America's favorite gelatin dessert." The ritual phrase that ends the program reassures the television viewer that his favorite show is a regular broadcast. But the play's audience is not fooled; for them a different sort of ritual has been created, and familiar characters assume new and disquieting roles.

To the stereotype of the good servant Jones has added the character of the trickster; the clever, deceptive valet, the criminal without scruples, is a popular hero that black spectators recognize. The play takes the plot of a well-known show and a situation common to theatre as well as to animal tales and folk ballads: the miser who is robbed and the servant who deceives his master. Racial implications add a new dimension to the theme. The humor of *J.E.L.L.O.* should get an easy response from the audience. Written in 1965, the play was not judged to be so innocent, for it was excluded by the publisher from *Four Black Revolutionary Plays*. In a note entitled "Why No J-E-L-L-O" at the end of the collection of plays, Jones complains: "In an era when Lyndon Johnson is accused in a dumb joke evenings of having knocked off the first Kennedy . . . this publisher has the nerve to censor and refuse to publish the play, J-E-L-L-O, as attacking a public figure's private life."[36]

The play was often staged before black audiences, and Jones made it into a prototype of the kind of street theatre he wanted to pursue, a revolutionary theatre inspired from *commedia dell'arte* as much as from agitpop. His project was similar to those of other radical groups like the Teatro Campesino and the San Francisco Mime Troupe. The dramatic complexity and ambiguity of his earlier plays thus evolved toward more popular forms, eliminating both ideological and emotional subtleties.[37]

Black collaboration with white power finds its most spectacular trial in the scenario Jones wrote in memory of Malcolm X. With *The Death of Malcolm X*[38] Jones attempts new aesthetic experiments and returns to the dramatic complexity abandoned in his agitprop plays. Far from an apologetic work, the play mentions militant nationalism only through the ironic allusion to the lack of support Malcolm found among his brothers. Malcolm appears only once, in a parodic scene. As demonstrated in his use of quickly moving tableaux, Jones is more interested in the wide coalition led by whites and their black allies to fight the revolutionary impulse. Images of America during the sixties are projected onto a screen as a counterpoint to the dramatic action. These varied techniques of staging in a firmly centered scenic space show the entire panorama of institutions that support repression.

The script uses more stage directions than dialogue to create its play within a play. Jones makes an obvious analogy between the political and the theatrical, as props and actors in both prepare for a dress rehearsal. One takes place in the wings while the other is rehearsed on stage. From his seat the omnipotent director, Uncle Sam Central, sees that each detail of the script and each episode are respected to the letter. The effectiveness of the political operation depends on the effectiveness of the production, and the force of Jones's argument depends on the entire production. Jones thus makes a fundamental point: whatever the stage, the black man is only an actor playing a predetermined script, controlled by an invisible director.

Numerous characters appear in the production. Some are anonymous, others can be identified by their costumes, gait, occupation, or some other symbolic detail. Whites are businessmen, doctors, teachers, military chiefs. The three white leaders are President Hippy in a beard, dark glasses, and blond wig; an obese Klansman with his collection of skeletons; and a bald, potbellied banker with his trophies. All these representatives of power lead a parade where symbols of authority from each historical period and every country march to join in the immense plot. Last comes a crowd of demonstrators. Within this white world blacks are subjected to mysterious experiments: hallucinations, drug addiction, being tied to operating tables or stretchers; dead people receive new white brains, schoolchildren are taught that "White is Right" and watch films caricaturing blacks, demonstrators carry placards that read "Please Cool Me Out White Daddy" or "Freedom or Death." Then Malcolm's face appears on a screen and his resounding voice is heard. Next come respectful defenders of Civil Rights led by an old man who preaches nonviolence in the midst of police brutality. Finally, four black traitors appear and get ready to carry out the orders they have received.

The procession depicts two Americas—Uncle Sam's and Uncle Tom's. The American myth is shown through stark images: the star-spangled banner, uniforms, the dome of the Capitol. In the background appears the grandeur of Europe and America with their institutions: church, government, stock exchange, courtroom, police. The presence of the Ku Klux Klan indicates how far racism has penetrated the national body. A medical metaphor, supported throughout the play by a pseudoscientific terminology, suggests that just as the United States manipulates people, using techniques from brainwashing to lobotomy, so too will theatre conduct an autopsy of the technological civilization which serves the American myth. "Operation Sambo," which prepares this spectacle, is compared to an atomic explosion. It is a matter of sophisticated lynching or of actual ethnocide.

Faced with this all-powerful machinery, Uncle Tom appears as a ridiculous puppet. Reduced to a state of incurable bewilderment, repeating slogans that glorify the United States, and suffering from "Ghandi's syndrome," he totally submits to whites. Without him, Operation Sambo would not have succeeded. This Uncle Tom is the creation of white America: fabricated from leftover pieces in its laboratories, trained to be a servant and traitor, he becomes one of the instruments of power. The caricature spares neither the ridiculous figures who are so feverishly agitated in Uncle Sam's world, nor Uncle Tom, grotesque in his fidelity to the nation that out of gratitude for his services awards him a gold watermelon studded with diamonds.

Between these two worlds and through the succession of images a new myth of Malcolm X is suggested. A television program shows him having breakfast with his family, giving a political speech, and finally being assassinated. In the midst of general hysteria, Malcolm is the only one with any humor: he refuses to be hurried "in order to remain faithful to the stereotype of the nigger who's always late." His legend is created according to the rules for all myths in America. His portrait is what the media presents of any celebrity: an exceptional personality who has the democratic simplicity of a man of the world. The large-scale plan to eliminate him is the only indication that he is the dreaded enemy of Uncle Sam.

Dialogue, which was so important in Jones' early plays, here gives way to a semiotics of body and voice, to songs and movements that are almost choreographed. We have seen the role of pantomime, cries, shouts, and an entire gestural symbolism in *Death Unit*, *Madheart*, and *A Black Mass*. With *The Death of Malcolm X* and especially the later plays, *Slave Ship*, *Bloodrites*, and *Ressurection in Life*, Jones's theatre goes further from dramatic literature toward basic ritual forms and an increasingly figurative language.

Slave Ship[39] retraces the historical voyage of black Americans from slavery to Black Power and the mythical voyage that initiates a spiritual renaissance with a cultural return to Africa. *Slave Ship* evokes the communal life of Africa and the rites that governed it. With the use of the slave ship Jones returns to images from his previous plays: the ghostly ship manned by the living dead in *Dutchman*, the shackled feet and howls in *A Black Mass*, the nauseating odors of *The Toilet*. These elements here recreate the pain of an uprooted people, penned like animals in the holds of a ship. Noises of chains and whips, roars of the sea, shouts of pain and anger, odors of bodies and vomit, with a background of drums and dirges, create an atmosphere of terror. Voices hurl their rage and hatred of the white monster; a woman kills her child before killing herself; bodies feel for their way, some of them mating haphazardly in the crowd; slaves in despair call for their country.

Incorporated into this production is another "pageant," which projects the people towards their past and their future. When the bent bodies rise up they will be not glorious African warriors but humiliated and comic slaves, no longer dancing but prostrated before the "Massa." This transition is achieved through pantomime without music and accompanied by an intermittent play of lights whose beams isolate certain symbolic shadows on the auction block. One traitor sells his brothers for a pork chop. Scenes of revolt alternate with scenes of despair. Uncle Tom reappears in the form of a servile preacher; he is Negro, Knee Grow, or Kneeling Negro, the conciliator charged with handling integration. While he remains motionless in the bent position of a sychophant, the slaves voice their complaints. What begins as a horrifying laugh becomes a melodic song inviting blacks to recover their identity as warriors. In the midst of a martial dance, the servile preacher and his perfidious god are killed. The head of the traitor is thrown among the dancers, ending the oppressor's myths and beginning the celebration of freedom.

This final celebration, in which the audience is asked to participate, should help the black community recover its former spirituality and strength. *Slave Ship* thus challenges the theory that slavery destroyed the soul of black people. The path is not irreversible; the final dance restores unity to the group, which recovers its original harmony after destroying the emblems of the oppressor. This sequence is also set aboard a ship, represented by the stage, where spectators are invited to join the actors. The joyous crowd transforms the ship into a cradle from which a regenerated people will be born. Through audience participation the theatrical event recovers its communal character; collectively forged, it becomes a ritual that creates a coherent myth from a fragmentary reality.

Like so many contemporary black plays, *Slave Ship* presents a twofold metaphor: a slave ship that holds black people in chains that will be broken by a liberating dance; and Afro-American theatre itself, whose history is retraced through character transformations. While other plays merely isolate the different episodes of this history, the action in *Slave Ship* is more complete.

Dance and song help to realize unity on stage. The use of folklore and the Yoruba language along with the presence of the drum (forbidden on plantations) reaffiirm the determination to regain a lost African reality and to turn away from Western cultural models. In fully integrating music and dance into stagecraft, Jones reminds us of their essentially expressive function in black experience. The dramatic development of *Slave Ship* sketches a cycle that brings theatre back to its dionysian vocation following the birth of tragedy on the cursed ship. Jones also recovers the mythic foundation that sanctions theatre's place beside religion and allows it to master "the worrisome and feverish agitation," "the unregulated wanderings of artistic imagination," and "the apollonian dream." Music and myth show the magical strength of their power: "One and the other exalt a reality where dissonance as much as the terrifying aspect of the universe are brought together in jubilant harmony."[40]

In *Bloodrites*,[41] song and dance triumph. The ritual killing of a chicken, whose blood is spilled into the audience, precedes a pantomime or circle dance. Bodies bend and convulse as they struggle against death. Other figures threatening them represent enemy devils while a voice spews out slogans from a loudspeaker. Racial brothers and sisters intone the same hynm: "Raise the race raise the rays . . . raise in the raze of this time . . . We are raised and the race is a sun son's sun's son's burst out of heaven to be god in the race of our raise through perfection" (pp. 29–30). This hymn to the sun, god of the new race, stages the message contained in Jones's volume *Raise Race Rays Raze*.[42] *Bloodrites* reiterates the importance of sacrifice, of blood as the purifying liberator of cosmic and human energy.

Jones's unpublished play without words, *Resurrection in Life*, shows the dynamism of regained energy and brings to an end the Manichean cycle begun by the victory of the beast in *A Black Mass*. Here blacks triumph over the white beast. But from this time on Jones will be more preoccupied with visual effects, using more action and fewer words:

"People *seeing* the *recreation* of their lives are struck by what is wrong or missing in them."[43] Defined in this way, theatre will recreate a collective experience. It reaches the listener more by example affecting the emotions than through a dialectical argument. Stirring up immediate reactions, this play belongs to agitprop and to guerrilla theatre without using their traditional forms. Like them, it teaches a truth that everyone can understand, but it does so by combining elements of the minstrel show, the morality play, allegorical "pageant," and ritual.

The theatre of LeRoi Jones is first of all a militant theatre. Created at a time when riots were breaking out in many cities, when militants like Rap Brown and Stokely Carmichael were calling for urban guerrilla warfare, and when liberation movements found a spokesman and martyr in Malcolm X, this theatre sent out a battle cry against white America and an alarm to blacks still threatened with pitiless repression.

In his proclamation for "a revolutionary theatre," Jones defined the functions this theatre must fulfill.[44] Its repertory follows the directives he outlined. It attacks first the cultural elite and those places cut off from reality where white theatre is developed; it then exposes the tools used to mystify the audience. Breaking into the home of Grace and Easley, falsifiers of knowledge, Walker Vessels symbolizes the intrusion of reality.[45] The rebel comes not to entertain them but to take action against them. The theatre should be one of the laboratories where black magic can be concocted to stop the ravages of the white beast, to frustrate the conspiracies against blacks, be they common citizens like Court Royal or leaders like Malcolm X. Faced with the bloody reality of an America where murder happens every day, the theatre stages other murders: applying to "ofays" the lesson of hatred taught by history, it makes the victims rise up and issue merciless decrees. It teaches whites their own deaths and chooses those who will be burned on its altars.

Accusative, iconoclastic, destructive, this theatre also builds the new nation. After showing the ugliness of monsters, it teaches the beauty of the righteous; after preaching hate, it advocates love. It gives form back to the world, restores the supremacy of the spirit over matter, of the soul over the intellect. "Businessmen of the world, do you want to see people really dancing and singing?" This parodic apostrophe defies white spectators to find in this theatre the exoticism and entertainment they seek. Jones promises them a total distance from familiar surroundings and a spectacle showing "the cruelty of the Just."[46]

According to this dual project as denouncer and regenerator, the theatre organizes around two types of rituals: rituals of exclusion and rituals of participation. The former should purge the black community of the evil acts propagated by whites, this evil of which Artaud says: "If we think that Negroes smell bad we are ignorant of the fact that anywhere but in Europe, it is we whites who smell bad. And I would even say that we give off an odor as white as the gathering of pus in an infected wound."[47] The rituals will exterminate whites and any blacks contaminated by them. As Clay says in *Dutchman,* "They'll murder you . . . they'll cut your throats and drag you out to the edge of your cities so the flesh can fall away from your bones, in sanitary isolation" (p. 36).

From this point on the complex relations between the individual and the group is emphasized by the theatrical ceremony. Just as white society tries to corrupt individuals in order to break up group solidarity, so will the black community isolate the guilty individual whose presence has become dangerous. Its actions are similar to rites of excommunication in Christian societies or perhaps the rites of purification by quarantine practiced in some so-called primitive societies. Often the individual thus punished endures his expulsion without understanding the reasons for it. These tests either inflicted by whites or imposed by blacks on their own are often interpreted in the theatre by a chorus. In its comments and laments the chorus represents the group contemplating its own situation through an individual who embodies those elements of the communal life which hinder awareness.

Finally this theatre invites us not only to contemplate the mystery of creation but to participate actively in it; in so doing it advocates close ties between audience and stage. Transcending the psychology of traditional Western theatre, it emphasizes cosmological and metaphysical dimensions; rising above the contingencies of daily life, it also goes beyond the rational in order to establish the dionysiac. Devoted to the supremacy of the group, it often condemns the individual while trying to abolish tensions between individual and group. The spectator is stirred out of his customary behavior and forced to take part in the disintegration of his individuality, then in his absorption into the community or universe of which he is a part. In Artaud's words, "In the true theatre a play disturbs the senses' repose . . . and imposes on the asembled collectivity an attitude that is both difficult and heroic."[48] Immersion, baptism, violent revelation, liberation of vital energy permit man to grasp his own potentialities. Such is the irreversible direction of "the theatre of cruelty" which "impels the mind by example to the source of its conflicts." In this sense the end result of Jonesian dramaturgy responds to the definition stated by Artaud. Because theatre is collective, it must be contagious:

> The action of theatre, like that of plague, is beneficial, for, impelling men to see themselves as they are, it causes the mask to fall, reveals the lie, the slackness, baseness, and hypocrisy of our world; revealing to collectivities of men their dark power, their hidden force, it invites them to take, in the face of destiny, a superior and heroic attitude they would never have assumed without it.[49]

This theatre develops its own language — a concrete language that addresses all the senses, incorporating voice, intonation, music, mime, and dance. Spoken language occupies a less important place. It becomes both a tool for profanation and the expression of profanity. As an expression of black experience, the voice of "blues people," this spoken language aims toward metaphorical connotation and circumlocution, not toward exact definition or direct expression, which in African tradition are considered signs of rudeness and lack of imagination. It favors paraphrase and slang. Jones has often been accused of obscenity, but he has refuted this charge: the only obscenity is reference to the norms of white culture. (Thus the term "motherfucker" represents in black expression a reality that cannot be denied.) Obscenity sets a whole emotional universe in motion. Accusing black writers of letting themselves be trapped in white language, Jones recalls that it is not enough to repeat that blacks are oppressed; one must examine the reality of the oppression in honest terms, not in the terms whites have used to describe it.[50]

Jones's style evolves from the discursive — in the earlier plays — toward the metaphorical; essentially lyrical and mythopoetic,[51] it relies on sonorous forms that orchestrate a dramatic poem. Jones's language is visceral; his humor is irreverent, fierce. The spectators, besieged by a multitude of impressions translated into a language for which they no longer have the key, may be upset and frightened by the production. The theatre of cruelty thus strives for a raising of consciousness. It imposes unavowed truths that disturb and destroy inhibitions while it uncovers the strength and the true role of the spectator. This knowledge can lead to a change in attitude about life, "something to get us out of our marasmus, instead of complaining about it," Artaud writes. Such is the point of *Slave Ship*. "The image of a crime presented on stage is in spirit something much more fearful than the crime itself."[52] The theatre of cruelty aims not at "realism" but at an image of reality as hallucinatory as the images of a dream.

Poems like Fists

Many dramatists who participated in the revival of black theatre followed the lead of LeRoi Jones. The new drama taking shape around the principles he had articulated in his essays and plays engaged in both the movement of revolt and in the creation of a unified nation. In the tradition of epic theatre and following the heroic example of African warriors, the people took up arms to crush infamy and to restore harmony. The new theatre thus followed Jones's lead: "We want poems like fists beating niggers . . . dagger poems."[53]

It is important to note the links between black poetry and black theatre: many poets, such as LeRoi Jones, Sonia Sanchez, and Marvin X, are also dramatists. In their work theatre and poetry exchange customary structures and images. Jones often presents in a poem the sketch or a synopsis of one of his plays, or he adapts one of his poems dramatically. One form continues to sing the blues; the other abandons its traditional structure to echo the phrasing and motifs of musical composition. Many of Jones's later plays are called "songs," and their lyrics come closer to poetry than to the theatre. Yet they are certainly dramatic: the poem-chant comes fully to life only through performance. The dramatization drawn from poetry and the use of lyrical modes on the stage are evident in the public reading. Read aloud, poetry becomes theatre. Black theatre thus embraces both dramatic poems and "pure" plays. Which form is used will be determined by the message the theatre wants to communicate.

The message of a play is determined by the nature of the discourse, be it conciliatory or accusatory, calling for revolt or simply revealing black experience. Rather than evaluating the new drama in the light of traditional genres, it is more useful to sketch out the typology of discourse it engenders. This discourse is articulated through three principal stages: the call, the denunciation, and the consecration. The first, characterized by a conciliatory and supplicatory language, is an appeal to a white audience, which is considered to be a sympathetic listener, an informed, liberal audience. Denunciation, in contrast, sets the theatre *against* the white audience, which is held responsible for centuries of oppression, and against the Negro audience (Negro as opposed to black), which is thought to be a traitor. In either case, the discussion brings offenses to light and renders judgment. Punishment will occur immediately on stage or sometime in the future. The third stage, consecration, means making a free choice to fulfill a particular mission and to become righteous. This message is addressed to a black audience exclusively, in order to separate the wheat from the chaff so that the healthy elements can be prepared for the regenerative struggle, or to make the audience the source of the black nation and the foundation of the new drama. Admittedly, this distinction among the three stages is reductive, but it can be useful in analyzing the plays created out of a language drawn from social or individual voices.

Allegory, Jazz, and Race Relations

Contemporary Afro-American theatre offers numerous examples of metaphors and wordplay concerning a minority's relation to the dominant culture. Relations between blacks and whites can be defined by means of an image or a rhetorical formula that develops dramatic structure—for example, the image of the cage in *The Bird Cage* by Floyd Barbour,[54] in which whites imprison blacks and set the birds free. In *The One* by Oliver Pitcher[55] a long monologue examines the possible uses of demonstrative numbering when a black man refuses anonymity and the role others have defined for him. Word games of rhymed monosyllables summarize his situation: his ambition "to get" is thwarted by constant postponement, "not yet." In the rhetoric of drama, relations between blacks and whites are reduced to those between dominated and dominator. This basic social reality is often transposed in an imaginary universe through a complex scenic structure. In proposing new forms to express a well-known situation, black theatre reverses traditional roles and genres. The tragedy of black people is often represented, paradoxically enough, by the modes of comedy or parody rather than tragedy.

Archie Shepp's play *Junebug Graduates Tonight: A Jazz Allegory* offers a burlesque representation of white America's relations with its black "children."[56] The characters are Uncle Sam, his daughter America, and a black youth and his family in which the father is a Black Muslim and the sister a prostitute. The play belongs to the tradition of *A Medal For Willie* and *Dutchman*. Junebug marches onto the stage to receive awards from his high school. The "medal" is not awarded to him posthumously as it is to Willie, but he is killed at the end of the ceremony. Junebug is seduced by Uncle Sam's daughter, America, and their relationship is as ambivalent as that between Lula and Clay:

AMERICA: I took you off the streets and fed you! I made you!

JUNEBUG: An ex-cannibal-turned-Christian. Son of Jessie the
maid and Sam the janitor. (P. 48)

America offers to initiate Junebug into the power and corruption of the
United States, but Junebug rejects her and says that he will one day kill
her. He is aware that he comes from Africa, which was raped, and his
new country attracts and repulses him. He agrees to help the pitiful Uncle Sam, who has lost his hat and shivers in the cold. In a symbolic
gesture Junebug offers him his shirt, and more: "When I took that shirt
off tonight it was like handing that old man back all the lies he'd fed me
all my life" (p. 56). Junebug's militancy is not stamped with rhetoric or
flourish like Purlie's, but he is too idealistic to heed his Muslim father's
warning. Chivalrous, he rushes off to rescue America and perishes with
her in a final explosion. The two fathers, Uncle Sam with his bomb and
the Muslim with his rifle, remind their children that it is useless to
dream, that blacks and whites can never come together. Junebug never
is initiated to either the corrupt white world or the militancy of his
father. During a last reunion in a banquet hall—a parody of the Last
Supper presided over by Uncle Sam, at which blacks and whites are
separated while listening to a speech about integration—a gunfight
breaks out causing the masks to fall and the real relations to be restored.

Douglass Turner Ward depicts race relations by playing upon the
customary roles of blacks and whites; he either adopts the conventions
in order to unmask them or inverts situations so as to reveal the per-
manence of behavior. The situation in *Brotherhood*[57] could have been
banal: a white couple invites a black couple to their home; the
American white middle class meets its counterpart in an effort to practice the ideals of integration as proclaimed by the Supreme Court. The
whites take the initiative paternalistically. To avoid shocking their
visitors by the luxury of their lifestyle or by racist objects in their home,
the whites set the stage: they dress modestly, stash away knicknacks,
hide their children in a closet, and place in full view a bottle of Black
and White whiskey as a symbol of the new accord. Enter the guests, who
are ecstatic over the originality of the warehouse decor and the furniture
draped with sheets. The white couple responds by complimenting the
visitors on their clothing, which they actually consider to be in bad
taste. To celebrate this symbolic reconciliation, the whites offer the
blacks some money for their children. When the visit is over, the masks
come off. In the house, the whites remove the sheets and reveal horrible
effigies of blacks. In the street outside, the black couple reverts to ritual
fantasies of vengeance: the woman pierces a voodoo doll with a hatpin;

the man stabs invisible white bodies with a knife. Their pretended admiration gives way to a liberating aggression. The blacks were never
fooled by the comedy of friendship, in which they joined only for profit.
The basic relations between blacks and whites have not changed: condescension and racism on one side, frustration and hate on the other.

Happy Ending, also by Ward,[58] unveils the reality of the master- servant relationship hidden under conventions and etiquette. Ellie and Vi,
two domestics, are worried that their employers, the Harrisons, will get
a divorce. Ellie and Vi's nephew, one of the new generation of
"liberated" blacks, is angry that they are so upset. Soon the nephew and
the audience learn the reason for their sorrow: Ellie and Vi are afraid of
losing the independence offered by their job. While young militants are
kept unemployed, the domestics enjoy a stable and lucrative position.
They help themselves to whatever material goods they want, and the
money they earn helps to support the nephew. Adept in the art of
manipulation like Cap'n Charlie's maid in *Purlie Victorious*, they are
the ones who run the household. The maids reign supreme and the
masters are fooled: "The victors and the vanquished, the top dog and
the bottom dog. Sometimes it's hard to tell which is which." Relations
between whites and blacks, boss and employer are not as simple or as
antithetical as they appear. By appropriating part of the whites' fortune,
blacks are only getting their due. In the end all is well; a telephone call
announces the Harrisons' reconciliation, and the servants can repossess
"their" house.

The couple in *Happy Ending* is similar to the one in Genet's *The
Maids*. The problems, however, are quite different. Unlike Genet's
Claire and Solange, Ward's maids do not feel a mixture of hate and
fascination toward their employers. The threat of divorce certainly plays
the same role in *Happy Ending* as the condemnation of the gentleman
does in *The Maids*, but here the blacks have no emotional investment in
their employers' lives. Ellie and Vi are more concerned about their own
well-being than about saving their employers from disaster. They do not
have to create a ritual to enjoy the illusion that they exist and exert a little power; their power is real. Ward's play reexamines once again the
servility attributed to blacks. It refutes the images proposed by white
society, which delights in visions of its authority, and by black militants,
who condemn any acceptance of the slave condition. Finally, the play
rejects the theory of alienation illustrated in *The Maids*. The domestics
of *Happy Ending* are not victims, and the title clearly indicates a lack of
conflict; there is no murder, no inclination toward vengeance; the
ending is happy. Yet the play does not avoid a certain ambiguity, for it

never questions the status of servants. Ellie and Vi have dominated the situation so well that they are no longer its servants, but neither are they part of revolutionary theatre. Ward is content merely to use roles well known to black audiences in order to invert the minstrel masks worn. The audience should recognize all the strategies for survival. On the level of theatre aesthetics the play announces the beginning of a drama in which humor and irony will take on a more subversive role.

Ward's *Day of Absence*[59] examines race relations in a more historical and mythical way. All the blacks in a small southern town disappear one summer morning as if by magic. The play opens and closes on an exchange between Clem and Luke, whose roles as observers and commentators reflect the role of the audience. Watching over the town as usual, they notice the absence of blacks: "Somp'ums topsy turvy." The blacks' new invisibility stirs up white anxiety and fantasy. A preacher suspects voodoo heresy. The President of the United States declares the town in a state of emergency and offers aid. Official speeches, in a parody of Booker T. Washington, call upon the patriotism of blacks. Flattery alternates with threats: if the blacks make honorable amends, no harm will come to them; if they persist, they will be crucified. The next morning the town returns to normal, believing that the day of absence was just a mass illusion, the nightmare of guilty consciences haunted by the fear of black revolt.

This satirical fantasy is a parody of the blackface minstrel. Ironically, the play discusses blacks but shows none at all. The black man has withdrawn his "grinning face" from the stage and, as a malicious spectator, observes the success of his improvisation from the wings or from the audience. Ward tries to duplicate the conventions of plantation performances by using a limited number of actors and props and no scenery; he creates the atmosphere of farce by suggesting loud, whiteface makeup, costumes, and wigs, and the color scheme of red, white, and blue.

First staged in Greenwich Village in 1965 before an integrated audience that was entertained rather than shocked, the play would eventually be performed by white actors "at their own risk." The subtle message did not provoke the white audience, for the actors were entertaining, not rebellious. As one of the first black shows, it seemed inoffensive. But would the more sophisticated and aware contemporary white audience react like the plantation owner who enjoyed seeing blacks (as he thought) caricaturing themselves? The new conditions of audience reception make *Day of Absence* an insidious invitation to imagine the possible consequences of such an absence; it could be seen as an incitement to strike. (Following the first performances, Harlem militants called for a general strike to be held every year on November 5.)

By relying on earlier traditions, Ward brings subversion back to the theatre, but taken out of context the play loses its duplicity. Today blacks would laugh at an audience incapable of unraveling the code of the slave actors, and the white public would easily apprehend the obvious message. Moreover, the satire directed against an already distant past seems to spare America from the sixties. The caricature of whites affects not a single character as in *Purlie* but a whole network of institutions. Ward is more successful in reclaiming the image of blacks on the American stage: although history has placed blacks in an inferior position, they have devised all sorts of strategies to turn less favorable situations to their advantage. Once again the trickster appears, and Ward draws superbly from a dramatic variation offered by the duped master. By recasting traditional roles and defiantly improvising upon already established scenarios, Ward takes a stacked deck and shuffles the cards.

Ted Shine's *Plantation*[60] repeats the situation in *Day of Absence*, but this time it is the master who is absent. While Papa Joe is off in New Orleans trying to stop integration, the servants quit working in order to obtain their own civil rights. The unexpected birth of a black son to Papa Joe's wife lends support to their cause. Shine is reminding us that black blood runs in the veins of many Americans. The union of Papa Joe and Mama Mina, of the paternalistic planter and the black Mammy, was well known. This unspoken historical situation is archetypal. *Plantation* underscores the debt America owes the black woman who not only reared many of its citizens but also provided descendants to whites. She was not just a companion for sexual play that was judged unsuitable for the too refined or fragile white wife; the black woman also took the place of the white woman when she was sterile. Papa Joe, who is proud enough of belonging to a superior race to crusade against integration, is put in his place by his "honest" servants. His warning to them to "remember your place" becomes ironic. The blacks require the master to fall into line, but he prefers to die rather than be displaced. His death allows the servants to become landowners. Their triumph is more complete than the one in *Purlie Victorious*, for the dangerous institution of the church is overthrown at the same time as the master. As fate would have it, justice is reestablished without revolt, and the birth of a black child in a white family, otherwise shameful and out of the ordinary, becomes part of the natural order of things. As a play about miscegenation, *Plantation* breaks with tradition. White theatre symbolically eliminates the mulatto either by supressing him or by assimilating him:

if the character is good, his positive qualities are attributed to his white ancestry. In the new black theatre the mulatto is returned to his true family, the black community. This reversal has the effect of defining America as a nation of mixed-bloods and, for the theatre, of eliminating "white" characters from a cast that becomes exclusively black. The perception of the racial composition of American society has changed completely.

Victims, Traitors, and Rebels

In contrast to the drama that gives strong roles to blacks and exhibits their small victories, another kind shows blacks as constrained by compromise, tempted to treason, or pushed to revolt. The images of the victim, traitor, and rebel are products of a climate of oppression. This theatre takes up the still active categories of protest from the thirties but goes beyond them. It points out the victims and enjoins them to see themselves as such, and it brings to trial the world that oppresses them. It exposes traitors and calls for their punishment. It presents examples of revolt and foretells the coming of a black nation that will devote itself to the building of a new world.

One of this theatre's first tasks is to show the chains: the physical chains that bind the feet of slaves and whose clanking merges with the moaning voices in *Slave Ship*, and the invisible chains that continue to strangle black people.

Ben Caldwell's one-act plays review the various mechanisms of oppression. Like Jones in *The Death of Malcolm X*, Caldwell reveals the systematic conspiracy of which blacks are the unsuspecting victims. Drawing from real or imaginary situations, Caldwell examines institutions and programs that, under the pretext of helping blacks, only increase their dependency. *Mission Accomplished*,[61] for example, whose title plays upon military and religious connotations, portrays evangelistic Christianity upsetting the small African kingdom of Baboza. Christianity accomplishes its goal, which is not to spread the message of love but to bring African treasures home to Rome. The verbal message is accomplished by sonorous and visual images and by a rapid tempo that reinforces the burlesque tenor of the episode. Just as the church corrupts Africa, white America pursues its "mission" with black people under the antipoverty program. *Riot Sale or Dollar Psyche Fake-Out* denounces this swindle by the government.[62] Cannons spew out money to placate demonstrators who have come to protest the murder of a black youth by police. The crowd grabs up the money and disperses; the weapons have purchased their silence and diffused their anger. Inspired by the ghetto uprisings, *Riot Sale* shows the violent confrontation between the forces of repression and black people, and exposes the duplicity of the system and the blindness of the crowd. The cannons dispense death as easily as they do money.

Top Secret[63] reveals a different kind of conspiracy and control. To limit the spead of the black population a program is started which smacks of both historical truth and science fiction. Physicians have for years been sterilizing black patients. Caldwell imagines the measures that could be taken on a larger scale, a thinly disguised genocide to stem the tide of "the black peril." This believable hypothesis places the black audience in a very real and dangerous position. And here lies one of the missions of nationalist theatre: to guard against threats to the biological existence of black people.

Using a different metaphor, *All White Caste*[64] offers another reflection on the risks of the disappearance of the black community and on the use of the ghetto as a reserve for "white Negroes." (We are no longer, as in *Day of Absence*, in the slaveholding South, but in the urban ghetto where blacks are indispensable to the economy of postindustrial America.) Caldwell denounces the politics of leaders who accept white control, manage poverty, and encourage the proliferation of degrading and carefully planned entertainment. Black capitalism, the attraction of luxury, and belief in an illusory independence are also debunked. The title refers not only to the social reality of a caste that practices segregation, but also to a theatrical situation where all the roles are white or whitewashed. *All White Caste* dramatizes the passage from revolutionary struggle to accommodation to repression. The revolution/repression cycle appears closed. For Caldwell, the metaphor of a black city empty of its inhabitants echoes a real situation: Harlem is populated not by blacks but by naive and manipulated "Negroes" who eagerly gather up the crumbs from the economic banquet table and who, like Court Royal, praise the good life without seeing the walls of their own prison.

A gallery of ironical portraits, *Family Portrait or My Son the Black Nationalist* measures the distance that separates "Negroes" from their black brothers.[65] Characters are identified according to the degree of their commitment to blackness, presented here as the only truth. They have names like Farthest from the Truth, Nowhere near Truth, and Sunshine on Truth. This typology corresponds to the rules of a truth game and to a common practice in black communities of nicknaming people after some physical or moral characteristic. But this naming also serves a symbolic funtion. The Uncle Toms are accused by the new generation. The revolutionary son incurs only the anger of his father whose arguments sound like a broken record.

For Caldwell, theatre must also show white aggression in the domain that concerns it most—art. *The King of Soul; or The Devil and Otis Redding*[66] exposes the conspiracy waged against the black artist. The devil is the white man, and his victim and adversary is Otis Redding. As Jones does with Malcolm X, Caldwell portrays Redding's death as an "accident" planned in detail, for the white world tolerates neither the black artist nor his attempts at autonomy.

The plot draws upon the Faust legend. The devil appears to Redding under different disguises and offers to market his voice, his art, and his life in this Manichean universe where "business" opposes artistic integrity. The devil uses every means to seduce Redding; in exchange for rights of authorship, he offers the singer the material symbols of success. Redding gives in, but refuses to hand over his voice and his life. The devil is relentless and takes his life anyway. The play accuses white power of deliberate homicide as it unveils its Machiavellian traits. It denounces the appropriation and destruction of black talent and the blindness of those incapable of recognizing the devil. *The King of Soul* gives the spectator enough keys to detect the devil under his masks. As required by the conventions of the genre, the play comes close to being a grand farce.

Federal job programs for blacks inspire another of Caldwell's fables, *Run Around*, a fast-paced pantomime that leads the black man in a dizzying course from office to office: from his hideout to the unemployment bureau, from the judge's chambers to the lawyer's office, from prison where he helps a Jew escape, to the courtroom which sends him back once again to his office. The game of "getting the runaround" is regularly used in theatre to evoke the vicious cycles in which blacks are trapped. The expression is also reminiscent of a phrase used in the thirties to describe the federal agency for relief for the unemployed; the National Recovery Act (NRA) was known unofficially as the National Run Around. The play's central motif of the racetrack evokes the game and illuminates the tricks of those who throw things into gear and make the wheels turn. The image itself is the system's game of sending blacks from one institution to another and of condemning them to an eternal wait. In pointing to the trickery at work, the theatre seeks a way out. In Caldwell's play a black actor in whiteface embodies all the interviewers to whom the protagonist is sent. Only the costumes and placards that designate place and function change. The uniformity of the white mask underscores the unchanging face of power. Like *Family Portrait*, the play invites the black audience to break the cycle and initiate a revolution.

In *The Job*,[67] Caldwell examines a government program called Project Negro Opportunity, and sets the action in a welfare office where unemployed blacks gather. A blond, blue-eyed journalist interviews five candidates in succession. The sixth, a musician, refuses this form of questioning and expresses his indignation through the music he plays. He answers the call for revolt by pouncing on the journalist and walking out of the office to the tune of Charlie Parker's "Now Is the Time." The message for revolt comes through the music, which enlarges the term *job* to mean both the *employment* the black man has to beg for in passing through the bureaucratic machinery and the *business* that he must from now on conduct himself. "Now is the time" — the time for physical assault against the oppressor, the time to refuse welfare palliatives, the time to take hold of freedom.

For Caldwell, a new art must have new objectives; and art must teach. The theatre should help the spectator to understand the mechanisms that affect his life. It must furnish the means to change the world for a better life. In this way the theatre approaches Brecht's idea of social function;[68] it is no longer an arena for entertainment as in traditional drama; it becomes a realm of experience. And if this central experience is victimization, then there can be no alternative but to change it. Theatre defines social process from a practical point of view; it teaches the possibility of changing socioeconomic and cultural conditions. The event becomes most important. Action is presented as an ensemble of gestures that demonstrate a situation. In Caldwell's plays there are no debates as in Jones's early works. Dialogue serves only to emphasize the gesture, which is action itself. Caldwell breaks with the discursive tradition of protest theatre to propose a framework that should make blacks aware of their condition as victims and instill the desire to transform the "Negro" into an authentic black man.

Where Ben Caldwell's characters are condemned to "run around" or to wait in vain in bureaucratic reception areas, Lonne Elder presents old men caught up in dangerous games in *Ceremonies in Dark Old Men*.[69] A former vaudeville artist and owner of a barber shop has gone bankrupt. Forced to find a job by his daughter, who supports the family, Mr. Parker refuses to enter the rat race of employment bureaus or to prostitute himself "downtown." The former actor agrees to play in a new comedy: he loans his shop to an illegal organization that competes with white exploitation of the ghetto by selling bootleg whiskey, running numbers, and betting on horses. The game is far more dangerous than the ritual checker match Parker plays with his old friend Jenkins; the whites are not so easily overthrown and the police keep watch. In the end Parker loses, for his son is killed during a robbery.

The metaphor of the game—"We acted out the ceremony of a game"—takes on many forms. Parker's sons and their partners want to put the whites in check, and the onetime comedian wants to get more fun out of life than the game of checkers provides. The "ceremony" unfolds not on a Charlie Parker melody but on a song by James Brown: "Money won't change you / But time will take you on." The protagonist returns to the solitude of his empty shop on a busy Harlem street. The play is a game directed against society and a performance of a vaudeville routine as well as the daily checkers match between two old friends which Jenkins always wins. The champion states: "One of these days you're going to beat me. And when you do it won't have nothing to do with luck—it just might be the unluckiest, worst day of your life."

The prediction comes true. Parker wins at checkers on the day that misfortune strikes his family. The daily ceremony protects the old man from the more dangerous games the young men wage against their armed adversaries. The final game is that of an actor yielding to the rules of the stage. Herein lie the two meanings of ceremony: a ritual that is repeated and a performance that follows certain conventions. Formerly constrained to execute gestures to make people laugh, the old performer is rejected by society. He cannot improvise the new role of a businessman or a gangleader. Nor will he be able to mourn the death of his son. From this character, who cavorts about on an empty stage and without an audience, gradually emerges the archetypal image of the black man whom life changes into a sickly, ridiculous figure condemned to repeat the same part. He is a clown, "an old crippled vaudeville man." At the end of the play, returning home after suffering many failures, Mr. Parker tries a dance step and collapses in the middle of the stage. This brief pantomime comments on the whole play, summarizing the vain efforts of a man who wanted to live but who was condemned to immutability and to silence. Parker's wish to dance and sing is his way of holding back the violence mounting inside him. The episode recalls Clay's claim in *Dutchman* that the black man became an artist in order to smother his rage: give him several men to kill and the "bluesman" will be silenced.

The ruses of blacks, which triumph in the plays by Ward and Shine, encounter a different fate in *Ceremonies in Dark Old Men*. One of Parker's sons asks him if he ever had any special thoughts while doing his comedy routine: "Didn't you ever go out on the stage with a new thing inside of you? One of them nights when you didn't want to do that old soft-shoe routine? You knew you had to do it—after all it was your job—but when you did it you gave it a little bit here, a little acid there, and still, with all that, they laughed at you anyway" (p. 35). With biting humor the play repeats the same message: whatever improvisation the black man brings to the ceremony of his life as codified by America cannot keep him from his destiny.

The Last Shine by Arthur Graham[70] enacts a different ceremony involving social misfits. After forty years as a bootblack, Hambone sees his profession die out. The metaphor of the stage is used once again: the bootblack is also an entertainer, making the rag dance on his customers' shoes while he tells jokes. The invention of synthetic shoes takes away his business and his audience, ironically, just as the Civil Rights Movement is beginning. Joe, a young militant, accuses the bootblack of scorning his black customers and of being just an Uncle Tom who has sacrificed his dignity for an obsolete job. Refusing to hear any more, Hambone strangles Joe, straps his body on the chair, and shines his shoes without sparing the slightest detail of his routine: "There's always a cheerful customer who pays more than the shine I give is worth." The final image sketches the portrait of a traitor who renounces his blackness and kills his brother in desperation. Much as Court Royal sacrifices his son in *Great Goodness*, Hambone sacrifices Joe, who wanted only to open his eyes. As suggested by the name Hambone, often given to good servants in nineteenth-century comedies, *The Last Shine* indicates a swan song, the last performance of traditional black theatre that is weakened by its persistent dialogue with whites. The multiple connotations that surround Hambone as entertainer suggest the theatre analogy and reveal it as a warning.

Herbert Stokes's *The Man Who Trusted the Devil Twice*[71] uses a similar situation: a father who is a school principal betrays his revolutionary son. The play makes an obvious point. A courtroom scene equates "white" with "just" ("white judge, a fair judge") and echoes the equation stated in Jones's poem "Black Art": we are black "and unfair." Through the assertion that whites are fair because they are white, the play ironically denounces an abuse. But it also states a possible reversal: a court of blacks is only a small step away from that of "just" whites. The metaphors of judgment are thus multiplied in order to prepare for an inversion of roles. Judgment by blacks can be as inexorable as condemnation by whites. At the last minute the school principal, who has all the characteristics of Court Royal, tries to keep the police from reaching his fugitive son. But like Court he is threatened by the police and condemned by the militants. Either group can decide his fate. But the theatre leaves nothing to chance: the father, punished by whites for failing in his mission, dies a victim of his error; his son perishes as a victim of the repression. Traitors and rebels end up the same.

In *The Breakout* by Charles Oyomo Gordon,[72] the traitor, Reverend Jackson, is condemned both by blacks who see him as an informer and by white power anxious to elminate him once his services are no longer needed. The action takes place in a "prison without walls or bars," a symbolic rendering of the ghetto, and weaves between the real and the metaphorical. Two prisoners, Slam and Feet, while awaiting "the breakout," dance with a white-faced doll, pretend to fight each other, and tell witty stories, jiving and cracking in the best ghetto tradition. They also replay the comedy of white justice by successively assuming the roles of judge and accused. While this Amos and Andy routine exposes the abuses of power, the Reverend Jackson gets special favors in a neighboring cell. During a conference with the jailers he affirms his faith in the American Dream and alludes to a secret mission revealed to him in a nightmare: he must assassinate Malcolm X. Slam decides to kill the preacher before he departs. But white power first manages to poison the traitor, who has betrayed himself.

Thus black theatre presents both positive and negative images, rebels and traitors. Some plays put them together on stage and define them by opposition. The rebel is often a young man who unmasks the traitors in his parents' generation. And although these antithetical figures meet the same fate, the meanings of their deaths differ: one is sacrifice, the other punishment. For the powers that be, these two kinds of death represent the same way of getting rid of obstacles since the rebel is by definition a traitor and Uncle Tom a disposable tool. But once conscious of being used, Uncle Tom can become dangerous. Dramas of vengeance show the consequences of his coming to awareness.

Rituals of Vengeance

Plays about the black revolution rarely depict educated or professional characters as traitors. Yet the rebels are almost always young. Their revolt is directed against power and its symbols or agents, an individual such as a father, protector, or patron, or an institution such as the police or the courts. The revolt usually follows an awakening of consciousness. Where an Uncle Tom mindlessly executes the orders of power, the rebel questions everything around him. The theatre bears witness to the small acts of resistance in daily life as well as the great rebellions in history.[73]

The poet-hero in Bill Gunn's *Johnnas*[74] launches a desperate revolt against the compromises accepted by the "niggers" around him and the frustrations imposed by "ofays." He refuses the roles his father accepted as singer, comedian, and chauffeur: "Finest blues and scat singer of his day, the 1920s," who entered show business by way of the cake walk. The poet's own career in the business is brief but shocking: poised on a roof from which he threatens to jump, he keeps the spectators breathless until his final act of suicide.

There are few suicides in black theatre. Characters do not die from natural causes or by their own choice; they are usually killed before they have a chance to decide. The stage fills with shocking murders perpetrated by whites and with revolutionary sacrifices.

In contrast to the hero in *Johnnas*, the young artist in *His First Step* by Charles Oyomo Gordon finds that rebellion does not end in death; it is the "first step" toward liberation.[75] The protagonist draws strength from his membership in a community and from the graceful black lifestyle emphasized by music and dance. The devil cannot tempt this new Otis Redding. And the play, like others, warns both the artist and the theatre.[76] The lesson is twofold: that artistic integrity is preferable to material success and that art is at the mercy of an exploitative commercial machinery which distorts it. The artist should not cater to decadent patrons but should seek his audience among his own brothers.

Revolt, which is often directed at the police, is a confrontation that can end in incarceration or in death. For the young rebels in *Flowers for the Trashman* by Marvin X and in *And We Own the Night* by Jimmie Garrett, the police are the first target.[77] This armed enemy requires armed resistance. The youths are often alone in their struggle. The father of one prisoner in *Flowers* refuses at first to aid his son. When he realizes his mistake and comes to the prison with bail money, he is killed. Father and son are separated forever, without understanding each other or fighting together. Where Marvin X offers only a glimpse of reconciliation, Garrett accentuates the conflict between generations. A young militant rebels against both the white world and his mother, who is its accomplice. He finds in the streets an identity that he cannot find at home. The play suggests that total liberation requires eliminating the mother, or at least putting an end to her emasculating role.

Another counterattack against police violence surfaces in an unusual ritual in *Charades on East 4th Street* by Lonne Elder.[78] The victims decide to end alienation through violence (in the same way that Genet's maids rehearse the death of Madam) by resorting to rituals that exploit the gap between illusion and reality — but this game of vengeance is real. The part of the policeman is not played by an actor/participant, but by a real policeman. His murderer, Adam, can no longer be seen as a mere walk-on part; his aggression against a flesh-and-blood enemy interrupts the play. Through the exchanges set up between the imaginary and the real, the theatre demonstrates the possibility of real action and criticizes the ritual for being incomplete. But are the rebels of *Charades* fully prepared to take such action? Adam does so, but only accidentally, and his friends quickly abandon him. The planned revolt is aborted and the ritual fails to produce a catharsis: the young men do not free themselves from the oppressive power or from the terror that inspires them.

Peter DeAnda's *Ladies in Waiting* stages a ritual of revolt and vengeance in grander style.[79] In a women's prison, the inmates and guards play cruel games, particularly sexual ones, which alternate the roles of seducer and object of desire. The relation between the prisoner and guard is the same as that of a white pimp and his black prostitute: a tyrannical person seeks to obtain total submission from the other. In prison the matron also represents white power. The revolt of prisoners against the society that has ostracized them is directed naturally against her. The ritual behavior between blacks and whites that animated Lula and Clay reappears here: seduction, threat, blackmail, aggression. As in *Dutchman* the underlying sexual metaphor completes the prisoner-guard relationship. Prison, however, is more than a symbol; it is a special place where rites of subjugation and revolt unfold. Sex is a more useful medium of exchange than money, particularly for the matron. The play attests to the demonstrative power of the theatre and its ability to define roles. Lana, the liberal, naive white inmate, leaves prison at the end of the play to reenter a world in which her place is assured, but for black inmates prison is a permanent state and society is just another prison. It is left up to Agrippa, aptly nicknamed The Bulldyke — "Bull for the man in me, dyke for stemming the tide of frustrated women folk" — to take vengeance with the only weapons she has against the double oppression of prostitution and incarceration.

The new black theatre also bears witness to the contributions of many blacks to the struggle for freedom. Each individual act of revolt leads some people to death and others to prison. Yet, the repetition of single acts in different circumstances demonstrates constant resistance. The steady accumulation of images of revolt in drama attests to the continuing effort to restore constructive black images. Individual contributions to the struggle vary. Sometimes very obscure characters improvise their own way of participating in the march of history. For those who are already committed, the new theatre offers new legends that enrich the philosophy of resistance. It also broadens the spectrum of characters to include the common people as well as better-known heroes.

One play that features the common people is Ted Shine's *Contribu-tion*, which pays tribute to an elderly black woman who uses well-worn strategies to conduct her own revolution.[80] In a small southern town, Mrs. Love does not participate in the demonstrations for civil rights, but on the day when whites prepare to police the streets, she slips poison into the cornbread she regularly bakes for the sheriff. This new Harriet Tubman will not go down in history, for unlike the demonstrators, who are exposed to repression, she remains above suspicion. She simply offers the delicious bread to the sheriff as she has done for the past ten years. Does she not deserve recognition? By killing the sheriff she foils the repression and contributes to the success of the desegregation cam-paign. Her eagerness to serve the enemy is part of a subversive strategy. The play ends with the simple question "Who's next?" Who are Mrs. Love's next victims, and who will take up her role?

It is important that this angry old woman acts on her own. Like Willie's mother refusing the medal, or like the woman who curses the audience at the close of Melvin Van Peebles' *Ain't Supposed to Die a Natural Death*, Mrs. Love alone decides which role she will play. She watches for the right moment, chooses her disguises, and lists her vic-tims (the doctor who refused to attend her husband, the state governor who reprimanded the student movements, and so on). Her character is even more interesting because it appears in the kind of drama that usually gives the best roles to the younger generation.

Through Mrs. Love, Shine reclaims the black woman and the Uncle Tom; but he especially poses the problem of the function of theatre in a struggle for liberation. Like Mrs. Love, the theatre must find its own way to affirm its commitment and its freedom. It can use strategies that are neither purely rhetorical nor entirely political. Its task is to create situa-tions and characters that play upon the gap between appearances and reality and thus to transform its audience into enlightened spectators.

Ideologies of Nationalism and Revolution

Heroic common people together with prominent historical figures such as Gabriel Prosser, Frederick Douglass, Marcus Garvey, and Malcolm X are part of the dramatis personae of the new theatre. These plays differ greatly from the historical pageants produced during the Harlem Renaissance. Playwrights Clifford Mason, Charles Fuller, and Norbert Davidson evoke various moments in the reconquest of lost freedom, begin-ning with slaves who escaped the plantation or who organized revolts.

Gabriel Prosser's revolt is the subject of Mason's play *Gabriel*.[81] Under ruse and secrecy, Gabriel organizes his conspiracy, but the prediction of his mother comes true: "You ain't gonna last long because you don't know how to shuffle your feet." Like Nat Turner, Gabriel is thoroughly committed to his mission, which is to return the land and wealth stolen by Europeans back to blacks and Indians:

> GABRIEL: But there is no justice, except what we make our-
> selves. The black man was in his home safe, and wishing
> for no man's country but his own. And the red man was in his,
> strong warrior of the north, ruler of the plains.
> BIG HENRY: And the white man came and took away both homes.
> (Pp. 193–194)

It is only natural that a suffering people rise up and spill blood and destroy the harvests produced by their labor: "I am . . . the son of a slave who tonight will fill his hands with death, black death galloping swift and furious through white Virginia to waste all the silken and linen that good brown sweat ever made." Planters discover the plot and foil it. After Gabriel's arrest comes the implacable white vengeance. The traitor is revealed, but Gabriel forgives him and refuses to make a spectacle of his anger. When he is given a last wish before execution, he defies his captors with his wit: "Give a nigger a chicken soup and he'll do anything for you, even die happy." Since he has failed he wants to be forgotten.

Mason's play undercuts the protagonist's wish, for it pays tribute to the rebel even while criticizing his action. Mason appears to be siding with the old woman in *Contribution* who links effectiveness with caution, but he reminds us that even the most spectacular failures can be instructive. The play examines the reasons for the insurrection's failure, showing all sides: the slavemaster's repression (ironically, the "good" master Prosser is more likely to be betrayed by his slaves than is his neighbor who is a hard master), the cowardice of the house slaves who internalize the paternalistic ethic, the rebels who think they can hold off an entire state. Despite its criticism, Mason's play reclaims the hero.

The Rise by Charles Fuller[82] depicts Marcus Garvey and the "back to Africa" nationalist movement of the twenties. Through the reactions of an integrationist leader, a black mayor of Harlem, and an elderly couple, Fuller shows how garveyism simultaneously stirred up both enthusiasm and hostility and was both supported and betrayed. *The Rise* is a more idealistic and ambitious work than *Gabriel*. While a common slave may see his plan for insurrection destroyed, the black masses in the nationalist movement will take a decisive step. Millions of followers from all walks of life gather around a leader with a solid socioeconomic program. Garvey's fall, caused by the hostility and jealousy of some blacks and the defamation of his character by whites, is all the more dramatic. Fuller is not pessimistic: the wait for a new prophet and the fearful possibility of white repression against him should not keep people from working together or from gaining new strength from each attempt. *The Rise* suggests a parallel between Garvey and Malcolm X and the periods in which they lived.

Rather than showing the rise and fall of a leader, Norbert Davidson's *El Hajj Malik* presents the whole spectrum of Malcolm X's career.[83] The biographical intention, characterized by a concern for sociological explication, is here given original dramatic treatment. Six male and four female actors exchange roles in order to embody all the figures, and a multilevel set allows smooth transitions from scene to scene that mark the crucial moments in Malcolm's life. His exemplary character is shown through the weight of circumstances and the unity of his destiny. Malcolm's experiences are like those of many blacks; the only difference is his revolutionary consciousness. In the fragmented style of the play, reminiscent of the "Living Newspaper" of the thirties, dialogue alternates with speeches and sermons, poetry with prose, lyricism with drama.

In addition to plays drawn from the high points of the black movement, dramatic panoramas are also created to describe more distant events or the different historical moods in a single production. This dialogue with history produces two trends: one emphasizes the basic rhythm and continuity through various breaking points in a dynamic "national' experience expressed diachronically; the other examines more closely the forces at work in a single event by initiating a debate and defining a problem. The protagonists are placed in difficult situations and faced with ideological choices.

Arthur Graham's *The Nationals*: *A Black Happening of Many Black Minds*[84] considers the multiple points of view within an emerging nation; it reveals the signs and structures of history that tend to be overshadowed by life itself. The play builds around three sequences: A Time in Hell, A Change, A Reorganization. Members of the black nation are presented through isolated images before they meet and share the same awareness. Graham presents Africa not as the model homeland to which Afro-Americans must aspire, but as a lost Eden where white corruption encouraged Africans to sell their brothers into slavery. The fate of black Americans must be played out in America and not repeat that earlier treason. The last two scenes symbolically depict new battlefields: the library, guarded by a sickly white man, where a cultural struggle must be waged, and the rooftops where armed revolution is prepared.

The final sequence shows the armed confrontation about to occur. The Nationals exhort their women to join them in battle and in the cultural awakening while the Rats (Senator Rat Fink, alias Uncle Sam) preach "Blessed are the Poor for they shall have rats" and that at the end of the world people will go either to a carefully guarded white Heaven or to a dark hell filled with "nigger lovers" and traitors. The Nationals delight in the first fires of battle. The vermin may be eliminated without a single shot being fired. The unanimous pressure of the people will stamp out the Rats, those absurd survivors of an oppressive ideology. The blacks then gather at a door that opens into a heaven of blackness, not hell.

Trying to combine all aspects of a militant interracial ideology, Graham fails to find a dramatic form suitable to his subject. The play nevertheless contains a host of images that express the turbulence of an era. The set design and staging abound with poetic and surrealistic notations while allegorical tableaux rapidly unfold to a grand finale.

Sonia Sanchez's *Sister Son/ji* evokes different moments in the Afro-American struggle through the life of one woman whose monologue affirms both the continuity and the irreversibility of time: "Today I shall be what I was/and have been and can never be again. Today I shall bring back yesterday as it can never be today, as it shd be tomorrow."[85]

The play follows the protagonist through several periods of change as a student at Howard University, a militant of the fifties, a civil rights activist, a nationalist inspired by Malcolm X, an advocate of black power, a mother of brave fighters, an ardent revolutionary ready to take up arms. She embodies the stages of the struggle and the roles women were asked to play. In her resides the promise of future generations; she raises hopes and gives meaning to the present pain; she is the one left behind and the one to whom a lover returns. She is expected to endure the harshest sacrifices: she offers her sons who leave and may never come back. Left alone with memories of a past she helped to create, she signs a pact with time: "Ain't time and i made a truce so that i am time / a blk / version of past / ago & now / time." Older than the Mississippi, she is the one whom the force of life wears down, but who nourishes repeated challenges. "Anybody can grab the day and make it stop. Can you my friends? Will you?" Through this character, Sanchez restores the black woman to her essential role. She is the protagonist of the drama being played and the consciousness that creates it and calls it into question. She is time and memory. In a sense she represents the same consciousness as the theatre whose function is to restore the past to collective memory, to seek with the audience the meaning of an event in a vigorously pursued reflection.

Sister Son/ji owes the originality of its monologue and the efficacy of its structure to the blues. The melody, with its interrogation, painful shouts, sweeping heights and depths of movement, belongs to a solo, and the "I" sings the sentiments of an entire people. The theatre does not only borrow its message and militant attitude from black music; rather, it integrates the very structure of a song into the dramatic monologue.

Many plays move on to perform the revolutionary act. From tragedy to melodrama, or from a serious dialectic to comedy, the theatre assumes different features. At times it becomes a conscience that questions as it narrates and dramatizes certain debates that invite us to judge the strategies and choices adopted. At other times it breaks away from referential situations in order to develop its own scenarios in full-blown fantasy on stage. It invents images and myths that underlie a theatricalized ritual.

In *Pig Pen* by Ed Bullins[86] events are seen through the eyes of an informed observer, a light-skinned mulatto with a Jewish wife. Len belongs to two worlds, the semi-assimilated and the intellectual, that are not directly concerned with revolutionary acts. Len is a potential traitor because he is in appearance a "white Negro." However, he does offer perceptive judgments about the action. Opposite him is the poet Ray, more sincere in his militancy. But it is Len who has the function of revealing the weaknesses of the movement. The major role assigned to the intellectual deserves notice, for he is rarely used in black theatre unless it is to show the failures of intellectuals as a group. Here Len is a guide, a seer and prophet; he unveils the essential truths rarely shown. Yet he remains a spectator, cut off from action. The theatre will tend to substitute for this kind of observer other protagonists who, engaged in the action, are limited to choices that directly involve them and that also compromise them.

Johnny Williams and his son Jeff in Joseph Walker's *The River Niger*[87] are too naive and inexperienced to comprehend the turmoil around them, yet they seek to play a concrete role in the revolutionary struggle. Johnny Williams belongs to the tradition of articulate characters that black theatre cannot afford to lose. He is an honest, good man, a little extravagant, but above all an artist who has sacrificed his ambitions in order to support his family. Somewhat romantically, he would like to do his part in the struggle. He wants to give this heroic time the poem it merits. But the inspiration for his poem—which he calls "The River Niger"—fails him. Meanwhile he uses most of his energy arguing with his wife and with his mother-in-law, who is proud of her Indian origins. Jeff, the son, engaged to a South African woman whose father died trying to protect his son from arrest, is torn between following the military career his father wants and joining his terrorist friends. Johnny Williams will share the destiny of his distant comrade when he is killed trying to defend his son. Ironically, his sacrifice comes just when Jeff rejects terrorist action. Johnny's real poem is his death, which the verses comment upon.

The play uses the modes of lyricism, comedy, epic, and melodrama without really finding its own tone or path. *The River Niger* is one of those rare plays where father and son are not divided by conflict. The father dies willingly, and his sacrifice bears no resemblance to other scenes in black theatre in which the son kills his father who has become too dangerous to the revolutionary cause. Nor does Walker's play join those which denounce whites. Audiences feel sympathy for this father who, as head of a household, wants to understand and protect his son. Johnny dies for this very reason and not to defend a cause. One may wonder whether he is not renouncing the values of combat that he attempted to proclaim on the artistic level. His act, which in one sense is a gift of self, is also a failure.

The play's content removes it from the category of revolutionary plays. First staged in 1973, it attests to a certain stagnation of the theatre in relation to the previous decade. The conventional charater of its dramatic structure, the lapse into melodrama, the desire for a clear-cut ending all add to the ambiguity of the message. *The River Niger* looks nostalgically upon the recent past of Black Power and evokes an earlier historical moment where heroism was more easily recognized. One cannot measure the impact of the play without placing it back in the context of its creation and production. First presented by the Negro Ensemble Company in the Village and next on Broadway, then made into a film, *The River Niger* spoke to a larger and wider audience, the majority of which is white. The play's commercial success is explained by the way such drama can sustain the intellect and gain the sympathy of the spectators: the twists of plot are carefully prepared, the protagonist is a good man and a victim, not of white society, but of an absurd situation. Far from the narrow dogmatism of Graham's *The Nationals* and the revolutionary theatre of Jones, Walker's play nevertheless offers an example of the dead end theatre reaches when it exploits a mode and tries to please everyone.

The protagonists in *We Righteous Bombers* by Kingsley B. Bass, Jr. (pseudonym of Ed Bullins) and *Black Terror* by Richard Wesley are not caught in the midst of revolutionary gunfire by accident; they choose to be there. The new generation accuses the fathers who serve as neither models nor allies. It seeks to eliminate them. This goal, however, is not easily accepted or fulfilled, and this problem constitutes the subject of the drama. While showing the revolution in progress, the plays raise questions about the targets and the modes of action it has chosen.

We Righteous Bombers[88] reveals the pressures endured by the militants and the conflicts among them. Bullins explained later that he tried to write the script as it would have been written by one of the victims of the repression, a young man killed in Detroit. Perhaps Bullins wanted to take shelter behind a pseudonym in order to broach a controversial subject without imposing his reputation on the work's reception (four of his plays had already been performed successfully). Perhaps he wanted to restore the revolutionary act to its true authors by a symbolic gesture. Bullins earns the right to show what the dead man felt only because he proclaims in the exclusive realm of the theatre the primacy of the creative imagination over lived experience. He organizes a structured world for the spectator where the forces at work stand out clearly. He distributes the parts and lays bare the conflicts, contradictions, and ambiguities. He finds a situation that serves as a catalyst, that stirs each character to unexpected reactions while revealing hidden virtues to the spectators. The whole pretension of realist mimesis is in this sense a hoax.

Black critics found the play guilty of another fraud: it tried to pass off as black theatre a situation created by a white playwright. *We Righteous Bombers* is a faithful adaptation of *Les Justes* by Camus, which was translated into English in 1958 as *The Just Assassins*.[89] A black Grand Prefect has been named to represent white power. Blacks are confined to the ghetto by a kind of apartheid. White supremacy is assured by the vigilance of black delegates who silence the artists and immobilze the activists while a military regime maintains order. The revolutionaries prepare an assault aimed not at the white world but at its black deputies. Each of the righteous bombers reacts to his mission individually: Cleveland is calm, Jackson idealistic, Harrison unyielding. Their campaign is filled with both realism and mysticism. Jackson, who is responsible for throwing the bomb, is troubled by the presence of children in the prefect's car, but loses this concern. Two days later when he commits the act, he is arrested and learns that he has killed an actor substituting for the prefect. He is offered a deal: release and the chance to save his comrades in exchange for serving as the prison executioner for the next six years. When the television announces to viewers that they are about to witness the execution of a revolutionary, the righteous watch with keen emotion, wishing to salute one last time their valiant companion, whose death means that he has not betrayed them. However, the image they see on television does not show that their friend is not sacrificed, and that the head that falls belongs to the first victim of the new executioner.

The play also displays the manipulation of the "niggers" by white power—the black prefect is charged with repressing subversive activities. The prefect, a clever, powerful man, cons Jackson into buying his freedom and that of his companions. Among the terrorists Harrison is the only disciplined one. Next to these two men, ironically situated in opposite camps, Jackson is just a vulnerable and ineffectual poet.

Bullins' play offers a less than glorious portrait of the righteous, for they are tricked twice: when Jackson kills not the prefect but his substitute, and when Jackson's companions believe he overcomes compromises by accepting death. None of their projects reaches fruition; neither killing the enemy nor paying for their courageous challenge with their lives. The adversary is not eliminated; his power is only enhanced.

Theatre's own mechanisms of simulation—tricks, illusions, disguises—play an important role in the machinations that foil the revolutionary project. The theatrical metaphor, represented by the second attack and by the televised execution of an unidentified victim, figures in the basic structure of the play. The second attack occurs when the prefect is assumed to be attending the New Lafayette, one of the most celebrated theatres in Harlem, the one where Bullins' plays are performed. This far-fetched allusion underscores the ambigious nature of a theatre that chooses its audience from among the "niggers" who have come to applaud their own misdeeds. This could be seen as a critique of the New Lafayette, which accepts the black middle class into its audience, or as a warning against the possible co-optation of all cultural enterprises. The presence of the prefect in the very theatre that points him out as the enemy of the people makes inoffensive entertainment out of a production that seeks to be subversive. Moreover, it is not the play that creates the show, but the arrival of the Grand Prefect at the theatre after parading his power through the streets of Harlem. A second detail also discredits the theatre: an actor was substituted for the prefect. Not content to play this character on a conventional stage, he has abused his power by going beyond prescribed limits. The confusion of rules is thus denounced: between the prefect and the actor, between the street and the theatre, between reality and staged illusion. Unconcerned about conventions, this theatre plays a game with reality to which spectators and Jackson submit. At the same time, the scenario prepared by the righteous is changed: Jackson kills not the prefect but his image, embodied by an actor. The world of appearances wins. Jackson becomes a victim; it is he, not the prefect, who will be sacrificed.

The last scene, in which the revolutionaries watch the televised execution, demonstrates once again how the "show" can be mistaken for the truth. For the righteous, the image is one of sacrifice — one of them pays for the cause he was defending — and they take pride in it. For the audience that knows about the meddling of the Grand Prefect, the image is that of a verdict carried out by an ex-revolutionary become executioner. It marks the triumph of an enemy who knew how to catch the righteous at their own game.

Theatre reference and the manipulation of power become metaphors for each other. Multiple relations are thus suggested between drama and the political scene where theatrical subterfuge is constantly used. Contrary to many works that present the "nigger" or traitor as an innocent, tricked coward, *We Righteous Bombers* makes more effective use of him. Neither blind nor innocent, the Grand Prefect makes remarkable use of his power. An expert director, he also knows how to improvise and prepare a deceptive script. The play also reveals the force of a well-structured society that delegates its power to deputies of unquestionable loyalty. As an intermediary appointed by power, the prefect in turn distributes parts to those who are devoted to maintaining order on all levels. Jackson, as a member of a squad of the righteous whose names ironically recall those of American presidents, becomes one of the subordinates of the penitentiary administration.

The play provoked strong reactions from black intellectuals. A panel discussion organized at the New Lafayette gathered together such theatre artists as Baraka, Robert Macbeth, and Marvin X, as well as theoreticians like Askia Muhammed Touré, Larry Neal, and Ernie McClintock, in order to right the balance of a play that presented too negative an image of the black revolution and that foretold its doom.[90] Two arguments emerged from the discussion: one raised criticism about the adoption of a psychology borrowed from Western drama, and the other concerned the ideological confusion at the heart of the play. Did it condemn revolutionary activity by showing the vanity of a rebel who helped reinforce the power of the enemy? In any case, the cynicism it manifested hardly encouraged admiration for the righteous. The most positive portrait was that of the prefect, and one suspects that he may be the real hero. The play can surely be seen as antirevolutionary.

As limited as these arguments seem, the controversy is interesting, for it reveals the preoccupations of black nationalist criticism and it poses a problem for revolutionary drama. The criticism bears mostly on the content, the signified element of the play, and is more concerned about plot and human problems than about methods of presentation, or the *signifiers*. These critics seem to require of theatre strict conformity to an ideology from which a normative typology of situations and characters can be established. These prescriptions are not unlike those which certain political movements impose on literature or those developed by totalitarian regimes. If the function of the theatre is to promote revolutionary action, these orthodox critics seem to be saying, then drama must incite the spectator to act. It must present unambiguous models, furnish clearly drawn images, so as to assure in the minds of the spectators, if not on the stage, the victory of the positive over the negative. The rehearsal of this symbolic victory builds up confidence and group determination. The major criticism addressed to Bullins in this regard is that his play plunges the audience into confusion rather than lifting them out of it.

In answer to those who felt that theatre should serve ideology, Larry Neal and Amiri Baraka spoke in favor of a more subtle drama that is not restricted to repeating slogans or stereotyped situations, but which shows conflicts of characters torn between contradictory allegiances. The role of drama is not, according to them, to resolve problems but to pose them; one must give back to theatre its subversive—indeed cruel—function. Instead of trying to please an audience by saying what it wants to hear, the theatre can make it think by unsettling its beliefs: "You can't have a revolutionary play that doesn't upset people." The merit in Bullins' play, for Neal and Baraka, lies in its examination of the basis of certain ideological postulates and of the nature of the theatrical enterprise.

Neal and Baraka, however, reproached Bullins for having created too intellectual a debate in the play, which does not affect the spectator as fully as it should. They believed the play talks too much and shows too little: action should be performed, not discussed. They also criticized the form of the play, which uses ideas to solve a revolutionary problem: "It's the job of the revolutionary artist to find out what forms in his culture are best suited to express a certain kind of idea." Thus, the unique aspect of black theatre is affirmed. It cannot use just any models of political theatre outside the ethnic cultural context. The adaptation of a play like *The Just Assassins* involves more than changing the content or casting the parts with black or white actors according to their relation to power or revolutionary action. One must also create structures and a dramatic language that take into account the group's own codes of behavior and forms of cultural expression.

A similar debate is presented in *Black Terror,*[91] a dramatic suspense play with a revolutionary theme, subtitled "a revolutionary adventure story." The play recounts a dangerous adventure that requires unconditional self-sacrifice in a universe that pits blacks against whites and angry youths against their moderate parents. For the young revolutionaries there is only one answer—weapons. But *Black Terror* exposes the weaknesses of a theory that favors mechanical rhetoric and forbids reflection or expressions of doubt and pity. Paradoxically, it falls to an experienced killer, charged with the most dangerous missions, to offer shrewd criticism of the organization. Keusi, a Vietnam veteran new to the terrorist group, is assigned with M'Balia to beat up the police commissioner, Savage, and the conservative black leader, Radcliff. After fulfilling the first part of this mission, Keusi suddenly doubts his comrades' project, which he sees leading to fratricide. For his doubts Keusi is expelled from the group. M'Balia accomplishes the second attack alone: without a moment's hesitation she kills her own father.

Black Terror raises basic problems about revolutionary ideology. Some concern the existence of the whole network: the role of the leader, the rights and duties of each member. Others examine the relation of the organization to the community whose interests it purports to serve. Are the people ever consulted? What is the group's relation to them? Will the masses support or condemn the terrorist activities? The role of women in the revolution is also questioned. But the heart of the discussion bears upon the relation between ideology and revolutionary practice. All the debates are integrated into the dramatic structure, not only because they oppose one character to another, but because they are presented through animated and intense dialogue in which retorts volley like gunshots. Accused of thinking when the moment called for action, Keusi reproaches the terrorist leaders for borrowing slogans from Western revolutionaries without adapting them to the circumstances of their own struggle and for hiding their own lack of thought under revolutionary ardor. He questions the fate that his comrades have decided for "niggers," and he disagrees about the educational value of these model executions. He disapproves of the choice of victims: the Radcliffs may be Uncle Toms, but the community thinks of them as heroes. Must the people be deprived of figures who bring them hope? If every suspect must be eliminated then the purge will never end. Keusi criticizes destructive nihilism: he sees in this cult of death a real fear of life; his argument for the survival of the black nation denounces the murderous and suicidal instincts of blinded revolutionaries, for their own conflict destroys them no less than does white repression. Keusi—whose role is to internalize the contradiction—figures as the solitary hero of the organization, but nothing is gained by his arguments. He is defined antithetically as the wise man who predicts the final catastrophe and the defection of the black masses. He glimpses the possibility of a struggle that is more moderate, but more rewarding in the long run.

The play is built around two scenes that frame its long ideological debate. A propitiary ceremony to the accompaniment of drumbeats, incense smoke, and songs that are plaintive and menacing gathers the fighters around an altar. From uncontrolled frenzy, the ritual leads to sermons and chants that express hope and determination before invoking the spirits of the ancestors: "And remove the fear . . . And remove the doubt/ Release the anger in our souls/ And give us strength . . . Place steel in the marrow of our bones/ Grant us inner peace/ To fulfill our terrible mission." The final scene brings an end to the terrorists' dreams. After a police raid in the neighborhood, the repression is unleashed. The revolutionaries, brandishing their fists, fall dead. In the midst of the dying people large figures rise up to recall the implacable and grotesque existence of a world that laughs at the carnage. A Klansman draped in the American flag parodies the Statue of Liberty. Other characters arrive on stage like victors; they are the sole survivors of a scenario prepared without their knowledge, but which reserves the triumph for them. A voice on the radio comments on this apocalypse: questions asked by a reporter who describes the state of the revolutionaries express not only the incomprehension that black militancy encounters but also a certain common sense that underscores the vanity of such a display of heroism. This ending introduces a note of doubt and derision, giving reason to Keusi's pessimistic prophecies. It is impossible not to see *Black Terror* as a response to *Righteous Bombers*. Wesley no doubt has tried to reckon with the criticism of the first play by creating a more complex dramatic structure. *Black Terror*, however, proposes no new elements for revolutionary black theatre, and it is closer to the kind of political melodrama of which *The River Niger* is the best example.

If theatre occasionally is a good place to express conflicts, one of its functions is to state certain facts. *One of the Two of Us* by William Adell Stevenson[92] presents one such fact, lyrically not dialectically. Only as free as he imagines himself to be, the black man remains a slave to power, and his destiny rests entirely in the master's hands. Let a man rise up to lead his people, and he will be caught, reduced to impotence or condemned to martyrdom. Revolution needs fighters not martyrs, action not sorrow. Black people lament the disappearance of their heroes and are subjected to an endless cycle, alternating between the hope that produces an exceptional leader and the tears that follow his death. The assassins chosen by whites are always blacks, traitors to their race, who are then condemned to death in the elementary law of retaliation. Stevenson's hero is killed by a spy, a member of his own revolutionary organization. The assassin is beaten up by another member, and this new "righteous" one is likely to become the next victim. Blacks seem destined to be victims or murderers. But the black woman in *One of the Two of Us* accepts neither this fatality nor the necessity of her companion's death. For her, the vocation of black people is not to cry, and that of theatre is not to dictate a funeral song from a chorus of women. She awaits the coming of a new era in which blackness will be celebrated. She announces the appearance of new rituals that affirm life instead of mourning death.

Model Punishments and Imaginary Games

Black drama often presents radical actions and spectacular feats directed against white power and its black accomplices. The denunciation of "white Negroes" sketched out in the theatre of Jones and Caldwell is pursued in parables, grotesque comedies, and scenarios where imagination restores to theatre its dual function to educate and to entertain.

In Sonia Sanchez's *The Bronx is Next*[93] the targets of the revolutionaries are a black prostitute and her white policeman client, both unaware of the unrest spreading through Harlem. The militants have decided to burn down the ghetto, and they hastily evacuate all inhabitants. Sanchez's prostitute, like the one in *Madheart*, is caught in the purifying flames. She pleads her innocence in vain, alleging that it was the black man who betrayed her by denying her love and protection. Inspired by the riots during the long hot summers of the sixties, the play offers no judgment on the desperate acts that filled the ghettos with fire and blood. It seeks rather to invest those acts with a metaphorical and symbolic intent. By destroying the environment in which they are confined, blacks expose the criminal behavior of whites; the violence they inflict upon themselves is an image of what they have suffered. Their spectacular gesture is liberating in that it abolishes the fears that made them incapable of action; it offers the white world the "show" of their challenge. The play also suggests a reversal of roles. The confrontation between revolutionaries and the police is reminiscent of the "ceremonies" of expiation and of vengeance that the young protagonists in *Charades* use on their hostage. Here again the white policeman is accused, brutalized, and reduced to silence. The "righteous" begin their own reign of terror and violence.

In *The Monster* by Ron Milner[94] militant students prepare a long ceremony—the annihilation of a dean at a black university. This creature, a tottering puppet manipulated by an invisible Frankenstein, is the incarnation of "the electronic nigger": his gait, gestures, and words embody the automatic behavior of a "guard dog" of power. The students steal the puppet and get ready to pull his strings themselves. Drugged with a magic serum, the monster submits to the new masters without realizing the substitution. His pseudo-metamorphosis reveals his deeper identity. Subjected to certain commands—a word, an order, a gesture—he responds predictably and mechanically. Before an improvised audience, he plays out the comedy of his character (the theatre metaphor reappears). When called upon to confront the demonstrators and give a speech, he receives a different message from his new masters and begins to preach insubordination and revolt. But just when the "Frankenstein Operation" is nearly over, the robot suddenly recovers his former nature. The foiled militants must yield to the evidence: the robot cannot be reprogrammed from one day to the next. They improvise a last scenario in which the dean accepts one last role—dictated, one thinks, by whites. The monster falls into a trap with a white cord wrapped around his neck. His execution could pass for a suicide.

A similar plan in *Prayer Meeting* by Ben Caldwell[95] is practiced on another Uncle Tom, a pastor comfortable in his ministry. Ironically, the plan succeeds this time although it is entirely improvised and its creator, far from being a militant aware of his mission, is a common burglar.

Caldwell presents his message in the burlesque mode. The conversion of the preacher happens unexpectedly; although the burglar wins the pastor over, he himself is not converted. Proud of his great trick, he leaves the parsonage with the loot after having done his part for the liberation of his people. *Prayer Meeting* borrows more from farce than from a demonstrated ideology. However, stated in terms of popular tradition that sees the trickster as a hero, the revolutionary message loses neither its relevance nor its impact.

In *The Gentleman Caller* by Ed Bullins[96] the comedy—in the course of which a mistress and her maid progressively change roles—unfolds under the silence of an unexpected visitor. Madame tries to define her relations to the mysterious caller. The gentleman gestures slightly and simply smiles. The master of the house, a Mr. Mann, turns out to be a cadaver. Madame and her maid try to devise an official version of his death. When the visitor steals the fake beard from the dead man, the maid seizes a revolver and shoots her mistress; she summons the gentleman to help her remove the corpses. Having gained her freedom, settled her accounts with the employers, the maid becomes mistress of the situation and of the house. She gets ready to start another war, for the call for liberation has sounded.

The theatre here offers an example of rapid simulation and instant change. The faithful servant is transformed into a militant and avenges all past humiliations. The explanation for this metamorphosis is offered by Madame herself in her stereotyped praise of a devoted servant, which here gains an entirely different meaning: "She was like the mountains . . . unchanging . . . like time . . . limitless. Always faithful . . . always the source of inspiration. Young . . . young man, you can be proud you sprang from her loins." The cosmic analogy in a cliché-ridden language reveals — through the words of her employer — the real nature of the monumental Mammy: mother of the revolution, harbinger of change, she is an inspiration for the struggle. Each term of the portrait takes on an ironic meaning. Madame thinks she is speaking about a servant who helped her get rid of Monsieur. She does not know that she is describing one of the "righteous" who will suppress her without pity. The ambiguous "gentleman," this elegantly handsome young man, who could be an incarnation of Clay in *Dutchman*, has no choice from now on; he must join ranks with the new mistress.

Dutchman, of course, presented the inverse situation; now blacks will gather up the dead bodies of whites and dispose of them with the complicity of silent witnesses. The allegorical mode emphasizes the character designations: Mr. Mann, with the false beard, who usurps authority and virility; Mammy, a "queen mother" who is kind and foolish; and the ceremony of the visit — an ironic term used to indicate this strange settling of accounts executed with all the style and grace of protocol. This ritual unfolds in an atmosphere of farce made all the more obvious by grossly symbolic scenery and costumes: Mr. Mann wears shorts made out of an American flag and star-spangled socks; the room is decorated with rifles, trophies, heads of blacks, Indians, Vietnamese, Chinese. The stage directions emphasize the caricature. The part of Madame is meant to be played by a black actress whose skin is painted silver and who wears a blond wig, or by a white actor in drag.

Here we find the classic situation of comic theatre: the valet playing the master — to which racial implications lend further meaning. And black revolutionary theatre adds to its traditional repertory scenes of punishment and death for the enemy.

These three plays by Milner, Caldwell, and Bullins have in common a subversive quality of language and an intentional parody. In *The Gentleman Caller* the visitor remains quiet, the maid answers with a definite yes or no. The silence is worrisome, and Madame uses all forms of discourse — orders, supplications, threats — which help her establish authority. The words and the clichés she uses appear empty of meaning, for they refer to a world which is collapsing, but their semantic potential remains intact: Madame speaks to say nothing, but she expresses truths which go beyond her understanding. The commonplaces refer to a situation she considers hers, but it is soon radically contested. In *The Monster*, the insurgents attack more directly the role language plays in the subjugation of blacks, for this language when exposed should give birth to a new liberating utterance ("In the name of the whites, the right and the fright"). Such word games are part of the revolutionary rituals: they express irreverence and a creative fantasy that parodies the games of power in order to bring a new power into being. As for the burglar in *Prayer Meeting*, the virulence of his speech literally steals language in order to tear the pastor away from his apathy. The prayer no longer harks back to formulas; it becomes an act, and the utterance is made event. The inflated language of the robber/God is not only a parody of the discourse of authority; it also corresponds to the dimensions of the event it predicts: the unheard-of word proclaims that the time of submission has passed. God is calling the pastor to take up arms, not to turn the other cheek.

In this drama, parody plays a major role and revolution occurs through irreverence. One must break the hold of official discourse, make fun of the superiors and institutions that limit free expression. One must also take hold of language as a weapon and an instrument of power. The game of parody amounts to this appropriation. Opposing this creativity are the Uncle Toms, the major obstacles to revolutionary action, and those who imitate without parodying, who repeat mechanically; they are the electronic niggers, the robot monsters.

The force of inertia is illustrated in a very simple parable, *Black Bird* by Marvin X.[97] Written for children, the play shows the "whitewashed" Negro as a blackbird caged in the master's house. He has accepted his captivity so well that he does not realize that the door to his cage is open. Other birds come to encourage him to fly away, but he remains obstinately faithful to his owner, who is grateful for his servility. One thinks of the slave character in *Gabriel* who comes back to the plantation after being emancipated by the master. In *Black Bird*, the bird refuses to leave even when the house catches fire, but his companions pull him out of the flames and reunite him with his family.

For the Uncle Toms, the theatre presents only two possible fates: redemption or implacable punishment. In *The Monster* the Uncle Tom who could not be converted had to be punished, and so will the "visitors" who do not wake up soon enough. The pastor of *Prayer Meeting* and the servant of *The Gentleman Caller* are converted into militants. But the many Uncle Toms who are already too corrupted and totally sold out to white power must be eliminated.

The trial of white Negroes is repeated in play after play. Those who plead to be spared from death come up against those who demand punishment. The conflict is situated either within the black community or within the family where choices are more painful and where retribution ends in fratricide or parricide.[98] Whether the act is committed or simply envisaged, the revolutionary theatre still assumes the primary task of choosing its victims.

LeRoi Jones has already defined the "theatre of victims." It remains to be seen what different interpretations can be applied to this definition, interpretations through which black theatre develops a whole repertory. During the thirties, it revealed to white America the racial and economic oppression of blacks and illustrated this argument through many situations. In the sixties, the revolutionary theatre was not content just to appeal to collective guilt or social humanism. Even less could it fall back upon religious ethics which postpone the punishment of the guilty to a distant future. Revolutionary theatre requires an immediate trial and model punishment. As an instigator of change, it seeks victims other than those offered by history. For the image of the black man chained by America it substitutes that of anyone, black or white, who helps to perpetuate crimes against blacks. The former victim rises up against his oppressors and deals them a mortal blow. The drama thus reveals two sets of victims: black traitors to their brothers, and all whites. And it develops around two types of rituals: the sacrifice of the black victim and the destruction of the white world.

Revolutionary Theatre and Promethean Consciousness

If the killing of racial brothers is sometimes called into question, the murder of whites is envisioned without reservation. A simple and unequivocal matter, it is dramatized in several ways. The violence blacks have suffered is now inflicted upon whites: this violence stems from "all that is scorned and hated in the enemy."[99] The white beast, created out of love by the magicians in *A Black Mass*, turns upon its creator and devastates the world; only its death can restore peace to the world.

Two scripts by Bullins once again stage the destruction of the white world. In *Night of the Beast*[100] the revolution triumphs over repression in Harlem in the course of a bloody night. With dawn comes a new hope. The revolutionary motto is taken from Fanon's words about the destruction of the oppressor, which Clay echoes in *Dutchman*: "Murder will make us all sane." Blacks choose violence to assure their mental health and survival. The ritual reappears in *State Office Building Curse*,[101] in which the dedication of a building becomes the occasion for the destruction of white power in Harlem. The "curse" cast by "black magic" comes true; an explosion destroys the building, and the people celebrate the advent of a new era.

In Val Ferdinand's *The Destruction of the American Stage*[102] a foreigner brings disharmony to a land where people live happily. The newcomer sets up a podium to signal his reign and reduces his hosts to impotence. He can be expelled only after the destruction of the podium and the gradual reanimation of the "actors" who must prepare themselves for new roles. The theatre metaphor once again represents the black condition: the alienating stage and the network of servile relations must both be destroyed.

The theatre metaphor is used by most plays that stage the ritual of destruction, whether in the most moderate or in apocalyptic forms. In *A Short Play for a Small Theatre* by Bullins[103] the actors exterminate whites in the audience. The ritual of aggression takes place within the theatrical convention of an actor confronting the audience. The whites are the new victims in this theatre, which aims at both the destruction of the stage and the purification of the audience, freed from the presence of whites. In *It Bees That Way*,[104] also by Bullins, the spectators should all be white. Black actors come among them as drunks, drug addicts, outlaws, playing the "nigger." They make jokes, secretly deriding whites who have come to be entertained by the show of their own downfall. Suddenly the scene changes: the actors arm themselves and shout a battle cry. They chase the audience into the streets where the real spectacle takes place: revolution. The theatre opens its doors to the outside world that invites the actors to become fighters and the whites to expect a decisive confrontation.

In this brief scenario, blacks are the only ones who speak, joking and threatening the audience. The silent whites enter and leave according to orders. The roles have been reversed, and the theatre convention of a "show" (black actors entertaining white spectators) indicates the more radical change to follow. As with theatre, life must change. Inversely, theatre (or art) follows life. Not content merely to submit to these transformations, it creates them; offering new representations, it instigates social change.

The theatre of agitation stages a brief and destructive action in a precise time and space. It owes its symbolic function to a fixed format of violent confrontation complete with victims and a final liberation. The forces are clearly antagonistic: good blacks against bad whites, the Manicheanism of a classic morality play. Undecided elements are eliminated, and those which present the least ambiguity are brought back to the principle from which they originated. The black traitor, for example, is either punished or brought back into the community, according to the degree of his corruption. Every act is thus accomplished with a dual purpose: to bring about change by inverting roles and to restore harmony. The destruction of individuals, institutions, and the social order becomes the means for change. It is a necessary stage in the reunification of the black nation.

The hatred brought out in the theatre is predictable; many black writers are encouraged by Trotsky's declaration: "Everything written in a state of revolutionary confrontation is inevitably fused with the feeling of hate." Plays that accommodate the oppressor at the expense of the victim are thus denounced as counterrevolutionary.

In analyzing the revolutionary theatre, African dramatist Wole Soyinka tries to extract its basic principles.[105] It is not a question of inflicting pain or pardon. Hate and anger are more dynamic than resignation and fear, and for this very reason they become the components of the drama of social upheaval. The theatre stages the play of forces that come into confrontation in a period of crisis, provoking a sudden and necessaray rupture. Soyinka, however, cautions against too literal an interpretation of the texts; he suggests that we see them as the working out of cosmic principles that he labels creators or destroyers of unity. Thus the murders acted out in this theatre—the murder of a black youth by a white followed by the murder of a racist by blacks (as in *The Fanatic* by Caldwell), or the murder of a father by his son—are all destined to evince the dynamism of revolutionary tension. The revolutionary theatre refuses the dimensions of tragedy or melodrama. These acts express the consciousness and the challenge of an individual who seeks to overcome his condition. Whether he turns against the white oppressor or against the traitor-father, the rebel breaks the law only to restore it. Human nature requires such transgressions or shows of excess. A superior wisdom teaches that destruction is often a phase of a regenerative and unifying process. What appears to be a fault or a blow to harmony is only a means to attain a higher level of existence. Man's repeated interrogation and excessive demands incite the cosmos to raise up once again a promethean challenge to mankind. In this perspective change does not come about as a punishment proportional to the offense; it happens only through a deep rupture that calls into question both man and the universe.

Although Soyinka advances an Africanist explanation for the cosmic dimension of revolutionary theatre, he does not encourage Afro-American dramatists to use African rituals. On the contrary, black American culture, in his view, is sufficiently rich in forms capable of showing the antagonistic forces in society. Ritual should allow an interchange between audience and stage. For Soyinka, the ritual contains its own dialectic—the complex evolution of tradition within history.

In the usual development of this "theatre of victims" there are three closely related steps: (1) an isolated individual chosen as the model victim; (2) the perceptions of a promethean consciousness favoring justified murders; and (3) the working of a certain magic that allows the audience to recover the meaning of its collective identity. An individual can be isolated from the group because of his role as traitor, accomplice, or victim, or because he has broken certain rules. This atypical character (because of his exiled individuality) is pointed out by the group and made to submit to rites of exclusion, excommunication, or expiation—which later can become rites of reconciliation and reintegration. The society thus contemplates its own situation through the fate of one of its members. It is not important that the individual be aware of having committed an error; the collective consciousness recalls the offense, often through the intermediary of a chorus that interprets the sanctions of the group for the excluded person and the solitude and suffering of the isolated person for the group. The community thus becomes aware of its own existence and of the need to punish infractions against it. The dramatic art becomes the show of an individual executed for his crime. By isolating the guilty party, society purifies itself of all temptation of complicity with him; it also immunizes itself against future infection.

Although the theatre is first concerned with the problems man faces in daily life, it is not restricted to reflecting them. It proposes neither an escape nor a liberation by catharsis; it necessitates a confrontation that clearly distinguishes the forces at work on the symbolic and the imaginary levels. Jean Duvignaud has shown how the social situation differs from the dramatic situation: the one invents social roles to affirm its dynamism and to modify its own structures, while the other *performs* action not in order to accomplish it but to assume its symbolic character.[106] If there exists a continuity between social ceremony and theatrical ceremony, each nevertheless is distinctive. Social practice contains many collective ceremonies characterized by strong theatricalization and role-playing. In society, as in theatre, an "effervescent" milieu (in the Durkheimian meaning of the term) comes into being through the playing out of the drama of its mythic cohesion or of its progress. Inspired by concrete situations, the theatre transfers them to the show, where they can be studied at a distance. Reality is directly involved, but it is sublimated. As Duvignaud argues, if the ceremony of drama can lag behind where life cannot it is because drama is a symbolic and metaphorical transposition and not simply an imitation of the real. The act of drama escapes from the constraints of ordinary life. It proposes imaginary solutions that may permit tasks in real life to be accomplished, but its goal lies elsewhere. Its effectiveness is achieved through a poetic language that is distinct from everyday speech by the power of the symbolic or by the rigor of an aesthetic that organizes reality. The theatre defines with symbols what in social rites is realized through concrete action. On the revolutionary stage, the conquest of and affronts to power are actions only through the performance that presents them.

The scenario is usually that of a crisis in the effervescent milieu of a given time and space. The group expresses its desire for intervention in order to create or to direct its future. The theatre has a promethean vocation, not only because it innovates but because it represents the action of a group at a precise moment in its development. It seizes upon action in that hour of revolution in which the members "glimpse," as George Gurvitch states, "the possibility of change after a concerted human action to tear down social structures."[107]

Unlike their predecessors who showed the tragedy of the black condition, unlike the type of drama that exploited this tragedy by imprisoning heroes in their destiny, the followers of revolutionary theatre create action aimed at making history, not succumbing to it. They draw man away from a metaphysical determinism and place him in a new determinism that can express an epic and historical dramatic attitude. Through the forms it creates, this theatre points out new models for human behavior and opens up areas of possibility larger than life. Inspired by real situations, "the promethean element of social reality," says Gurvitch, in turn sublimates the real in order to reveal unexplored regions of experience.

The efficacy of revolutionary theatre cannot be proved in the context of social change. It rests in the conjunction of two rituals: the production itself and the exchange between the audience and the stage. The dynamism of the dramatic art, according to Soyinka, aims at creating "a communal cementing factor" by involving the actors and the audience in an "operational totality." It puts the audience under the "magical jurisdiction" of an experience that attempts a collective purge and liberation — the working out of this magic rests on the exchange set up between the audience and the forces represented on stage, between tradition and history. The spectator is projected both into a kind of atemporality and into a historical present, into the perpetuity of community and into a future open to change. Anchored in tradition and the past, the performance proposes through dialogue a change however momentary or limited. This finality must be analyzed as a ritual of liberation and also as a ritual of reinsertion into group origins that reconnect a common past and future. The tensions and conflicts shown on the stage offer the spectator a microcosm of his cultural universe.

Black theatre thus uses ritual for very precise artistic purposes: to integrate the fragmented consciousness of black people and, above all, to free the theatre from decadent dramatic forms. It involves both a systematic subversion of Western dramatic language and form and the search for a medium capable of healing a wounded and often denied consciousness. This quest has led playwrights to African culture, but also to the very sources of theatre craft: in other words, to its beginning in ritual. (The Haitian Frank Fouché reveals the same point of departure in his *Vaudou et Théâtre*.)[108] The use of ritual entails certain risks, but black American revolutionary theatre appears to have avoided them; in fact, it has searched for a dialectical relationship between ritual — in its traditional meaning and influenced by myth and magic — and the dynamism of history, which is to say a conflict of forces staged at the heart of the construction that is the play. It has integrated, or very nearly, ritual and revolutionary potential.

Seen in this way the production must simultaneously plunge the spectator into terror and reassure him. Fanon has described this effect: "The atmosphere of myth and magic frightens me and so takes on an undoubted reality. By terrifying me it integrates me with the traditions and the history of my district and of my tribe and at the same time it reassures me; it gives me status, an identification paper.)[109] In terrifying the spectator, the production brings back reality which is no longer doubted, for the performance must go beyond the domain of "magic" to reveal an order that is not dominated by the forces of destiny but regulated by the laws of history where change is necessary.

The theatre exists only by virtue of the exchange established between audience and stage, but the nature of this exchange must not be misunderstood. Revolutionary theatre does not seek to charm the spectator taken in by the "magic" of the production. It seeks to startle him without invoking the notion of an irrevocable fate, for it questions the inevitability of the evil it denounces. It exerts a maieutic or dialectical power by expecting participation and judgment from the spectator. As a *passive actor*, the audience is involved in the performance, plunged into identification with victims or with blind, misled traitors; but at the same time the audience must be an *active spectator*, capable of reflecting upon and debunking the fatality that is presented. This is not a drama of abdication but of reflection: to use Brecht's terms, not a theatre of contagion but of solidarity.[110]

It is no surprise that in examining the principles of revolutionary theatre one cannot help speaking about Brecht. Contemporary black dramatists who refuse Western models will perhaps be irritated by such a connection, but the manner in which they explore the problem of audience participation comes close to Brecht's reflection on the subject. Like him, they want to restore the social function of theatre. They want to create a *civic* theatre which engages the critical judgment of those who participate. The development of a "spectatorial consciousness" is particularly evident in a play like *Great Goodness of Life*, where the audience is invited to consider and correct the judgment proposed on stage. The aberrations of the protagonist's character and those of the executioner must be clearly evident in order for the spectator to substitute his own interpretation for the explanations given by the playwright.

Spectator awareness is developed on two levels: identification (the spectator identifies with a character-victim, subject to the same ritual of violence/persecution/inquisition; he also recognizes neither the place he is in nor the voices he hears) and aesthetic dissociation (the spectator seeks out causes and remedies; he judges and adopts uncompromising measures; he is offered several clues and keys but must draw his own conclusions).

The great lesson this theatre imparts is that man's troubles, like his salvation, are of his own making. The dramatic heightening of consciousness must sweep away the melodramatic illusions of an unexplainable destiny, of an insurmountable fatality, of salvation brought by some *deus ex machina*. The latent drama of black life resides less in the oppression suffered than in complicity with the oppressor. The drama exposes excuses, lies, and illusory sublimations that have passed for consent.

In one sense the theatre aims at revoking the "false dialectic of consciousness,"[111] obscured by illusions, in order to reach a true dialectic about real conditions. The theatre must elicit truths, however briefly, that are not always well defined or easily translatable; it offers the promise of another world. The spectator's emotions are born from his yet unconscious perception of the profound meaning of the drama. Destiny is never shown to be universal, but distinct and specific. Black revolutionary theatre rejects the concepts of the universality of suffering and the uniformity of human destiny.

The spectatorial consciousness examines a deeper meaning which is not evident in the language or gestures of characters on stage. Many black plays do not resist the temptation to didacticism and techniques of agitprop. But the real criticism comes through the dramatic structure itself, favoring the awakening of an authentic and active consciousness, which must break certain mirrors in order to know itself. Questioning the myths black consciousness has been subject to and has accepted, it reveals the relations between alienated consciousness in a spontaneous ideology and the real conditions of its existence. As Althusser writes:

> This relation — abstract in regard to self-consciousness — . . . can be represented through the characters, their gestures, their actions, and their "story" only as a relation that, while involving them, exists apart from them . . . This relation is necessarily a latent one to the extent that no one "character" can fully express it without ruining the whole critical project: this is why if it remains involved in the action, in the existence and gestures of all characters, it represents their innermost meaning, transcending their consciousness — and therefore remains obscure to them, visible to the spectators inasmuch as it is invisible to the actors — and therefore visible to the spectators in the mode of perception that is not granted but must be discerned, conquered, as if drawn from the original obscurity that envelops and yet engenders it.[112]

Black drama breaks away from the forms of classical theatre, which reflect the entire play through the mirror awareness of one or several central characters. It calls into question the principles of theatrical catharsis, desperate pity or complicity. It puts the audience in a position where it cannot escape the representation (it should feel involved) or participation in it (it is not entertainment). Putting the spectator at a distance does not depend on technical devices such as the Voice in *Great Goodness* or the introduction of the spectator/traveler in the antechamber of history in *The Death of Malcolm X*; nor does it depend on psychological modalities of a positive or negative hero. Rather, it rests on the internal structure of the play. And it does not exclude identification: in judging, the spectator not only accuses the blind or weak character on stage, he also encounters his own blindness.

One must take issue with both the total separation that reduces the spectator to the role of a detached judge and the total identification that makes any critical view impossible. The ties of empathy, which are easier to establish when the character is familiar, must be doubled by analysis and exegesis. There is no real separation between the stage and the audience; they do not have well-defined complementary roles such as, for example, the lucidity of the audience and a character's lack of awareness on stage. The spectator's behavior can no longer be reduced to a psychological attitude. The audience's first step is cultural recognition, which is thus ideological: before identifying or not identifying with a protagonist, it must recognize the myths, aspirations, and ideology that govern him, even without his knowledge, and that unite spectators and actors in the same essential identity. Yet, the object of this theatre is not a game of mirrors that forces the spectator to a set self-awareness. The vocation of revolutionary theatre consists, on the contrary, in upsetting this "immutable sphere of the mythic world from illusory awareness."[113]

Black theatre sets out to change the world view developed by the dominant society and expressed through the image of an inexorable destiny. Enclosing the hero in unhappiness and lulling the spectator into passive contemplation would encourage resignation, not action. Thus it is not astonishing that black playwrights have not been following the aristotelian models that serve as the basis of Western theatre. They refute this tragic system proposed by a tradition that serves white political power; they refuse a catharsis that would correct and purify human actions. Analyzing the ultimate objective of tragedy, they deem it repressive; impurity must not be purged, as the aristotelian concept of catharsis requires, because it is a necessary assault on the social body whose order is imposed by those whom revolutionary theatre exists to challenge.

If the spectator's empathy leads him to delegate his powers to the hero, how can theatre stop serving that established order defined as desirable social harmony? How can it inspire those whom that order oppresses with examples of revolutionary action that the conservative theatre points out as failures? Aesthetically and ideologically, the fundamental opposition is between a drama of order (some would say of oppression) and a drama of liberation (some would say of disorder)—the definition of which is a matter of irreconcilable political choices.

The Theatre
of Experience

 THE THEORIES that influenced the Black Renaissance of the sixties called for a theatre of "black experience" as well as one of struggle, a theatre no longer dependent on white liberals or black militants but created from the most fundamental aspects of Afro-American life.

In the 1968 essay "Black Theatre—Go Home" Ron Milner enjoins his fellow playwrights to create a living art from material and techniques within the community. "The further you go home, the more startlingly new and black the techniques become."[1] He defines theatre as a prism of light that projects warnings, directions, memories, or exemplary creations. Milner envisions a theatre that "displaces and replaces" ideas, concepts, images, and symbols in order to translate the rhythms of black life: far from being a simple reflection of experience, it should give organization and meaning to the confusion of reality.

Five years later, in a manifesto published in the *Village Voice*, Ed Bullins called for an art free from Western tradition and renewed by contact with black people. "We don't want a higher form of white art in blackface: we are working toward something entirely different and new that encompasses the soul and spirit of black people and that represents the whole experience of our being here in this land."[2]

Bullins sees theatre as a monument built from "black awareness," "a citadel of evolving consciousness . . . a sanctuary for the recreation of the black spirit." Defined in such nationalistic and religious terms, art becomes sacred; the theatre is transformed into a place of communion and of celebration dedicated to the creation of communal forms. The promotion of this theatre condemns both borrowing from white theatre and confusing art with politics. Using the Arab proverb "the dogs may bark but the caravan passes on," Bullins calls for an end to the ravings of political theatre; it is time, he argues, for theatre to stop wasting its breath and follow the slow but sure path of the caravan. In this period of profound change and dangerous manipulation, the artist should "hold onto his own." His vocation is not to serve politics but to dedicate himself totally to his people. "Black theatre is not a Theatre of the Lip . . . hustling America, but a people's theatre, dedicated to the continuing survival of black people."[3] Sounding the death knell of an imitative theatre, Bullins reclaims one that articulates the enduring truths set forth by the community. He proposes a rhetoric of love as opposed to superficial political rhetoric; he champions the artist who listens to the will of the people, not one who merely mouths slogans. The theatre draws its true inspiration from black people, assisting and protecting them against leaders who deceive or mislead them. The only engagement art should endorse is the reciprocity between the theatre and the people.

For the playwright and theoretician Paul Carter Harrison, theatre should express as fully as possible the spiritual reality of Afro-American life.[4] The artist should be reunited with the sensibility of his people, revive collective memory, and restore a vision of the world that brooks no compromise. This theatre should be more than simply a theatre of the oppressed, for oppression encloses art in the restrictions of the oppressor and limits the theatre of experience to exposing threats directed against blacks. The theatre must attest to the beleaguered but resilient spirituality of black people and define itself as a spiritual experience.

Militant theatre and theatre of experience should not be seen as successive stages in the development of black drama—one could say that the second was born out of the impossibility of making performance into a tool for struggle, or out of the disenchantment caused by the defeat of revolutionary fervor. It is true that the beginning of the seventies saw both the weakening of the Black Movement and the progressive disappearance of works it inspired, and that the decline of revolutionary black theatre accompanied the decline of radical theatre throughout the United States. However, even if one form did dominate a period, both types of theatre coexisted throughout. Both can be found within the repertory of a single company, of an individual playwright, or even within the same play. They are not mutually exclusive, but complementary. In examining the struggle of blacks, militant theatre intensifies the conditions of victims, but also shows the possibilities for change; it revives the earlier traditions of slave narratives, popular epics, and abolitionist literature. The theatre of experience finds its roots further back in African oral traditions. The two developments nevertheless reveal two very distinct perspectives when one considers the place each gives to the theatrical act. One subordinates theatre to an action foreign to its nature by making it serve the revolutionary cause; the other restores theatre's primordial function and autonomy.

Yet in black theatre, every creation is political. In its own right, the theatre of experience is also revolutionary. It offers blacks an image of themselves that disputes the validity of images offered by the white world. It reveals the dynamism of a culture whose importance and authenticity have been denied, and attempts to develop structures from models within Afro-American culture. Psychologically and aesthetically, the theatre moves far away from the artistic values of the dominant society. In so doing it establishes a different dialectical relation with the reality it examines. It does not pretend to act upon reality, but seeks to apprehend it. Although less critical, its vision is more open. As a theatre of truth, it seeks to integrate all aspects of black life, particularly the most neglected ones. Finally, out of its concern for a new language, it is preoccupied with the modes of discourse that develop from dramatizations found in black tradition—religion, rituals, narrative forms, and music. If it borrows most of its elements from popular culture, it does so to enlarge the culture by proposing specific models, images, and a new representation of reality. The theatre of experience offers a more radical and total definition of black theatre; "coming out of the life experiences of black people in America; its focus is black people and comes exclusively from black playwrights with black audiences as references."[5] This ideological choice merges theatre of experience with revolutionary theatre, a merger that is dictated by the nature of its signs and references. It presupposes that the playwright must be black and eliminates whites as spectators, critics, readers, or audience. Ceasing to antagonize whites, it simply ignores them and addresses a black audience that knows the sociocultural context and the linguistic, visual, auditory codes being used. It is with this audience that communication must be established. The theatre endeavor thus grows out of the participation it encourages.

Finally, the theatre's role in the creation of cultural unity amid militant nationalism must be emphasized. The playwright should both represent the tensions that characterize relations between the races and that tear apart the black community and suggest their possible resolution. The language of this theatre departs from the argument about these conflicts in order to affirm a "blackness" that is shared by all.

The surge of black expression on the stage was considered a revolution in theatre. Ed Bullins has searched for his own symbolic formulation in a brief skit with few words called *The Theme Is Blackness*.[6] The stage and the house are left completely dark; spectators are physically confronted with "blackness" and it is up to them to give form and voice to this entity whose presence is signified by silence and darkness that gradually become unbearable. In this way Bullins symbolizes the movement from militant theatre to theatre of experience: silence sets the stage for another kind of discourse. The created darkness prepares the senses to perceive a different reality that takes form progressively as black theatre itself moves on.

LeRoi Jones/Amiri Baraka, *Dutchman*. Production at the Cherry
Lane Theatre, New York, 1964. Photo Alix Jeffry.

Ruby Dee, Ossie Davis, and Sorrell Booke in a performance of Ossie Davis' *Purlie Victorious*, 1961. Photo Friedman-Abeles.

Louise Stubbs, Donald Griffith, and Claudia McNeil in a performance of Ted Shine's *Contributions*, 1970. Photo Bert Andrews.

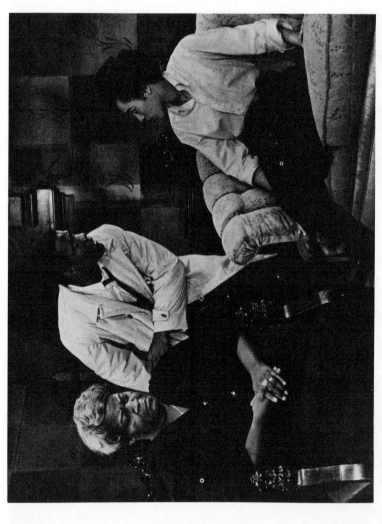

Claudia McNeil, Sidney Poitier, and Diana Sands in a performance of Lorraine Hansberry's *A Raisin in the Sun*, 1959. Photo Friedman-Abeles.

James Baldwin, *The Amen Corner*. Performance at New York's Lincoln Center, Black Theatre Festival U.S.A., 1979. Photo Bert Andrews.

LeRoi Jones/Amiri Baraka, *Slave Ship*. Performance at Brooklyn Academy of Music, 1969. Photo Bert Andrews.

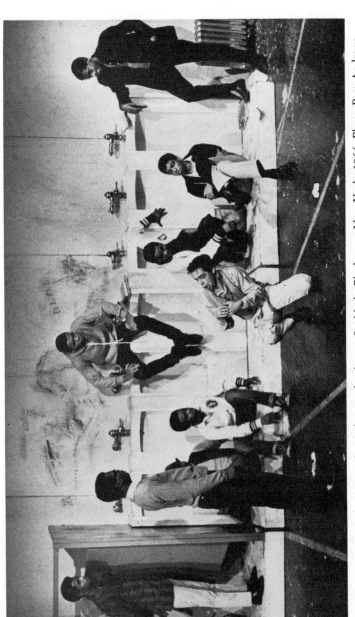

LeRoi Jones/Amiri Baraka, *The Toilet*. Production at St. Marks Playhouse, New York, 1964. Photo Bert Andrews.

Joseph Walker, *Ododo*. Production by The Negro Ensemble Company, St. Marks Playhouse, New York, 1970. Photo Bert Andrews.

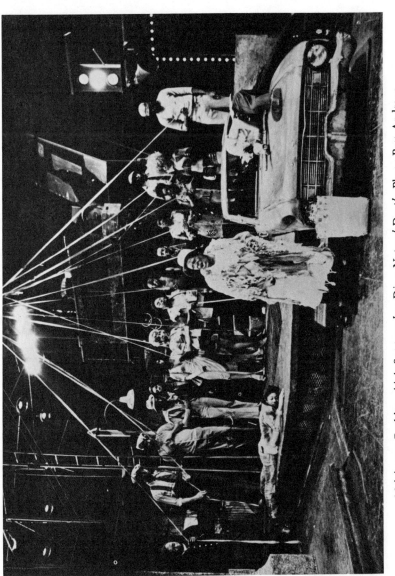

Melvin van Peebles, *Ain't Supposed to Die a Natural Death*. Photo Bert Andrews.

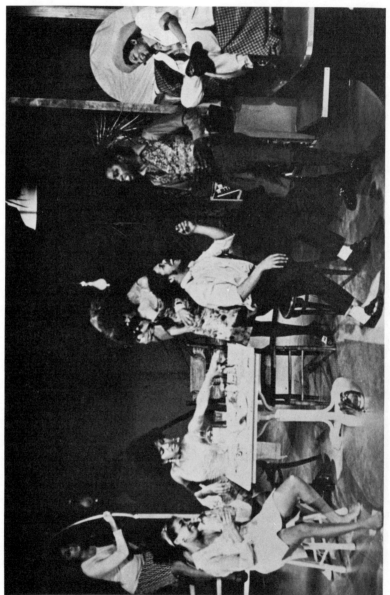

Ed Bullins, *The Duplex*. Photo Martha Swope.

Douglas Turner Ward, *Day of Absence*. Production at St. Marks Playhouse, New York, 1970. Photo Bert Andrews.

Micki Grant, *Don't Bother Me, I Can't Cope*. 1976 production. Photo Bert Andrews.

Metaphors in the Titles of Plays

Theatre begins with confrontation. Black people come face to face with the reality of their experiences in America, and are reminded of how Africans were enslaved and how they migrated from plantations to ghettos; in short, how they became victims.

The most ambitious play among those that revive the past is *Ododo* by Joseph Walker.[7] The play follows the prototype of Baraka's *Slave Ship*, but uses music to evoke the major movements in Afro-American history and to reveal truths: *Ododo* in Swahili means "truth." A succession of songs and scenes presents the genesis of a people in a land ruled by gods long before history was recorded. Foreigners, who do not have "the color of the earth," arrive suddenly on the scene and are offered food and shelter. After a symbolic night, the people awaken terrified to find themselves bound together by their hands and feet. Their long and harrowing imprisonment is marked by separation, chains, revolt, and for some, a fiery death meant to destroy the conqueror's ships.

With slavery begins a life of trial that continues well after Emancipation. "Let me tell you about slavery and what it did to you and me." Reconstruction results in the displacement of blacks to northern ghettos, where they still search for their own voice and for freedom from white paternalism. Blacks thus recognize themselves as victims in order to stop wallowing in their defeat and to take charge of their destiny.

These basic experiences in the lives of black people recur in the theatre whose goal is to show not the mechanism of exploitation but the common features of black life and perspectives. More dialectical than didactic, the theatre forges new metaphors whose meaning goes beyond the single event, seizing upon images that stimulate reflection and anchor the collective memory.

A brief look at the titles of some plays reveals a concern for metaphorical representation and illustrates the varied aspects of black experience. Some titles refer to maxims borrowed from the blues or from popular speech and are readily identified by black audiences. Thus *Trouble in Mind* by Alice Childress recalls the tribulations evoked in the heyday of the blues. *Who's Got His Own* by Ron Milner brings back Billie Holiday's famous song "God Bless the Child Who's Got His Own." Other titles like *It Bees That Way* and *It Has No Choice* reveal resignation and disillusionment, while some express the rejection of a condition and the hope of changing it. Many titles come from popular sayings: *Ain't Supposed to Die a Natural Death*, *Don't Play Us Cheap*, *What If It Turned Up Heads*, *Don't Bother Me*, *I Can't Cope*, *Don't Let*

It Go to Your Head, Gettin' It Together. Often a poetic image will serve as a point of departure for a metaphorical development (*And We Own the Night* derives from a poem by Baraka). Other titles allude to the ruses of slaves or of trickster figures; *Wine in the Wilderness*, with its biblical resonances, speaks about wine as a form of nourishment and revival; *This Bird of Dawning Singeth All Night* depicts secular patience. *The Drinking Gourd*, taken from a slave song, contains a double allusion to nourishing water and to the seven-star constellation of the "dipper," an image of hope for fugitive slaves who used the North Star as their guide. Other titles recall cultural practices and contemporary verbal games: *Cop and Blow*, *The Mummer's Play*, or the dramatized rituals of *Charades . . .* , *Parades . . .* , *Ceremonies*.

Metaphors of place are common, as in *No Place To Be Somebody* and *The Meat Rack*. Images of exclusion and imprisonment or of garbage are striking. Blacks are condemned to live in degradation, close to sewers and toilets. "Everything's a gutter," says Jude, a bitter old man in *Requiem for Brother X*. Many plays return to images associated with filth, stench, ruin, to describe not only the sordid places where blacks are forced to live but also the contaminated latrine which is America itself, "a great unflushed toilet," as Edgar White says in *The Mummer's Play*. Rats and roaches are inevitable companions for humans who end up identifying with them. The two protagonists in Melvin Van Peebles's *Dont Play Us Cheap* enjoy dressing up as cockroaches in order to upset a family gathering. In *A Rat's Mass* by Adrienne Kennedy the characters see themselves as rats. Clay Goss's *Mars* shows a roach-man who wants to join other blacks on the planet Mars in order to know real life. In *Roots* by Gil Moses an old man finds near a rat trap an image that resembles his own existence. Alice Childress's *Mojo* presents a couple who grieve over their inability to verbalize love when they are surrounded by rats and garbage.

Next to sewers is the underground world of basements and cellars where blacks are kept from the light. The hospital, the prison, the funeral parlor all figure prominently as symbolic places. In *Mojo* the hospital with its immaculate whiteness indicates the exile and physical deterioration of blacks. The funeral parlor in Edgar White's *The Wonderfull Yeare* becomes a metaphor for the courtship of death, not because all blacks will someday end up there, but because all blacks are incarcerated. "All black people are in prison," says a protagonist in White's *The Life and Times of J. Walter Smintheus*, in which both prison and hospital suggest containment.

Black experience is also represented by images of movement: forced mobility in migration, departures, returns (*A Son Come Home*), followed by farewells and new discoveries (*His First Step*). Feverish movement and never-ending quests oppose forced immobility and offer proof that one can go somewhere. Character movement in the stage directions can take on considerable importance. In *Requiem for Brother X*, for example, only Nate moves about on stage; his brother, an Uncle Tom taken with the promises of whites, remains glued to a stool, and their tired and disappointed father is riveted to a wheelchair. Other plays denounce the motions of an infernal cycle of routine. In *Black Cycle* one generation is forced to accept the lies and compromises of a previous one, unless of course someone can escape (*The Break Out*) or break the cycle (*Take a Giant Step*). The dominant language also becomes a prison, especially as blacks are taught to stay in their place, to repeat lessons learned (*A Lesson in a Dead Language*), to become robots (*The Electronic Nigger*) or well-trained puppets (*How Do You Do*). The rewards are certainly absurd (*Junebug Graduates Tonight*; *A Medal for Willie*). Other plays warn blacks about the difficulty of breaking away (*On Being Hit*) from the relations of master-slave, employer-domestic, teacher-student, guard-prisoner. Those blacks rejected by the world like a bad hand of cards (*Dirty Hearts*) can escape only through parties, dreams, or the cruel games of the imagination, as in Adrienne Kennedy's plays. Still, the black man can become a pilgrim in exile, wandering in search of his lost identity. Condemned to live on credit, he expects what will never come; cursed from birth to death, as in White's *Crucificado*, he is forever in the wrong place at the wrong time like the hero in *The Mummer's Play*. The black man is a "bastard" who is refused any home. He can seek to relieve his solitude in dialogue with stuffed owls (*The Owl Killer*), birds of wisdom and of death whose response (*The Owl Answers*) can be full of anguish.

This metaphorical discourse unfolds in play after play, title after title. Each work is part of a vast intertextuality that takes up earlier images and continuously reinvents them. Reading these associations, repetitions, and complementary oppositions produces a polyphonic scenario.

Race Relations

Race relations lie at the heart of the theatre of experience, which does more than simply illustrate basic metaphors; it develops new scripts, creates new situations, and casts roles differently. Two major kinds of plots emerge: one shows blacks confronting a white world in a different way from that in revolutionary theatre; the other shows blacks confronting one another and depicts whites only parenthetically.

Every image of race relations draws upon the efforts of whites to establish and maintain their superiority. Whether in the segregated South or in northern ghettos, the white man appears as The Man, Mr. Charlie, Uncle Sam, or the Great White Father; he is a master, an exploiter, and often an executioner. Despite these barriers, whites and blacks come into contact and confront each other. The theatre holds the white man responsible for the misfortunes of the black community and puts him on trial. Through him, the white audience is interrogated, attacked, and, if possible, eliminated. This symbolic aggression reaches beyond the audience and to the whole of American society.

The first voice emerging from the theatre of experience is that of the blues, the blues of anger and resistance, not of resignation. James Baldwin's *Blues For Mr. Charlie*[8] is the outcry of a community revolted by a murder, the clamor of a people fed up with being brutalized. "It's that damn white God that's been lynching us and burning us and castrating us and raping our women and robbing us of everything that makes a man a man." From the perspective of the theatre of experience, Baldwin's play is remarkable for showing whites not through the unequivocal character of a cruel master but through a liberal who calls himself a friend of blacks and through a poor white who is exploited by his own people. The play tries to show the ambiguous relations of class within conflicts of race: discord between "niggers" and "crackers," aborted alliances between well-to-do whites and blacks. The wealthy Parnell is rejected by the white community because of his interest in blacks, and by the black community because of his paternalism and his failure to honor commitments. Parnell cannot do anything without appearing as a traitor to one or the other group. The play's message — that the two worlds are irreconcilable — leaves no hope.

Beyond these acts are the taboos inscribed in the collective unconscious, which eventually come to light. Blacks are stereotyped as violent primitives or as beloved mammies betrayed by the "dirty niggers." On a deeper level, the antagonistic communities are siblings (born of the same white father, raised and nourished by the same black mother) and this biological and emotional tie underlies the conflicts presented in the play. Parnell is the rejected father; Lyle and Richard are rival brothers. Whites will make the black brother pay for his individuality as if he were a "native son" whose return from exile constitutes an unacceptable challenge. In this way Richard is a marginal figure both as a black man and as an artist. His sexual exploits with white women spark another provocation. Between Richard, who seduces white women, and Lyle, who rapes black women, the taboos of the dominant society can be fought reciprocally.

The play thus seems to exceed Baldwin's intentions, stated in the preface, to paint a universal portrait of a murderer in socioeconomic rather than racial terms. *Blues* remains primarily a testimony about *race* relations in the South, not only because it relies on actual events, but because its very images and structures are documentary. Indeed, a third of the play takes place in a courtroom, which is an image of what black theatre should be: the place where the truth is told.

The Bird Cage, a little-known play by Floyd Barbour,[9] is part of the same repertory of plays about blacks and whites in the South. In a land where birds are set free and blacks imprisoned, whites make a sport out of mocking then killing an old errand boy, one of the "coon niggers." The anger of the victim's son goes much further than that of Rev. Meridian in Baldwin's play and becomes a symbolic revolt.

Langston Hughes's *Mother and Child*[10] examines the consequences of a rich white planter's wife giving birth to a mulatto. Hughes does not attempt a sociological analysis of miscegenation; he simply dramatizes the reactions of the people, represented by a church choir of black women. The dramatic interest rests on a series of interrogations not about the identity of the father but about the consequences of illegitimacy for the child, the mother, and the entire black community, which is held responsible by whites for the "crime" of one of its members (for although sexual relations between a white man and a black woman are tolerated as long as they are kept secret, relations between a black man and a white woman remain taboo).

If sexual relations between the races are criminal in the South, they have been better accepted in the North, particularly during the Civil Rights era. A whole decade was swept up in the vision of a unified America where whites and blacks would struggle side by side for a national ideal. This hope is denounced in a short play by Paul Carter Harrison, *Experimental Leader*,[11] in which a conflict arises between the leader of the black community—a homosexual who wears a white mask—and an interracial couple who want to save blacks from disaster. The leader opposes the couple's intervention because he feels that the union of blacks and whites cannot end discrimination. The black man refuses to follow orders from the white woman. When it is discovered that the homosexual is attracted to the husband, a struggle ensues and the leader is killed. The use of a homosexual character, whose racial identity is ambiguous (since he wears a white mask) complicates the usual scheme of race relations; Harrison wants to remind us that racial conflicts are often subsumed under sexual rivalries. He delights in refining, not muddling, the elements of a situation that border on the stereotypical. Here, race relations no longer constitute a source of tragedy but offer an occasion for games.

Harrison's *Pavane for a Deadpan Minstrel*[12] also depicts the crucial problem of ambivalent racial identity, but in the mode of farce and parody. In a cafe, black Mr. Brown and white Mr. Smith exchange masks and racial identities and set out to seduce Miss Polly. They compete in song and dance, using styles suggesting the other's race: the black man dances ballet, the white man a jazz rhythm; they exchange insults drawn from one another's culture. The competition ends when the white mask seems to accept what the black mask (worn by the white actor) brings to the pantomime by the exotic beauty of its movements. However, the black mask has taken the white girl by force and strangled her. True to its "historical imperative," the white mask must punish the savage who has dared to violate the white woman. Yet when the masks fall the playwright poses the ironical question: Who is dead? "The white mask is removed, thereby exposing the features of Mr. Brown, and Polly remains stretched out on the floor, prostrate, next to a dead Mr. Smith. Or was it the 'black stud' myth that was dead?"

The interpretation given the ending of this play in a performance at the Actors Studio in 1963 caused much controversy. Did the final murder mean that a stereotype had disappeared? Or did the "event" itself constitute a ritual meant to eliminate clichés attached to the mask? Removing the mask from one protagonist also unmasks its double. The answer to the question of who was killed remains purely academic, if we are to believe the playwright: "Mr. Brown, the bad nigger, is alive and well and ready for other conquests, while Mr. Smith has died from the weight of his own oppression."

The sexual metaphor is frequently used to comment on interracial relations. Definitively presented in *Dutchman*, motifs and figures of seduction, rape, and castration constantly reappear in this theatre where interracial couples are usually composed of white women and black men.[13] Ed Bullins' *The Taking of Miss Janie*[14] (first staged in 1975) varies the format. The play takes place in the sixties when all optimism about race relations was shattered by the murder of Martin Luther King. Morty, a young black, meets Janie in a creative writing class; years later, he rapes her brutally. For Bullins, this rape expresses the end of hope, the destruction of a dream.[15] The black man refuses the role of eunuch that white America has granted him. Rape is committed here as a statement of refusal to be emasculated and is presented as the culmination of black evolution from integration and separation to self-determination.

Attempts to destroy and seduce blacks are shown in Archie Shepp's *Junebug* in the mode of allegory and burlesque, as we have seen in chapter 2. The graduation ceremony where Junebug receives a prize is both a rite of initiation into American society and a sacrifice that is the price of citizenship. The beautiful America offers him a deal ("give me your love and I will make you a rich nigger"), which Junebug accepts by stating another promise ("one day I will come back to kill you"). Putting himself in the service of America-the-protector, whose goodwill he is never supposed to forget, Junebug can see neither this decoy as a mother nor Uncle Sam as a father. The violent end in which Junebug and America are killed reveals the absurdity of any attempt at alliance between the races.

The title of Charles Gordone's play *No Place To Be Somebody*[16] summarizes many plays in black theatre. The title also comments on Richard in *Blues for Mr. Charlie* and on Junebug. The play pits blacks against each other in an America that has no place for them. Here three characters search in vain for a role to play: Sweets, a dying bum who embodies the "bad nigger," wants nothing more than to ward off Charlie fever; Johnny, caught up in ambition, wants to counteract white power by organizing a black mafia. But the game is lost before it starts. Sweets dies trying to defend Johnny, while Gabe, the third figure, prefers to shoot the frustrated mafioso rather than see him engaged in a lost cause. He fires the weapon that Johnny gave him and places it close to the dead body to suggest a suicide. As a writer and unemployed actor, he entones a hymn about the destiny of his companions: "You are black. But you ain't goin' git no chance to prove it. Not on no stage, you ain't. You remin' whitey o' too many things he don't wanna look at" (p. 114). After acting out the role of destiny, Gabe must grieve, and in the play's epilogue he reappears as a woman dressed in black. "I will mourn a passing, yeah, the passing, the ending of a people dying."

Gordone's play, which won a Pulitzer Prize in 1970, shifts from realism to surrealism and to melodrama without fully examining any of these modes, thus diminishing the plausibility of the characters. In a tirade punctuated by a phrase which has since become famous ("There's more to being black than meets the eye") Gabe states the basic components of blackness:

Bein' black is like the way you walk and talk!
It's a way of lookin' at life!

. . . . .
Bein' black has a way of makin' ya call somebody
a mu-tha-fu-kah, an' really meanin' it! An' namin'
eva body broh-tha, even if you don't. (Pp. 79–80)

Yet Gordone never reaches the point of theatricalizing what he
celebrates here as the distinctive trait of "soul."

Paul Carter Harrison's *Tabernacle*[17] offers a different kind of performance than either the drama of *Blues*, the allegory of *Junebug*, or the
melodrama of *No Place*. "I am not interested in the duplication of oppression on the stage," Harrison has stated. "I am interested in
heightening what oppression means on stage, in trying to touch another
sensory level of experience, what it looks, sounds and feels like."[18]
Tabernacle is a Passion play and "a play within a play." The production
takes place in a church and is presented by a minister who combines the
talents of an African sorcerer and a Baptist preacher. He tells his congregation that several parishioners are about to perform a mystery play.
The spectators are seated while the performance gets under way and the
actors are introduced; the chorus of mothers is played by men wearing
masks, in order, Harrison explains, "to raise up the image given to the
black woman and disengage it from a too sociological context." The
mother should be considered a force, not a character. Two teenagers,
Adam and Ham, are accused of killing Anna the Panhandle, a Jewish
woman who sold clothing at exorbitant prices. A trial takes place,
followed by scenes that mime different moments of the event: the
murder, the sessions in court, the pleas of the lawyers.

Performed in a grotesque manner, these scenes emphasize the farcical
aspects of every trial in which the lawyer becomes the accuser. The
masks worn should be taken off at the end of the mystery to suggest a
dynamic relationship between masks and real faces. The facade of life is
accepted only to strip it better of pretense.

Edgar White also broaches the problem of justice for blacks, through
the trial of the Scottsboro Boys, young men falsely accused of raping two
white women in the thirties. *The Burghers of Calais*[19] takes place in a
prison. Six visiting couples are offered a show put on by the inmates in
which each inmate plays himself. Here the narrator, like a ringmaster,
presents the protagonists, comments on the action, gets carried away in
digressions, serves as the author's intermediary, and finally gets angry
when characters take liberties with their lines. Seated among the
onlookers is the author, who intervenes from time to time to give advice. The players carry placards to indicate a place or announce an inten-

tion: "The author says the sun was shining." There is no pretense of realism in the setting. The plot closely follows the tribulations of the young inmates during their nineteen-year incarceration. The play's strong base of accusation is subtle, and its interrogation occurs with care and precision. The incongruity of the questions suggests the incongruity of the trial, which never establishes the guilt of the accused.

Several protagonists are presented: Bagatelle, a sensible figure whose only weapon is his wit; the accused, who are still in prison; Club Hawk, the sheriff; Leiby, the lawyer who arrives in a white suit to claim his clients ("Where are my Negroes?"); the liberal Lazorillo; John Day of the NAACP who aids the victims only to enhance his prestige; Miss Twitromp and her friend Susan Docile; the Inquisitor; Bella Donna, the mother of Bagatelle. The burlesque character of this *commedia dell'arte* is underscored by the choice of names like Bagatelle, Nicknack, Quid and Proquo, and even the judge Pudic, the alleged victim Twitromp, and the deputy Cormorant. Behind these innumerable characters and interminable scenes of a recalcitrant and defective justice, groups from the NAACP to the Communist Party get involved in the notorious case, mostly to get publicity.

In the course of the performance each actor rehearses the part he is given by the author, who is congratulated with ardent kisses and compliments from several spectators. Only Bagatelle and his mother manage to make changes without the author's approval. Bella Donna recalls that her life has been nothing but a series of lies, and that their only sin was being born black. The son argues that nineteen years of prison has only helped to serve the Fourteenth Amendment. He states that the sympathy and generosity of whites can be just as dangerous as their fear. These subversive intentions are not part of the scenario, but Bagatelle refuses to take on the role assigned to him. He insults and challenges the author and offers his own version of events as the scenes progress.

Burghers thus offers a new metaphorical representation of theatrical creation. The underlying theme (injustice) and the characters (the accused) are at the mercy of those who interpret their story and of a public that judges them. The author disposes of his text just as white power disposed of the nine suspects and of blacks in general; neither will accept alterations in the script. As a last resort, aesthetics has priority over truth, as the narrator tells the players: "The Author says that he couldn't care less if you all killed each other one second after the play is over, but now you're interfering with his sense of the aesthetic."[20]

In this alienated universe, the sane become insane. Lazarillo offers to have Bagatelle examined by a psychiatrist, and each time unpleasant truths are presented outraged visiting spectators leave the prison. The last one walks out in anger when Bagatelle alludes to failures in his life. Not only does Bagatelle appear out of place as a character commenting on his destiny, but he has the audacity to try to make the spectator feel guilty for events that happened thirty or forty years ago. Bagatelle is reminded, ironically, that the function of theatre is to entertain, not to disturb. White uses this inverted image in an effective if not totally original way. The playwright is interested in examining the possibilities of theatre, not in the revision of history. White's denunciation of injustice toward blacks occurs indirectly in the mode of farce and parody which, on the manifest level of the production, concerns the domain of justice as a metaphor of white America, and on the latent level, the world of theatre.

Whatever the scenario's central image or metaphor, the basic relationship between oppressor and oppressed is always examined. Relations of power usually place the black man in a subordinate position. All of Philip Hayes Dean's plays, for example, revolve around the single message that white America needs "negroes," not authentic blacks. This negro, a longtime figure on the American stage, is as hard to get rid of in black theatre as old clothes or masks. Dean tries to show certain parallel behaviors: on the one hand, the various manifestations of a superiority complex among whites and their pretensions to define black soul in terms of psychiatry, entertainment, or ethnology; on the other hand, the different rituals blacks undergo that attempt to humiliate or emasculate them. *Thunder in the Index*, which along with *This Bird of Dawning* and *Minstrel Boy* makes up the trilogy *American Night Cry*, presents the realm of psychiatry.[21] Dean's counterpart to White's author in *Burghers* is a doctor who interprets the characters and their illnesses.

As omniscient as the playwright, the doctor establishes once and for all the criteria of normality for the characters. Joshua, his patient, shows symptoms that make him interesting but incurable. His own language (ghetto speech) is proof of his imbalance. The clinician uses a technical jargon that is incapable of conveying the subtleties, symbols, and truths of his patient's responses. Any sign of difference indicates inferiority. Patients are forced into a treatment that annihilates them, unless, following Joshua's example, they revolt, reverse the roles, and send the therapist off to enjoy the delights of electroshock.

Dean's *Minstrel Boy* and *The Last American Dixie Band* show the progressive dehumanization and exploitation of black entertainers in American show business. Rainbow, like other Toms, coons, mulattos, and mammies on stage, is a figure without a face, an oddity inviting laughter. Everywhere the black man is examined by "experts." *The Dream Time* presents the rape of Africa by missionary ethnographers who bind and gag the Dark Continent, reducing its inhabitants to categories of good little negroes, crazy negroes, and dirty negroes. Every black man is thus confronted by this frightful expertise which strives to define and label him, and the theatre continues to stage these confrontations.

While this situation provokes humor and sarcasm from Philip Hayes Dean, it remains painful for Adrienne Kennedy's characters, whose prototype is the bastard mulatto woman. Torn between the inseparable yet irreconcilable black and white worlds, Kennedy's heroine identifies with one then the other, alternately merging past with the present, personal destiny with history, America with the continent of her ancestors. Unlike most authors who view Africa as the motherland, Kennedy turns toward England. Her journey, similar to Edgar White's, opposes Anglo-Saxon heritage to Afro-American tradition. The symbolism in her plays extends the surrealistic limits of a hallucinatory universe peopled with figures from a nightmare.[22]

Kennedy's first play, *Funnyhouse of a Negro*, staged by Edward Albee,[23] was inspired by an amusement park attraction whose gates are flanked by two enormous grimacing figures—a metaphor for America "where real places don't exist, only bizarre houses." Two white characters, the landlady and Raymond Mann, play these frightening sentinels who guard against self-knowledge in the sardonic and exaggerated manner of carnival monsters. An expressionistic setting suggests the queen's chambers, a student's room, a ballroom, and a jungle. Except for the young girl, her father, and Patrice Lumumba, the characters are in whiteface. The heroine seeks her identity in this baroque setting peopled with historical figures (Queen Victoria, Jesus, and others). She questions the creatures that share her solitude: the white doves, the sinister ravens, and an owl whose cry echoes her concern, "Who am I?" Born of a black man and a mulatto woman, she imagines that her mother wanted her to be the New Messiah who returned to Africa in order to save the race. She imagines various fates for her father: either she herself kills him for having given her a taste of the jungle, or he commits suicide upon hearing of the death of Lumumba, or again he lives with a white prostitute. Between the *murder* which punishes him for giving her an undesirable heritage, the *suicide* which unites him with a great historical figure, and the *treason* which unites him to the white world, the heroine seeks her own voice. She hangs herself as the curtain falls, and her death becomes as real or as imaginary as the games she has just played.

Kennedy's play can be related to Dean's *This Bird of Dawning*, in which a young black woman talks to her white twin, whom she eventually kills. The heroine of *Funnyhouse*, however, commits suicide because she cannot reconcile the different poles of her being. Her absurd death is preceded by much laughter on an empty stage. Her corpse balancing above a void is the image of a life that wavers between a rejected past and a confused present. There is no place for blacks to be somebody. In this play color symbolism is determinant. Whiteness attracts and repels: it evokes leprosy, and the plaster statue of Queen Victoria, the pale light "unreal and ugly," and wan masks are all symbols of sterility. In contrast, the darkness of the jungle teeming with life is overwhelming. The props have the vulgarity of a carnival setting, underscoring the absurdity of the place and the ritual.

In the same atmosphere of fantasy and gloom, Kennedy's *The Owl Answers*[24] presents the drama of a young girl torn between the body and the spirit, the past and the present. Clara Passmore is the illegitimate daughter of William Matheson, one of the wealthiest whites of Jacksonville. Her mother probably killed herself after giving birth, and Clara was adopted by a white Baptist minister and raised by his unfeeling wife. When the pastor dies, Clara is forbidden to attend the funeral. Later, she resigns her teaching position in order to make a pilgrimage to Great Britain, the source of her paternal heritage. Except for scattered details and fragments of memory, she knows little about her past. Her wild imagination recreates her childhood by merging it with history: Clara's mother is successively the Black Woman, Anne Boleyn, or the pastor's wife. Her father is "the Richest White Man in Town," the Reverend Passmore, or the dead father. The white mask he wears hides a black face whose skin in turn comes off. Racial and historical identities blend: alternately bastard, Owl, and Virgin Mary, Clara is both living and dead, man and woman, black skin and white mask, a child bearing the body of a dead mother. Enamored of a culture she wants to join, Clara arrives at the home of her white ancestors and visits places and people named Big Ben, Shakespeare, Tower of London, Dickens, and William the Conqueror, but at each turn the gates close in order to imprison or exclude her. Her plea to enter St. Paul's where her father is buried goes unheard because a black woman cannot possibly have white ancestors. But is she white or black? Is she, as the dead man says, only the "daughter of somebody that cooked for me"? Is she the descendant or the bastard of a missing person? Is she in front of the gates of the Tower of London, or in a New York City subway about to pick up a black man? This whirlwind of hallucinatory questions signals the vicious cycle of a present that is totally incongruous. The scenes telescope. The mother kills herself with a butcher knife, and a white bird carries her body to the dome of St. Peter's in Rome. The father, suddenly dead in London, dies a second time. At the altar where Clara takes refuge and where her father has just died, she rebuffs the black man and tries to kill him, but prefers instead to kill herself. Like the owl, she stares into empty space: "I call God and the owl answers." A ghost in death as in life, she is now condemned to wander in a world of darkness, pierced by the cries of birds, shaken by the flapping of their wings like the pages of the notebook where she recorded events in her life. In this last scene, Clara connects to the symbol of the phantom ship developed in *Dutchman*. The doors open and close on emptiness, the borders between the real and the imaginary worlds disappear; the ambivalence of the protagonist's emotions responds to the ambiguity of the play's metaphor.

The reference to the owl organizes the symbolic structure of the play. Characters frequently assume the posture of night birds: the black mother is "perched like an owl," and when Clara dies her look has the open fixed stare of a nocturnal predator.[25] Haunted by the belief that all living creatures are part human and troubled by the frequency of animal references for blackness, Adrienne Kennedy explained her choice of this bird to evoke the sounds of the African jungle. Owls are the companions of solitude and the friends of darkness. Their cries are also the distress call of blacks who seek their identity in vain—"Who am I?" Other characteristics make the bird an appropriate symbol for blacks. Its dark brown color makes it almost invisible to careless eyes; but it has, in fact, a changeable color, suggesting that blackness is a more complex reality than has generally been admitted. Kennedy questions the whole black/white symbolic structure presented in theatre and improves upon the metaphor of invisibility. She thus calls attention to the American tendency to consign the mullato to obscurity and marginality.[26]

In Kennedy's *A Lesson in a Dead Language*[27] a large white dog teaches the lesson "I am bleeding" to seven schoolgirls surrounded by statues of Jesus, Mary, Joseph, two Wise Men, and a shepherd. The blood that the children must learn to recognize as a fact of life is not only the symbol of the female but the sign of sexual games that end in death. All the images of birth are conveyed with visions of death, and every game leads to an inevitable fall. The "dead" language of this exchange is borrowed from parental authority, Christian dogma, Roman history, and is stated in a monotonous tone, evoking scenes of punishment and murder in which life courts death. The rejected identity is disguised as frustrated sexuality. The lesson for women is the impossibility of achieving anything without being wounded with humiliation or rape.

No matter where her plays are set, Adrienne Kennedy's theatre unfolds in a closed world where the character is a prisoner of creatures that violate her privacy. Insane asylums, cages in a zoo, gates of a palace convey imprisonment, as do rats and pestilence. Before launching her metaphors, Kennedy grounds each place and reference in real experience. The stage is thus transformed into a closed space where the forces of a divided self confront one another. In this space are elements that the audience should recognize in order to rebuild the image of the black psyche. The bastard is the symbol of an aborted identity: in order to avenge the shame that stigmatizes her, she must kill the parents who repudiate her or the man who humiliated her, commit suicide, or get rid of the illegitimate fruit she is forced to carry.

Sun, a poem dedicated to the memory of Malcolm X,[28] completes the cycle of Kennedy's plays and offers a vision of a bloody world where the limbs and entrails of mutilated animals are tossed about. Yellow, orange, and red suns fight over this territory with a black star of death and the moon to which the black man is attached. The world knew a moment of hope, of seeing the truth triumph from Malcolm's example, but it explodes with his assassination; the suns and moon fly about with his scattered remains, spilling bits of color and blood until nothing is left of the man except his voice, which is finally silenced.

Adrienne Kennedy's theatre makes an eminently symbolist contribution to the new drama of black experience. This esoteric universe, in a frenzy of visual and auditory images, surrenders to impotence and the wildness of the imagination in a nightmare of intolerable reality, which uses fantasy to reveal a hidden truth.

Dramatizing race relations has led black playwrights to grapple with a multitude of themes. Interracial relations, manifestations of oppression, forms of injustice, manipulation of ethnic identity by white institutions are boldly and pitilessly analyzed. Characters who are marginal in everyday life, as in traditional drama, are introduced in the new repertory as victims, prisoners, inmates, the dead, and those to whom Adrienne Kennedy gives new voice: the mulatto bastards. Most of the plays are not content merely to state this message, to diversify the thematic situations, or to widen the range of possible roles. They also strive to surpass theatre's tendency to bear witness or stage demonstrations: their forms are primarily farce, burlesque, allegory, and fantasy. In these plays, the central message is developed out of an analogy to the world of theatre in which the white man has traditionally been either a despotic director or an omniscient dramatist. These images of theatricality serve the dual function of representing the manner in which whites have treated blacks in real life and the fate of blacks in the entertainment world. Both the roles that blacks have accepted and the different masks they have worn are revealed simultaneously. If the dramatic forms that have had the most success in American theatre (farce or vaudeville, melodrama or minstrel) reappear, it is most often with a subversive intention: parody shows these forms to be just another kind of deception.

The Family and the Community

The Arab proverb "the dogs may bark but the caravan passes on" announces Ed Bullins' call for theatre that is attentive to the passing caravan, to the struggle to ensure group continuity and cohesion. This kind of drama is dedicated to the community; white power appears indirectly, by the distortions it creates in the behavior, tensions, and frustrations that pit blacks against one another.

The theme of this theatre is "blackness," or black experience as it is lived, not abstracted into an idea. The scene shifts to northern and midwestern urban centers, the ghettos where blacks gather after migration from the South and await the fulfillment of the American Dream. Time stretches toward a slow and uncertain future. This theatre celebrates what is basic to black experience, while taking into account the flux and flow of events that modify it and alter the course of history.

In this kind of theatre the home and the street become protagonists and poles around which the cultural models in the community are structured. Each has its own set of characters and a variety of relations: couplings and separations, cooperation and discord, love and hate. The home is depicted more as an extended rather than a nuclear family. The street is described through diverse individuals who are marginal to society (prostitutes, con men, drunks, and drug addicts); they are the misfits of the larger community, products of the so-called culture of poverty. In this way the home and the street appear as antithetical spaces. One is a structured institution organized around certain values which it helps to preserve despite rivalries between men and women, children and parents. The other is a world that appears too heterogeneous and anarchistic to be called a social institution but that possesses nonetheless a structure, conventions, and rules.

It would be too simplistic to see the opposition between the family and the street as one of contradiction, for these two entities are parts of one social structure. Some white sociologists have gone so far as to deny the existence of a black "family" according to the definitions of the dominant society, and to ignore the "community" created by the dispossessed who crowd the streets of the ghetto just because they have no real social status or clear identity or share in a recognized culture. In this perspective the street appears even more picturesque and exotic. It is hard to dissociate the theatrical characterization of the street and of the family from the images associated with them. Here again the theatre discards the popular images and offers new ones.

To outside observers the street and the family have provided a wealth of stereotypes. The chaotic world of the street has been held responsible for the lack of cohesion in the family; inversely, the dissolution of family relations has been blamed for the predominance of the street. Many myths have formed around the image of the absent father, the angry, domineering matriarch, depraved prostitutes, and proliferating drug addicts, pimps, and criminals. The theatre examines these stereotypes carefully, before allowing them to depict daily life. It offers no analysis of the "incurable pathology" of a deprived community, nor any explanation of behavior to aid arbitrary programs. It plunges us into the depths of an experience in order to ferret out the authentic manifestations of an environment that is naturally complex, diversified, and infinitely rich. In a sense, theatre, like unprejudiced ethnology, has the single aim of rigorously restoring culture.

But theatre develops from other goals as well. By giving due recognition to a barely explored reality, it establishes a new system of values and formulates an aesthetics that runs counter to the American ethos whose "experts" are content merely to "rehabilitate"questionable social elements. The theatre proposes different criteria to those of the dominant society that measure what is normal and what is pathological. The creation of drama helps raise up an alternate image that defines the collective values and ideals, the conflicts within the group as well as its desire for understanding and freedom. Theatre seeks to reconstruct a system of signs, to reunify group symbols, and to formulate them into a language or a model situation.

Theatre's search for an ethic doubles as an aesthetic aim. Models for drama can be found in all modes of behavior and expression found within the ghetto and even in the discredited culture. The intensive representation these modes and rites receive on stage establishes their legitimacy. What happens on stage cannot be ignored. From there begins the rich exchange between black experience and dramatic art. Theatre draws from real life, and in return offers multiple meanings of that life.

The Family: Hero or Anti-hero?

"Expert" studies of the black family such as the Moynihan Report describe the persistent failure of blacks to create stable family units;[29] if the entire society depends on the institution of the family, then the "deterioration of the black family" leads to the demise of the community. Paradoxically, the benevolent attitude of liberal scholars toward blacks has led to the same conclusion. The stereotypes have only been rationalized and the image remains negative. The Moynihan Report is a startling example of the way white liberals have tried to legislate on behalf of the black community while remaining ignorant of its culture and social fabric. Black theatre could neither ignore these attitudes nor remain apart from the debate; indeed, the issues theatre tries to raise are central to the whole question of the black family.

The debate follows two different paths. The liberal approach shows how the black family conformed to models of white society and attributes its alienation to socioeconomic factors that handicap blacks. The other approach seeks neither to rehabilitate nor to explain, but to present the family as a group of individuals both united by ties that have nothing to do with legality and profoundly divided by conflicts. The family appears as a dynamic unit, a cultural entity gifted with its own vitality; what must be dramatized are the dialectical relations it maintains with other elements of the community and with the dominant society.[30]

Undoubtedly, Lorraine Hansberry's *A Raisin in the Sun* (see Chapter 1) provides the most interesting prototype of the black family ever developed in contemporary theatre. It has served as a paradigm for a whole series of representations, in which this model is sometimes amplified and diversified, sometimes radically contested.

Hansberry endows the Younger family with characteristics that stem from contradictory intentions. She sets out to challenge existing stereotypes by retracing the important episodes in the history of this exemplary family. However, the situations in which the Youngers are placed and their behavior show them to be exceptional and separate from the mass of family "types" in the ghetto. Instead of destroying the stereotype, the play only shows how the Youngers escaped it.

Like those of many Afro-Americans, the Youngers' forebears left for the North in search of employment and a life free from racism. Just as in *Our Lan'* by Theodore Ward, the family epic begins with dreams and hopes, despite inevitable setbacks. In the Chicago ghetto, the Youngers subsist in poverty. One is tempted to see the absence of the father as typical desertion until it is learned that the head of the family is dutifully dead. To make the relations between the characters more dramatic, Hansberry introduces a moment of crisis when each dreams of spending the dead father's insurance annuity in his or her own way. The different aspirations reveal diverging ethical choices and become sources of conflict. The daughter wants to continue her medical studies; the mother wants to buy a house in a white suburb; Walter, the son, wants to open a liquor store. Concerned about respectability, Mrs. Younger opposes Walter's project and forbids him to accept a deal offered by their prospective neighbors who want to keep blacks out of the neighborhood. No doubt, *Raisin* illustrates the social and racial relations in America, which promises integration in theory only. On a more profound level, however, the Youngers' victory is due to the fact that they are different from others in the ghetto: they "deserve" to move into the white suburbs because they have adopted the values of the middle class that they hope to join. Hansberry's hope for integration for the Youngers and for black theatre can pass as a concession to the tastes and ideology of Broadway audiences. The Younger family's aspirations—to get out of the ghetto at all costs, to satisfy basic needs and eventually "plant a garden"—characterize many ghetto families. But the Youngers' entry into an all-white neighborhood does not portend a bright future. Perhaps it is on this point that the play is dishonest: in its depiction of integration as salvation and in its happy ending.

The test of blacks desiring to integrate a white neighborhood at the end of the fifties is depicted somewhat more realistically in *Take a Giant Step* By Louis Peterson. This play can serve as a follow-up to *Raisin*, since it shows the life of a black family after the move. Yet neither Hansberry nor Peterson states openly that integration is often a trap for blacks. In effect, if social mobility allows them either by accident or by exception to better their condition, it also leads them into a hostile environment and exiles them from their community.[31]

Raisin, however, marks an important step in the direction black theatre will take in its image of the family. The play sets characters in specific roles that serve as a basic pattern: dominant women and unscrupulous, immoral, or ineffectual men. Constantly nagged by the women in his family, Walter serves as a scapegoat for their frustrations. In a world of criminals and victims, possessors and the possessed, he wants to possess, not for respectability but out of a need for independence. Walter's complaint is that of the black man who forever endures the harassment of a society that leaves him nothing but dreams, and the nagging of women in his family who do not want him to dream. The opposition among the characters expresses an opposition among value systems: conflicts between the mother (work ethic and merit) and the son (materialism, success that comes from money); conflict between brother and sister (who wants an education and who substitutes African references for the American Dream). Yet the play's interest lies especially in the representation of relations between the man and the woman and in the contradictory images Hansberry proposes. The portrait of the mother underscores the qualities of honesty and endurance, but Walter points out the way the woman begrudges her companion the respect and attention he needs:

> Man say to his woman, I got me a dream. His woman say: Eat your eggs. Man say I got to take hold of this here world baby. And a woman will say: Eat your eggs and go to work. Man say: I got to change my life, I'm choking to death, baby! And his woman say — Your eggs is getting cold . . . That is just what is wrong with the colored woman in this world . . . Don't understand about building their men up and making 'em feel like they somebody. Like they can do something.[32]

One cannot ignore this criticism of the down-to-earth woman who keeps her man from dreaming and realizing his dreams, criticism that is presented alongside the image of the generous, strong woman who cements family unity. In the theatre of the sixties this role will be more clearly defined as a castrator, and the woman will appear quite often as the major obstacle to the man's affirmation of virility.

Ten years after *Raisin* the plays of William Wellington Mackey offer an uncharitable view of the black bourgeoisie. Mackey closely examines the qualities Hansberry presented as desirable for the working class. The Youngers, who yearn to escape the ghetto, have little in common with the Vanderkellans, Mackey's family, whose notion of "nobility" comes from several generations of university administrators.[33] Three generations (the grandfather, founder of the college, was a former slave) have built the dual monument of a black university and a dynasty by applying virtues extolled by Booker T. Washington. A riot on campus threatens to shake up this patrician family and its apparent security. The exterior revolt provokes an unexpected confrontation within the family in which each member reveals his weaknesses, sexual or moral faults, and hidden hypocrisy. The virulence of intention and actual violence culminate in a kind of dance of death where parents and children tear off their masks as the fragile edifice starts to crumble.

Instead of a realistic or moralistic theatre, Mackey prefers a theatre of cruelty where drama borders on farce and exposes fantasy. In his play *Family Meeting*[34] he goes all out for caricature. The family structure falls apart following an imbroglio of national and domestic events: the death of Roosevelt, the March on Washington, a grandmother's death, the Korean War, the assassination of John F. Kennedy. In the pleasant neighborhood of Heavenly, members of a black capitalist family trade bad jokes and dance around the grandmother's coffin. To reinforce the caricature, Mackey gives his characters incongruous names like Father Love, Lilly of the Flowers, and Hopeful. Precise stage directions regulate the choreography of this pantomime in which black and white actors alternate in the same roles, underlying the racial ambivalence of their behavior. Following a hallucinatory and quasi-mystical scene, the dance ends with an apotheosis of madness and the family members are escorted one by one toward gates that close with a sinister bang.

Charles Russell's *Five on the Black Hand Side*[35] also places respectability on trial through a moment of crisis in a bourgeois family. Halfway between the moralistic perspective of Hansberry and the zany parody of Mackey, Russell uses light comedy. The upheaval that unsettles the Brooks family is short-lived. And the satire of the ideal petty bourgeois and the black nationalist, both in their intellectual comfort, remains benign. Order is restored and roles are redefined without stripping the characters naked.

With the exception of plays that criticize the middle class, the theatre turns more willingly toward the underprivileged who can take no "giant step" across ghetto borders. Here the manifestation of cruelty needs no artifice of the stage: it is found in the very environment, and realism alone gives it life.

Following his farcical images of the middle class, Mackey goes on to depict the ghetto in a more macabre manner. *Requiem for Brother X*[36] explores the notorious places in Black Alley, to which the bourgeois characters in the other plays could not help alluding. Locked in the same room, different members of a family chant a "requiem" to express personal frustration and resentment: Matt, an employee of the post office, is condemned by his job to remain seated on a stool. Jude, the father, rolls about the stage in his wheelchair. Bonita, his daughter, is no more than a mammy to whites, and the son Nat, caught between hatred and love for whites, between his emotional dependence and his wish for liberty, knows he is castrated. The family awaits the birth of Nat's child by a white girl who is in labor in a back room. Powerless old Jude helps his sons bury the coffin that reigns in the middle of the room and which contains all their disenchantments and the threat of death that each tries in vain to overcome.

In the same mode of the blues, *Roots* by Gilbert Moses[37] also presents a slow agony, a wake. *Roots* takes place in the southern countryside where life dies out in the same cotton fields evoked by Nat's monologue in *Requiem*: "We're just a stone's throw from the cottonfields. Yesterday is but a fart's smell away. Strong black guts will be needed again, those strong black guts that picked all that cotton and sweated in those fields will have to bleed again." Events transpire as if the future of blacks were fixed between the ghetto where Jude and his sons are imprisoned and the cotton fields where Gil Moses' elderly couple withers away. The life of Dot and Ray, protagonists of *Roots*, has drained away monotonously and joylessly. Dot has smothered the hope of ever having a child and Ray laments being left without descendants. He sees death approach and does not understand what has become of his life: "I'm dying and don't even know who I am . . . My feet feel like boulders in the cottonfields." Dot still holds onto the dream of the life she could have had if she had remained a maid to whites, or had been chosen as "Queen of the Delta," or had known better than to marry the darker-skinned Ray. As for Ray, he feels neither a past nor a future; his death, from stepping into a rodent's trap, mirrors his life.

These "family meetings," whether they occur around a coffin or a cradle, assume an absurd character. Members are united by the same lost illusions, and each generation suffers the irreducible misery of the previous one. There is no real reunion, only a juxtaposition of lives confined to a space that closes up again from one play to the next. Images of closure, of coffins, prisons, traps, appear everywhere in a time without past or future. All the people can do is tear each other to pieces. The history of the black family, as presented in the theatre, is characterized more by divisions, ruptures, departures than reunions and reconciliations. The theatre presents a whole series of oppositions that shape the trial of a father or mother, a husband or wife — or, to the contrary, their rehabilitation. At the same time, play after play sets up the family and its members in a variety of dramatic relations.

Parents: Targets of Criticism or Rehabilitation

The Amen Corner by Baldwin sets a strong and capable woman against a weak and misled man.[38] However, the play's ending shows an abrupt change in the relationship between the two protagonists and the values they hold. The usual situation of a man deserting his family is reversed: Margaret has left her spouse. As head of the family and pastor of a church, she devotes herself to both tasks with efficiency. The unexpected return of the husband Luke suddenly brings disarray. She reproaches him for living in sin and loving music and liquor too much. But Luke refuses to feel guilty. He does not care about salvation, but about getting back the woman he loves. The son seeks the help of his long-absent father in getting free from the maternal bond. While the two men join forces in refusing to say "Amen" to Margaret's wishes, the congregation turns away from their pastor as they begin to see her as just another woman.

Through the conflict that divides the couple, Baldwin introduces the church as another rival. The black woman seeks it first as a refuge, than as a territory to dominate, but it ends up being her prison. *The Amen Corner* brings an end to the accusations brought against the deserter-husband or the castrator-woman. The trial of Sister Margaret becomes that of the system of values she adheres to unquestioningly: The church is the final authority. The male characters reclaim their right to live a hedonistic and libertine life. The woman also ends up finding satisfaction in a life that rejects puritan values.

Ted Shine's play *Herbert III* presents a similar drama of a woman too submissive to the church and too convinced that her children need its protection against a hostile and dangerous world.[39] The play is one of the few that shows the hope of new solidarity among young blacks, less broken by circumstances than their parents were. While the mother worries about her son leaving her and risking danger, father and son, as in *The Amen Corner*, join forces. In light of the usual representation of the black family, the father's role in *Herbert III* is unexpected. His world view opposes his wife's, and he offers his sons the support and encouragement they need to become men.

The theatre often presents the woman as a major obstacle to the black man's endeavors. In this role the woman receives support from both the church, which teaches her that she is made to suffer, and white society, which continues to deny blacks happiness. The mother in *The Sty of the Blind Pig* by Philip Hayes Dean,[40] for example, devotes her life and her daughter Alberta to the church. When a blind man from a brothel in Alabama comes looking for a woman he once loved and wins the heart of Alberta, the mother drives him away. She sends her daughter to the church to find refuge and realize her femininity in the shadow of God, sheltered from desire. For Alberta, the unknown man from afar was a kind of Messiah who offered her the image of a different life. The stranger made her dream for a moment; now her dreams and illusions will be extended by the church. By repudiating the world the stranger represents, the mother prescribes for her daughter a happiness divorced from the adventures of life. In the inverted pattern of *Amen Corner*, the two women are placed under the protection of a religion more blind than the stranger they reject. Thus the deep solitude of the black woman who chooses God over man is revealed.

Beyond the condemnation of the women, the play criticizes conformist attitudes that lead to sacrificing life to an artificial ideal. In the black community, it is usually the mother who restrains the man's or child's desire for adventures or their more anarchistic instincts. She seeks to create a world without surprises in order to eliminate trouble either by leashing her spouse or by throwing him out when his outbursts threaten the equilibrium she has set up.[41] The man is not only a companion—lover, spouse, procreator—but also a son. Conflicts, ruptures, vengeance, rivalries are the situations through which the black family is represented. One must also note the role theatre gives to music and the church in these conflicts between the sexes. Music and religion are presented as being just as irreconcilable as the masculine and feminine worlds to which they are related: the woman disapproves of the man's love of music just as he disdains her submission to the church.

Two plays with strangely similar titles, *A Son Come Home* by Ed Bullins[42] and *Soul Gone Home* by Langston Hughes,[43] belong to a group of plays that explore relations between mother and son in an unusual way. Bullins' play is less interested in presenting a conflict than in orchestrating emotions by dramatizing tensions. In a complex interplay of scenes, the mother glimpses her old age through memories of her youth as the son sees different moments of his life through that of his father. Bullins specifies that the play should be acted by four actors (son, mother, young girl, young man), embodying different moods and figures. In one sequence the boy plays a father who encounters his son at a bus stop; in another, the girl acts the mother telling her lover that she is pregnant. Beyond the intentions exchanged between mother and son lie all the episodes of a shared life evoked through metaphor.

Soul Gone Home depicts a confrontation between a mother and her son who has just died. The dead son accuses his mother of not loving him, and the mother reproaches him for dying just when he could begin to earn a living. At the end of the play, two porters come looking for the body and leave without paying any attention to the mother. By this indifference, the outer world seems to bear some responsibility for the lack of communication between son and mother. The son dies not only because of his mother's negligence but because of all that contributed to alienating one from the other. Before leaving to prostitute herself, the mother whitens her face as the dead boy throws off the coins that cover his eyes. As ritual funeral objects, these coins are symbolic. Death teaches the son the secrets that life hid from him and allows him to admit truths and to return "home" to the fold.

Children in the black family are often caught in a desperate situation. The mother may obstruct their emotional or sexual development by depriving them of a home (*Soul Gone Home*) or by setting up an exclusive model for salvation (*The Amen Corner, The Sty of the Blind Pig*). And some plays replace the authoritative mother with a tyrannical father. The dramatic structure in both types of plays centers around a debate that oscillates between trial and rehabilitation, between rupture or reconciliation.

The family in Philip Hayes Dean's *The Owl Killer*[44] has already come apart. The son and daughter reject their father, Noah, who keeps reminding them of the sacrifices he has made to raise them. Characteristics usually given to women—conjugal fidelity, abusive authority, conformity—are given to Noah, whose respectability gives the lie to the stereotypes of black men. But this perfect man gets no appreciation from his children, and he disavows them when they fall by the wayside.

The son, the "owl killer," never appears in the play. He prowls about the house hiding from the police and the wrath of his father; he prefers the company of stuffed owls. The son takes revenge on the father who disowns him. Knocking at his parents' door before finally disappearing, he leaves them a message: the body of an owl—both an image of the life they have lived and an omen of death. The bird becomes an instrument of fate when the father gets his own head caught in the furnace he has lit to burn it. The wish to destroy the bird expresses the father's refusal to understand his son's message, and the accident that unites father and animal in the same death identifies one with the other. This ending can also be read as a last vengeance of the son who brings home the instrument of his father's death and of his own freedom.

Written in 1957, well before the publication of the Moynihan Report, and then titled *Noah's Dove*, revised the following year under the present title in a version that gives the principal role to the son, Dean's play seems to refute the sociological arguments that gained currency during the sixties. This family departs from the usual model, for the father is always present and is hardly irresponsible. It is interesting to note that when Lorraine Hansberry was courting the favors of Broadway, Dean was addressing a different message to another audience — which may explain why his play, performed in Ernest McClendon's small theatre, passed practically unnoticed. The spectator is not asked to be entertained by the merits of a respectable black man. Noah's alleged qualities appear to be his unrewarded concessions to bourgeois values. He is caught up in demanding recognition from whites and in the end he sacrifices his family.

Dean's play is at once realistic and symbolic: through the trial of the father it also accuses society. The deterioration of the family is imputed to socioeconomic conditions that control the lives of the black midwestern urban laborers Dean knows so well. At the same time, Dean's symbolism, as suggested by titles like *The Sty of the Blind Pig* or *Noah's Dove* and by the metaphorical role of the unseen son in *The Owl Killer*, expresses his message: Is Alberta or her mother more blind than the vagabond blind pig? Is the occupation of the owl killer any more absurd than the conscientious labor of the good-citizen father? Noah's son is just as invisible as the owls the father refuses to see, and in white society Noah himself is no more than an "invisible man."

Dean's view of life in the ghetto as defensive or compensatory behavior may seem outdated. The environment is held responsible for oppression and frustration. Black culture, as it is expressed in the characters' actions, is not seen as a specific reality, but as a response to conditions in the dominant society. It seems tolerated more than freely chosen. Yet, the theatre will move ahead to reveal an internal dynamism in the communtiy apart from environmental factors. Dean's plays suggest nonetheless a more complex reality than the single perspective his theatre seeks to illustrate. He extends his analysis well beyond those of a *théâtre à thèse* precisely because he is not content merely to show how blacks deal with oppression; he moves beyond social realism through the symbolic extensions that clothe the dramatic action and the atmosphere of dream or nightmare evoked in his plays.

The father also appears as a tragic figure in Harry Dolan's *Losers Weepers*[45] in which a man, accused by his mother-in-law of causing the death of his wife, is sent to jail. When he is released after seven years, his mother-in-law, whose hate has not subsided, dies from the emotions caused by his unwanted return. The protagonist surrenders to the police, knowing that he cannot prove his innocence regarding this second death. His children do not even try to defend him. The grandmother's mission seems to be accomplished — she has totally alienated the children from the father — but the children do not mourn for her either.

They have learned to expect nothing from others and are ready to challenge life alone with two toys as souvenirs, one of which contains the old woman's savings, which they greedily appropriate. Through a melodramatic plot that accumulates calamities, the play presents a pessimistic view of the family: with emotional ties broken or nonexistent, the only thing that matters is material survival.

Losers Weepers presents an argument directly opposed to that of *The River Niger* (see Chapter 2), in which the family comes through a series of tests without losing its unity and the father dies a hero in a last, somewhat grandiloquent scene. It is easy to see why New York audiences preferred this colorful paternal figure to the dull and broken character in Dolan's play.

The message of *The Owl Killer* is made more explicit in a work by Ronald Milner set in a similar midwestern ghetto. The father in *Who's Got His Own* has just died, and the action takes place at his funeral. When seen through the perspectives of the son, daughter, and wife, the father's life takes on new dimensions. Death shows Tim Senior to have had qualities that his wife barely perceived, and through the interplay of memories the entire genesis of the family is recreated.

The title, taken from a song by Billie Holiday, concerns Tim Junior, who reaches maturity on the day of his father's death, as he questions himself about the father he never really knew and tries to unravel the meaning of his father's life and the reasons for his death. This confrontation is more conventional than the face-to-face one between mother and son in Hughes's play. Milner presents the young man's feelings on the day of the burial: his irritation toward family members and the pastor who have come to mourn, his resentment against the father who gave him only beatings, his pity toward those who spend their lives in menial jobs, finally his recognition of love in an outburst of unifying tenderness. Two images of the father are superimposed: that of a fearful and distant god who terrifies his family and that of a poor fool humiliated by his white boss. Tim Senior's children reject their identity as members of a community without ideals and repudiate the black world, seeking refuge in personal relations with whites or in revolutionary ideologies. This rejection of "the black thing" sets them apart from the father's world of violence and frustration as well as from the mother's world of submission.

The identity crisis provoked by the father's death brings a resolution. The mother and sister tell young Tim the truth about their lives, thus delivering the important message that there is no isolated destiny. The mother's intervention brings about the children's reconciliation with their condition and their blackness. Unlike her more negative roles in other plays, the mother here functions as memory and as the repository of memories she knows how to arouse and endow with meaning.

As a story of reconciliation, *Who's Got His Own* is the antithesis of *Losers Weepers*. Awareness triumphs over the paralyzing fear and hatred of others and of self. This message, however, was not understood when the play was performed at the American Place Theatre before a largely white audience that saw it as a reflection more on race relations than on black consciousness. Moreover, the problems presented in the play, through the ethics of the Baptist church, are really those of a black family whose divisions are not solely due to pressures from the outside world. The truth emerges only when Tim and his sister stop questioning the world and discover answers in themselves and in the secrets of black experience.

From *The Owl Killer* to *Who's Got His Own*, from *Soul Gone Home* to *The Sty of the Blind Pig*, black drama multiplies images of the family through the trial and rehabilitation of a contested institution. Above and beyond the debate established by white sociologists, the family is described from within, as intimate, lived experience. One by one, the stereotypes are taken back and reexamined. And in place of the image that white society wants to give the Afro-American family, another image surfaces, or rather the two views are in constant conflict. In this respect, the dramatic event in *Who's Got His Own* is not the father's death but the confrontation of the two images Tim Junior has of him, the movement from one to the other, the elimination of one by the other. Readers must also take note of the role this conflict plays in the model proposed by the theatre, which rather than emphasizing destruction or deterioration shows that conflict itself is a dynamic generator of change.

The Ritual of the Dozens

The theatre offers its most original presentation of the family not through dramatic conflict but through dialogue that displays such verbal rituals as "the dozens" (see Chapter 2). The challenge and derision in the dozens place the family in constant performance. This verbal game, especially as practiced by adolescents, proceeds by obscene references aimed at a particular relative of the opponent or at his entire family. The game expresses a complex network of emotions in a form of ryhme that appears to be spontaneous but is actually highly codified. This game involves the confrontation of two opponents before spectators who encourage and judge the assaults. The presence of the group is as essential to this verbal joust as an audience is to a theatrical performance.[46]

The dozens dramatizes the relations between the players and thus the relations between their families. The objective is to affirm virility and to prove one's mastery of language. The dozens also fulfills other functions: it allows taboo subjects to be broached—sexual infidelity, homosexuality, incest, illegitimacy—and emotions to be expressed. By insulting the family of the other, a player may be attacking his own family, which he then defends by responding to his opponent. The game thus exposes an ambivalent relation. While each player must defend the honor of his own kin, he must also show enough aggression to free himself from frustration; by this means he can get even with his close relatives. Thus it is the son who abuses the family, most often the mother. In the theatre the scope of the dozens is enlarged by reversing the roles (a daughter may accuse her father) or by diversifying the situations. However, the dozens bring to light relations between the sexes that are ordinarily kept in shadow—even in the theatre. By allowing violent feelings to be expressed, this ritual exchange imposes strict rules on violence and, especially, forces it to remain verbal. The recourse to words offers a chance to expose and resolve conflicts. The theatre here finds its match.

Another feature of the dozens is that it makes no allusions to whites. The group thus authorizes forms of aggression directed at itself. Yet the dozens must not be seen as a simple diversion that allows blacks to inflict on themselves the aggression they cannot exert with impunity on whites.[47] A creative and recreational game, the dozens is also a ritual that establishes group cohesion by the acceptance of a strict code that affirms the solidarity of the players and their loyalty to the institutions of family and community, or to what Richard Wright in *Black Boy* called "tribal bonds."

The dozens thus codifies and ritualizes tensions by centering them around the adolescent and the family, which takes on a symbolically feminine role and which the adolescent attacks in order to affirm the existence of an emancipated masculine world. This function shows the dozens to be a rite of initiation.[48] When the game is played among girls, as in the first scene of Ron Milner's *Warning: A Theme for Linda*,[49] it develops mostly by allusions to puberty, contraception, flirting, the loss of virginity, abortion, or hidden pregnancy. When boys play the dozens they not only attack the sexual mores of the mother but also accuse other males of impotence and homosexuality (*The Toilet*). The adolescent asserts his virility and his ascendance either positively by announcing his sexual relations with the mother or sister of his opponent, or negatively by dismissing the virility of the other player and his family. This perspective places the dozens beside other adolescent rituals that link the player to his peers and declare his independence from the women in his family.

The dozens reveals a way of thinking that characterizes not only youths but adults as well. Indeed, it is drawn from attitudes young people observe in their elders and expresses the values and problems of the community. This verbal confrontation has a variety of functions: dramatization of family conflicts concerning sex, initiation, a head-on revolt against the adult world, a challenge to feminine or maternal authority, but also an affirmation of family and tribal ties.

It can easily be seen that the dozens furnishes the theatre with a wealth of dramatic situations and structures. Often a parallel exists between the structure of a play and that of a game of dozens. Provoked or attacked, the protagonists must counterattack. Players are forever on the alert. Their reaction to the world is thus defined, for this world requires them to have defensive strategies and ready repartee. Also defined are their relations with others (players-characters) with whom ties of complicity or rivalry are established. Each member of the family is called upon to respond to his role, and to reassert himself through the dialectic of insult.

The dozens serves as a model for theatre by having the dialogue refer not only to a specific cultural context but also to the deeper structures of the play. In the theatre as in the dozens "signifying" occurs: addressing someone in order to manipulate him by indirect and witty mimicry and gestural language. The spectator becomes a participant in a ritual from which he cannot withdraw without losing face. Each "actor" takes part in the ritual of insult that the theatre organizes around the family so maligned. Far from contesting the existence of the family, this ritual helps to reaffirm its reality. One of the main interests of the debate set up by the theatre of experience lies in the fact that this debate occurs in terms of the very structures the community has developed in response to its own problems. The most successful plays are those that free themselves from psychological or sociological discourse and find models of theatrical discourse among the cultural forms in the ghetto and in the black community at large.

Man and Woman: Myth and History in the Theatre

The relations between the sexes govern the network of relations in the black community. On the basic union between man and woman rests the cohesion of the family and, more important, the nation. The theatre explores the experience and sentiments of blacks through two poles of sensibility and consciousness, the masculine and the feminine, which create and sustain life. At the core of the conflict of drama lies the contest between man and woman, either as parents or as mutual antagonists or complements.

In their characterizations of black men and women, playwrights struggle against images anchored in the collective American mentality that fixes roles at each stage of history. The black couple exists in a double dimension in myths and in interpretations of history.

The most persistent myth concerning the black woman places her in a privileged position and claims to draw upon specific observations: on the plantation the woman is given certain duties (as concubine, wet nurse, cook) and lives in the "big house." Forced into sexual relations with the master, she gains various advantages in return. This situation, however, alienates the man from the home, and the woman becomes head of the family, responsible for the children. The usual economic roles in a patriarchal society are reversed, and the man begins to see his wife as an accomplice of the oppressor. From then on it is easy to understand how historical circumstances established the attitudes that marked relations between the sexes. The man's resentment and his repeated accusations fall upon the woman who has assumed masculine prerogatives. For the woman, her accusations and rancor are directed at the man who fails to protect her from the white world and who forces her to prostitute herself. She is bitter about having to satisfy the white man instead of her racial partner. The black man and the black woman are no longer a couple.

This mutual indictment imprisons the man and woman in two processes that give rise to the stereotyped conditions of prostitution and castration. The first places the woman in an active though negative position, since sexual relations should be a matter of choice not imposition. The other places the man in a passive situation. White men see him as a sexual rival, and the black woman accepts his emasculation and judges his impotence in one area to mean failure in all others.

Theatre sets up an argument that opposes man and woman on two axes. The man holds the woman responsible for his castration because she has never given him a chance to affirm his maleness. The woman holds the man responsible for her prostitution because he has never fully recognized and protected her femininity. The dual metaphor of prostitution-castration not only serves to define relations between blacks and whites, it also signifies relations between the sexes in the black community. The image of the dominating matriarch is replaced by that of the whore who after being sold to whites prostitutes herself in the ghetto for a black pimp who has become the absolute master of her body. The image of the emasculated and bullied black man gives way to that of a supermale who makes his partner submit to all his desires and become the source of his income. The revenge is accomplished; the score between the sexes is settled; but the permutation of the roles does not make the conflicts any less violent.

The theatre serves two other functions. It stages the opposition but also the reconciliation between man and woman, and it allows them to confront each other and to patch up their differences without any intermediaries. Beyond the contradictory images that the myths project, the theatre seeks a more hopeful truth.

Sonia Sanchez's play *Uh Uh, But How Do It Free Us*[50] picks up the dialectic of the couple through a series of tableaux. Each scene is followed by a dance sequence that mimes the previous action. The language of the body movement adds to the words; the tableaux depict different moments in the ethnic consciousness and the antithetical aspects of black experience. On one side of a triptych are a young actor, Malik, and his two pregnant wives who live together in spite of their rivalry. In the second tableau five horsemen, one of them black, are flanked by two prostitutes, one white and one black. Compared with the first scene of relative domestic bliss, this scene is a violent episode in which sadomasochistic relations between the sexes are shown through the image of the horse and rider. The characters retrace the course of time toward a countermyth: the black prostitute predicts the coming of a new era that will transform the black woman into a queen, thus ending her prostitution and freeing the man from his complacent self-image. His virility will be debunked. The men respond to these predictions with derision by crowning the black prostitute and making her share her reign with a white horseman masquerading as a "queen" or homosexual. Having exorcised their fears through this parodic ceremony led by the inoffensive "queen," the cowboys proclaim the continuity of their reign. A third tableau, with one man and two women, shows the partial realization of the black prostitute's prediction. The man is a young revolutionary who lives off money from his white mistress's inheritance. His other partner is a militant black woman. Rivalry breaks out between the women, then eases. The white woman recognizes the man's need for a black woman at his side who will bear his children, but she refuses to let herself be totally supplanted. Through this character, Sonia Sanchez presents a Lula who is intelligent, manipulative, but more human and who realizes that her reign is ending. The black woman must calm her jealousy toward this rival. Asserting her black and female identity has not been easy, and the black woman agrees to remain with her man in order to bring about the changes she has awaited for two centuries.

Through a succession of symbolic images, *How Do It Free Us* evolves through scenic movements which are as precise as choreography. The play suggests the hope of a reconciliation between man and woman. It also suppresses the rivalries between the races. The white woman is no longer the lovely object on whom the black man takes vengeance through sex. Nor is she any longer the feared rival who effaces the black woman; she is an ally and a companion. In the future community glimpsed here human beings are freed from images imposed by others and able to live in brotherhood.

The theatre thus replaces the old myths with new ones. Describing the long march that came before the building of the black nation by the reconciled couple, drama reconsiders past mistakes when blacks served only as tools for the building of white America. In that kind of exploitation, man and woman remained mutually ignorant of their desires and visions with still a long way to go before encountering each other.

Ron Zuber's *Three X Love*[51] evokes this long path in a male narrator's lyrical homage to woman as the "creator of black love and black life . . . the natural, unifying force." Inviting us to hear the voice of black love and affection, the narrator lets the woman take the floor in a litany that evokes the destiny of her race and asks her descendants for help in building a strong people:

> Mother of warriors, kings,
> Mother of slaves and freemen
> Mother of niggers and black men
> I black mother seek to be free
> . . . . .
> I mother of traders twisting their own souls white
> Free me
> Sons, sons, sons
> Black manhood I know I've given, RISE.

After the mother's song, the "sister" implores her racial partner to see her as an equal and a companion who will let him become fully his own man. It is from him and not from whites that she expects her freedom, for the liberation of one depends on the emancipation of the other; the happiness of one must be assured through the other. Successive separations have given way to mutual rediscovery and to marriage.

In representing the genesis of the new nation that follows this wedding, black drama becomes less intellectual. It uses ritual to release pent-up energy. The dialogue gives way to songs, an orchestration of calls and responses, invocations, lamentations, questions. The play moves from realistic domestic drama to incantatory lyricism, from rhetorical explication to polyphonic evocation. This sharp change corresponds to a breaking away from the narrow strictures of the traditional family and toward encompassing the nation, which is apprehended as a tangible physical and spiritual reality, not just a concept. In this way the theatre retraces the epic of blacks in exile. After the wrenching cry of Mother Africa, whose children were stolen, come the plaintive chorus of mothers and the impotent cries of fathers, then the curses that announce the new era.

Blk Love Song #1 by Val Ferdinand[52] orchestrates songs and cries through a long movement that has led the pilgrims from their lost country to another homeland which must be conquered. "Where has the seed of Africa gone?" is the anguished question underlying the evocation of their deportation to American soil:

And they whipped us in America
And seized our bodies with terrible afflictions
. . . . .
They hung me in a tree
. . . . .
they stretched my body out
and ripped it open
they set me afire
and I blazed till my guts fell
out.

The man has not heard the cries of his wife:

Where were you when I screamed
. . . . .
Where were you nigger.
Parading around the streets in your sharp suits
or was you hiding somewhere.

The woman does not understand the man's distress, and he accepts the accusations brought against him:

We have come to be the lies that
they told us we were
. . . . .

> We have denied our mother [Africa]
> We have denied the body that borne us
> . . . . .
> We have died the silly death
> Our women lost, gone, taken from us
> Raped and made over into the image
> of filth, into the image of fairy tales.

Constrained to wander far from home, the man proclaims his faith as an expression of truth and beauty. But his wife refuses to be taken in by pretty words and vain promises.

To the unsatisfactory union formed between Peaches and Beat succeeds that of two other characters, Sarah and Jethro, whose biblical names contrast with those of the first couple. In their search for a different identity Sarah and Jethro refuse to be mutilated or humiliated, to become a raped and reified woman or an emasculated man. They are going to awaken captive spirits and exorcise the demons that linger in white people's fantasies.

Emerging from an ice age in order to enter a regenerated world, the black couple become the living force of a cosmos where they will blossom. In this new cosmology the man is the sun, the woman is the earth. The universe is reborn with the first couple who give it life.

In this symphonic construction, male and female choruses by turns interrogate, accuse, reassure, and guide the central couple. Their anguished quarrel evolves into a serene quest. In the seclusion of a wedding night, spouses will conceive a regenerated nation. Their mutual rediscovery thus predicts the reunification of black people.

From *A Raisin in the Sun* to *Blk Love Song* the theatre moves away from domestic chronicle and melodrama towards cosmic ritual. The principal protagonist in this theatre, the place where crises form and unravel, where recurrent confrontations are played out and rehearsed, is the family, which also undergoes profound changes. The family is the microcosm in which antagonisms that divide the community appear with dramatic intensity. By examining the roles white power forces onto members of the black community, this representation of the family allows the exploration of a multiplicity of images and their insidious penetration into the psyche. The family is the point of intersection of social roles and the most secret emotional relations. Caught between the need to conform and a desire for freedom, each individual struggles to accept one without sacrificing the other. The theatre strives to proclaim the reunification of the black nation and the vitality of the family reborn from the ashes in which the ideologues and experts of the dominant society tried to bury it.

From this point on, the family becomes the hero of the new drama. Between the poles of triumphant virility and femininity, it is no longer the battleground of man and woman but the matrix in which they come together to create a new life.

Thus, in *Blk Love Song*, Jethro and Sarah leave the historical realm for the universe of myth: "I speak of the beginning and how it was and how it will be again." The play proposes a ritual of creation which starts with a search in the primordial time of the original couple before the slave trade began. It evokes the stages of the progressive alienation of black men from black women. Through the epic of these protagonists with biblical names Val Ferdinand develops a myth that shows white power to be responsible for the "fall" and projects the possibility of regeneration. Just as in *A Black Mass*, the play dispenses the poison as well as the antidote. Similar to the rites of faith healers who bring illness back to its source in evil, *Blk Love Song* shows the long submission of blacks to whites as an illness that generates bitterness and anguish. The threatened equilibrium is restored by the participation of each person in a ritual in which he becomes one with the cosmos and which also restores balance to the community. The exchange of magical formulas and the symbolic abolition of a previous condition permit the transition from chaos to cosmos and the reintegration of a legendary past. The chosen couple recovers, in the edenic state before the fall, an idealized image of life in Africa before the arrival of whites. With no apocalyptic cataclysm, *Blk Love Song* stages the end of a world and the beginning of a new order recreated from the first man and woman.

Heroes and Rituals of the Street

The life of the ghetto is organized around the poles of the home and the street. These are complementary and rival spaces not only because individuals constantly come and go between them but because of the cultural models each offers. Each space has its own modes of behavior, and each determines the roles particular characters will play: a mere passerby in the street, for example, can serve an important function in the family. The street favors chance encounters and adventures. It is more dangerous than the home, and its unpredictability offers more diversity and openness. The street is most often associated with a masculine world, and this feature has important consequences for the development of black drama.

Theatre draws partly from the tensions exerted between life in the family and life in the street. Often, family crises put the undesirables out into the street. Or the street becomes an outlet for those who are inhibited at home. The family is thus defined either as a smothering, enclosed space or as a haven eagerly sought (the return "home"). In *Five on the Black Hand Side* several characters leave home temporarily to mount a revolution in the street; conversely, the young militants in *The River Niger* take momentary refuge in the home of one companion. Whereas the street can be a place of change and revolution, the home is a shelter from turmoil and a reserve of traditional values. The street is hazardous and uncontrollable territory, open to every vice; this is the way the bourgeois Vanderkellans view the sinister reputation of the "square." Since respectability for the middle class comes through the family, the street is repudiated, kept at a distance as a place of temptation and lawlessness; it is approached with trepidation, for therein teem marginal and vulgar people. The choice of the street as a major environment and as one of the protagonists of the new drama involves problems. For, like the black family, the street has been represented through a great many stereotypes.

Black writers have always been somewhat reticent about describing the low life of their community. To portray this so-called "sordid" reality by showing irresponsible and depraved characters is to play into the hands of whites and to offer them new grounds for racist statements. Negative images of blacks sap racial pride and deprecate blacks in their own eyes. An implicit consensus seems to imply that writers should work toward rehabilitating the image of blacks. On this point, curiously enough, conservative authors agree with militant nationalists in their determination to show only the most noble aspects of the black "soul." This reticence can also be seen as a reaction against the way white authors have exploited exotic images and stereotypes perpetuated since the minstrels in shows like *Porgy and Bess*.

Yet a certain ambivalence can be found even among artists opposed to showing the less flattering aspects of black life. Something authentic about ghetto life both attracts and repulses them. The prescriptions of conformist or militant ideology run counter to aesthetic intuitions that perceive an unsuspected richness in the ghetto. In order to reconcile extremes, a new aesthetic was developed to encourage artists to defy the taboos and assail the sectarian directives of nationalism. This aesthetic proclaimed the right of the artists to integrate even the most forsaken aspects of black experience into their own vision.

When "Black is Beautiful" established blackness as a value, the artist could not neglect any aspect of this reality. The street, usually shunted aside, became a sort of melting pot where black popular culture thrived, since it was protected from the cultural imperatives of whites. The street became the property of the people. It is also in the street that "blues people" are most present. Nothing that is black could be foreign to a theatre that sought to be popular and ethnic. Moreover, situations associated with the street and its inhabitants fit into the realm of drama. This territory had to be reconquered by the black artist who was the only one capable of understanding it and transcribing it accurately. Whites, from now on, would be relegated to the role of observers or trespassers.

The Theatre in Social Science Discourse

Since the emergence of the Chicago school of sociology in 1940, the ghetto has been the object of numerous studies. From *Black Metropolis* (1945) by St. Clair Drake and Horace Cayton to *Dark Ghetto* (1965) by Kenneth Clark, the emphasis has alternated between socioeconomic conditions and pathological behavior. But the principal theories have been developed from the ideology of the dominant society, which views the streets of the ghetto as filled with a large underworld brought there by rapid industrialization and massive immigration. The ghetto inhabitants are thus presented as the dregs of an industrial society. Abandoned by a system that has "colonized" them, they are held responsible for their own condition. In a country whose ethos favors natural selection and the puritan ethic of merit, poverty and indigence become faults, indeed, punishments for those who show themselves neither desiring nor worthy of joining the "mainstream." Indifference toward the poor is thus justified. And those few who still have a bad conscience can always practice philanthropy, but only for the "worthy" poor.

The early studies of the ghetto were limited to examining the socioeconomic conditions and came to the same conclusions about the predilection for pathological behavior in the ghetto. More recent analysis conducted by urban cultural anthropologists has questioned those theories and centered the debate on the existence of a popular or ethnic culture. In this perspective the street appears as a cultural space where certain kinds of behavior arise that differ sensibly, not pathologically, from the dominant culture. For some, this marginality makes for a simple subculture, often characterized as "the culture of poverty." For others, ghetto culture is authentic, not a by-product of American culture or a pale imitation that suggests an inability to create a different model. Rather it is an autonomous phenomenon. For ethnic minorities, this culture tends to preserve those characteristics which, threatened with extinction when the group is transplanted or tempted to assimilate, are revived through segregation; the distance created by separation allows differences to flourish.

Two studies of masculine behavior in the ghetto, *Urban Blues* by Charles Keil and *Tally's Corner* by Elliot Liebow,[53] well illustrate the clash of these two theories. Drawing upon the same need to correct existing stereotypes, these works follow very different paths. Keil substitutes a cultural interpretation for the narrow sociological perspective that often leads to psychological misinterpretation. He argues against the idea that a black man's behavior manifests his anguish over his virility. Liebow believes that the parallels encountered in the ghetto between the behaviors of fathers and sons are due not to cultural transmission but to the repetition of failure from one generation to the next. These acts are signs of failure and of compensation through which the black man seeks to abuse himself. Whereas Keil studies the black man within his community taken as a separate entity, Liebow seeks to tie the ghetto to the larger society that furnishes the cultural models; according to Liebow, the obstacles the black man encounters working through these models and the awareness he has of failure determine his behavior.

Black theatre is placed in this double perspective, alternately adopting the socioeconomic deterministic explanation of culture and the theory of an autonomous ethnic entity. Militant theatre favors the former viewpoint by holding the white world responsible for a state of affairs that must be changed. The latter view is embraced by the theatre of experience, which sees the black community as the principal body of references and microstructure;[54] the cultural models gain new currency as protest gives way to a celebration of the intrinsic values of the group.

The Semiotics of the Street

The street appears in black theatre as a semiotic entity whose language must be decoded.[55] It is a text whose grammar must be constructed in order for the message to be read. By offering a reading of the street, the theatre strives to free it from all ideological discourse based on concepts of alienation, promiscuity, and poverty. The ghetto inhabitants are not represented as people resigned to the space where they have been segregated, but as people acting on a space that they structure and organize. They are no longer a people who endure their environment and deteriorate along with it—then their only salvation would be the escape recommended in *A Raisin in the Sun*. On the contrary, they form a group that reacts meaningfully to the demands of that space. The group changes and manipulates space through acts that are both functional and recreational: functional, because they permit adaptation and survival; recreational, because they take the form of ritualized play. The theatre's goal is to show street life as a cultural space where lifestyles, models of conduct, and linguistic behavior develop. The decoding of messages that occurs leads to a suggestive cultural typology and meaning that show the street to be a totality or a universe.

The street-as-space qualifies as a topic-space to the extent that a syncretism exists between the place of *énonciation*, or speech event, and the place of *énoncé*, or narrated event, between the place spoken about and the place from within which one speaks. This space is taken over by its occupants and given meaning through the language they construct. They first work through disjunction, exclusion, or through opposition to everything outside the street community. The language is not simply the expression of a social morphology, offering both the inscription of a particular society in space and a reading of this society through space, but a means through which this society thinks about and signifies itself. What must be signified first is both the presence of blacks, in a reversal of the metaphor of invisibility, and their duty to inform and transform.

The street is an important place for the theatre because life there is highly dramatized.[56] For the inhabitant of the ghetto the street constitutes a stage that demands a performance. There he becomes an actor; his gestures, his walk, his manner of moving, greeting others, and speaking exhibit all the elements of a performance, a stylized game that mixes improvisation and calculation. The performance aims at very specific effects and develops along certain codes that are not that different from the conventions ordinarily used in theatre. A greeting, an altercation, everything is ritualized; the least incident can become a dramatic event. The many annexes of the street — public areas like parks, or semipublic bars, pool halls, or barbershops — are also places for encounters and exchanges. This is the arena where the black man acts out the image he wants to give and be given, where he builds character in scrupulous detail without making the role correspond to his social function or status.

The street thus becomes a world of reflections, of mirrors, of illusion. At the least occasion, a situation is created that recalls the exact basis of theatre: an actor appears, takes hold of the stage, and transforms it; an audience gathers around him in wonder; a complicity binds them together. The actor also shares with the audience some codified norms that determine the nature of the show he will improvise. It can be said that in the streets of the ghetto each person is a spectator and a potential actor, a participant. Everything contributes to the show: the taste for action or for the unexpected, the availability of people, the creativity of those who improvise as actors, and their eagerness to exploit any occasion and to respond to expectations. Everyday life is charged with theatricality, and the audience is everywhere. The dramatic situation is maintained thanks to the full participation and adaptability of people: exchanges are established that turn spectators into actors and vice versa. The ability to arouse and sustain a theatrical situation is a gift each person possesses to one degree or another. This talent is not limited to blacks, but among the values of the ghetto, it is cultivated with care and confers enviable prestige. Historically, the gift of repartee, of "style," and the ability to step into the better roles in all situations have proved important in a community where "performance" has stood for victory over one's adversary and has been a strategy for survival.

The Bad Nigger

Old stereotypes made the black man into a born actor and entertainer. Like all stereotypes, they contained some truth. The black man became an actor at the request of whites whom he had to entertain. But he was also an actor by necessity, since his survival depended in part on his ability to pretend. He was very early led to play roles and wear masks. The servility and flattery often attributed to slaves can be seen as the result of deliberate training. Paul Carter Harrison has shown how the "good slave"—the Uncle Tom or Sambo prototype of the black actor—knew how to harmonize the forces around him, to feign complicity with a skill that was more effective than overt aggression.[57] On other occasions, this inoffensive figure could change his smile into an angry grimace and become a dangerous adversary. In the daily life of the ghetto, each person wears a mask or plays a role even to friends, who either accept or reject it.

Some figures in the ghetto—junkies, delinquents, drug dealers, pimps, gamblers—are defined by illegal or marginal activity.[58] They glorify idleness, licentiousness, a certain kind of hedonism, and they develop an ideology borrowed as much from the code of the outlaw as of the middle class, combining audacity with a reverence for money and material things. They scorn equally the police (The Man) and the rich. Through dreaming or drugs they escape their feeling of impotence. They exalt their virility, affirm their independence and their contempt for all who would enslave them to an occupation or a personal relationship.

The "tough guy" of the ghetto is thus gifted with qualities that build up his prestige. This cultural hero is not really a despicable figure; only in the eyes of liberal humanism or capitalist puritanism is he seen as improvident or overwhelmed by a hostile environment. For his peers, he is an exceptional person, one who knows how to appropriate the space around him, take stock of danger, and exploit any situation. He adds wit to know-how without worrying about scruples.

An actor par excellence, the man of the street can easily be stereotyped by his picturesque dress, speech, and gestures. But by taking hold of this character, as part of a world of victims, the theatre of experiece seeks to inspire neither anger nor pity, nor to present the picturesque fauna of the underworld. By including him in its universe, black drama establishes him as both subject and hero.

Each person in the street freely emphasizes a gesture or an utterance, and the theatre increases this emphasis tenfold. The dress, walk, and voice, and all the negative characteristics—indolence, idleness, irresponsiblity—are reassessed according to the person who exhibits them. The man of the street embodies a wisdom, a way of being in the world and an art of living. His aggression is seen as a way of gaining respect. The theatre takes no notice of those sociological or psychological concepts against which Harrison launches his battle cry: "Look out, Niggers! Freud will get yo' Mama."[59] The theatre does not seek to explain, it shows: the "bad man" is a hero and his "badness" is a means of affirming his blackness. What is categorized as bad is reclaimed by blacks as a mark of their uniqueness: "We are a Baad people," proclaims Sonia Sanchez. In this slogan are the traits of the Afro-American writ large. "Bad" is associated with "beautiful" and becomes a synonym of "black." The terms "bad" and "good" are placed outside the usual categories of ethics or aesthetics. The audience is asked to recognize and admire this new hero of the stage. He is the bad nigger, a rogue peculiar to the ghetto, who embodies the wickedness that becomes a virtue.

In response to the simplistic image of the bad nigger presented on the traditional American stage, the theatre of black experience strives to make him a complex and representative dramatic figure. It thus debunks theories about deviance and the categories of normal and abnormal, sane and pathological. It also sets forth an artistic challenge by unsettling the audience's expectations. The "bad man" enters the repertory of drama in the same way that he joins the pantheon of heroes in black folklore.

This character also becomes an archetypal figure. The "bad man" can be apprehended negatively by the white world, for he fully possesses that ethnic quality of soul which is the hallmark of blues people. As analyzed by Lee Rainwater and Ulf Hannerz, the concept of soul is the key to the value system of black culture.[60] To understand this notion, one must first disengage it from the jargon imposed by the media. Unlike the terms "blackness" and "Afro-American," which indicate the physical or historical identity of blacks, "soul" designates a spiritual quality. Applied to a way of cooking and to a style of life in the rural south, the term refers to a common past and an intrinsic cultural quality of a people that has endured despite enslavement and migration.

Soul and the adjective "soulful" indicate attitudes that are not resigned to the unhappiness of life. Whereas the blues arises from a sense of loneliness in search of community, soul proceeds from a communal spirit and explores the cohesiveness of a group in spite of the isolation of its members. One can see why a militant perspective often judges the idea of soul to be more effective than the spirit of the blues: it is more of a mobilizer since it creates a climate of confidence and fellowship and recognizes a control over destiny.[61] Soul thus becomes a gift that whites cannot possess. What was once a handicap is now an asset. Recognition of this quality in a person is conveyed through a revealing expression: "He's a people." He is a member of the black family, no longer marginal to an unstable community threatened with extinction, but rooted in a social and ethnic context. The concept of soul seeks less to interpret reality than to describe it, to prophesy a future state and to propose an ideal. A black person cannot be a bad man in the traditional sense, which explains why there are no villains in the theatre of experience, unlike the militant theatre which argues the necessity of eliminating traitors.

The concept of soul also includes a reality which is felt more than intellectualized: it encompasses opposite characteristics such as melancholy and exuberance. "The most valuable quality of life is the will to live."[62] The desire for life leads to a certain idolatry of the transitive verb and of action in which a person is both subject and spectator. It is not enough for the hero to appear; he must create himself through acts and words.

Starting with qualities deemed universal among blacks, with reexamined stereotypes (badness) and specific ethnic traits (soul), the theatre of experience develops a diversified typology in which the principal social types from the ghetto and archetypes from black folklore can be found. The theatre's task is both realistic, in that it considers life in its sociohistorical context, and symbolic, through its reference to a cultural base and a common myth.

Pimps and Hustlers: The Swindle and the Swindler

The theatre divides characters from the ghetto into "squares" and "dudes." A square follows the rules of the dominant society and stays "on the right track." He is usually treated with a degree of irony and condescension, since he has opted for an uninteresting life of security without adventure or risk. Dudes, by contrast, are the audacious and hardened and more authentic masters of the street who are protected, according to Clay Goss's metaphor in *On Being Hit*, by a shell.[63] They learn to defy everything and to see each person as an enemy until proven otherwise. Such is the function of "sounding"—a ritual of probing another through speech. According to the age of the participants, this verbal challenge may assume many forms, the best known of which is the dozens. In the street as on stage, the phatic function of language and the rituals of recognition occupy an important place. In drama, these dialogues of identification are numerous and precede or accompany other exchanges.

The action of the dudes is directed toward a search for material needs of life ("bread" in both meanings) and a search for excitement. The pursuit of the first must be undertaken with caution, for one should avoid trouble with the police; a taste for adventure mixes with the quest for material gain and one must remain alert while taking risks. Vinnette Carroll and Micki Grant's *Don't Bother Me, I Can't Cope*[64] explores in this way the implication of the saying "compete in order to cope." The will to survive is not incompatible with the spirit of competition advocated by capitalism. But it is important that each lucrative activity also bring pleasure; the theatre continues to oppose the hedonism of the ghetto to the puritan ethic. One must have fun, live well, laugh and sing, drink and make love. Improvised partying among friends and neighbors plays an important role.

Ideally, the protagonists divide their time between two activities: making love and making money, both referred to by the same expression, "taking care of business." The action is structured into time devoted to serious matters and time for pleasure, romance, or dreaming—time to be drunk, which Ed Bullins calls "in the wine time." This temporality certainly includes empty moments, such as days or months spent in prison; the weekly cycle is organized around lively and unrestrained weekends from Friday night to Monday morning ("Stormy

Monday"), when one pays for the excesses of enjoyment. Far from the time clocks and work days that rule production among whites, time in the ghetto surges and dwindles according to the richness of pleasure.[65] The theatre tries to give appropriate artistic expression to these rhythms of life: free time, waiting, restlessness. A play may have no plot other than a preparation for a burglary — as in Bullins' *Goin' a Buffalo* — or the planning of a party as in Melvin Van Peebles' *Don't Play Us Cheap*.

Relations among characters can start with two types of activities or with the split between dudes and squares. Between them come false friends, adversaries or accomplices, or hypocrites who betray the group. But these deserters are not like the traitors in revolutionary theatre. There are no truly bad people; each person acts according to the law of the jungle in order to survive. Interpersonal relations are marked simultaneously by sincere bursts of brotherly concern and solidarity and by selfish and petty reactions. And if the strategy of pursuit necessitates careful planning, friendly conduct is more spontaneous. Aggression is always in the air, but it rarely leads to open hostility.

The modalities of exchange between protagonists are expressed through two functions — pimping and hustling — which describe ways of earning a living outside the legitimate world of work, but also a means of manipulating others.[66] The street, which in ghetto language is referred to in stage terms as "the set," is transformed into a marketplace where merchandise is purchased and money changes hands. People bargain and negotiate for other people as well as for objects. In one sense the hustler corresponds to the boss. The hustler is also the last entrepreneur according to the judicious slogan, "free enterprise for the poor and socialism for the rich." He manages his accounts and, like the petty capitalist, has the illusion of a certain power. The hustler's client like the prostitute's is often a white person, who loses his money. Hustling is not only a job, it is an *art*, practiced and perfected out of a taste for refinement and performance. In a sense the white man is also a hustler par excellence, for he is the supreme exploiter; yet he is a brutal, unwitting hustler, whereas the black pimp makes skillful use of his resources in order to get his money's worth from whites. Thus the reversal of roles settles the score: the white man must pay his dues.

In the theatre of experience many plays use the hustler or the pimp as a paradigm. In *The Reckoning* by Douglas Turner Ward,[67] for example, the hero, who stands up against the hypocrisy of a southern leader, is a hustler whose ruse ensnares a victim deserving punishment. This character serves both a referential and a poetic function: his acts and words reveal the cultural model he represents, and he becomes part of a complex network of meaning; he is not simply an imitation of a known type through mimesis, but also a symbol.

In the broader sense, hustling evokes the form of power that any individual can exert on others. A chain of relations is established among different subjects, since to one degree or another every person is a manipulator. Each intermediary has his victims, but each victim is also a hustler in a chain of relationships that extends *ad infinitum*. This ambivalence and this permutation of roles become important pivots for the drama.

The secret world of hustling has always engaged the curiosity of makers of theatre because it is the key to many situations and possesses a strong symbolic resonance. It furnishes paradigms that not only designate the conditions of life for ghetto inhabitants but also recall the historical situation of blacks in America. If sociologists consider pimps and hustlers excellent informants and subjects for studies,[68] for the theatre they are repositories of ethnic culture and sources for drama. As expert directors, they rule over a rigidly defined space that exists only insofar as the conventions they prescribe are followed. Like the world of theatre, their universe is made up of illusion and artificiality, and the manipulative power of the hustler can serve as an example for the manipulation of the audience. The analogies between the hustler's world and the theatre can be multiplied. The vocabulary is revealing: the Black Player, as he is called, is a perfect actor. He enjoys an uncontested reputation, for the black popular audience remains loyal to its heroes, and the theatre can find no better figure than he to represent one of its goals.

This metaphorical function of the hustler is best served by none other than the master pimp, the king of the urban jungle who draws his personality both from his milieu and from the dominant society, whose values he parodies without really rejecting them. This businessman sells expensive pleasures. His profession is called The Game or The Life. As head of an organization that gathers prostitutes, clients, intermediaries, hotel owners, police, and drug dealers, he often considers his profession a kind of sacred mission; combining charm and authority, he talks about moving the world, waking it up. As a sort of magician, he makes a business out of dreams and fantasies. His income derives directly from whites or from the black bourgeoisie, "Mr. Charlie" or the "boojies."

The act of pimping draws upon a particular kind of relations between the sexes. The theatre reveals the complexity of these relations by coming back to the polarization already established between the home and the street. In the street, the man, who has often been forced out of the house, tries to reconquer his power. Just as the dozens is a ritual of emancipation for adolescents, pimping allows the adult to avenge his castration. Humiliated by the black woman because he is a man and by white society because he is black, he regains possession of his virility as arrogantly as he can. The principles of his emancipation are spelled out in his "bible," or "The Book," and they allow him to inflict upon women the dominance that they have exerted on him. In The Book can be found the characteristic ambivalence of the dozens: the pimp sees his woman as both an opponent to be mastered and an indispensable collaborator. Yet the status of the woman changes when she passes from her kingdom of the home to the man's domain of the street. Aspiring to honest and respectable work, she sees herself constrained by a less glorious profession which totally subjects her to the male; she is reminded that since she has freely prostituted herself to whites in order to survive, she can just as well serve a black master who will use her to get back at his white rival.

Paradoxically, by reducing the woman to servitude the man becomes dependent on her again: no prostitutes, no pimp. The permutation of roles thus leads to no radical change. The male's reign is established only by a game of appearances; he must have the look of a master. In order to signify his ascendancy, he cultivates his body and emphasizes his sexual prowess. In the hierarchy of pimps, the most respected is he who can best impose his image. The best "actor"—the one who can display all the signs of power and prosperity—has the surest gait, the most irresistible voice, the most flamboyant clothes, the most beautiful cars and women.

Generally, adding white prostitutes to his "stable" increases a pimp's prestige. By putting a white woman to work, he is ravishing the mate of his oppressor; he breaks the greatest taboo by degrading the woman whom southern society had made into a symbol of purity. Part of his superiority lies in permitting her to have white clients, for he can then preside over the sexual fantasies of both.

The pimp prepares his strategy with the same care that an actor brings to his part. In his performance nothing is left to chance. The pimp's life is thus structured around two scenic spaces: the backstage, or bedroom, where he prepares his show, and the proscenium—the bar, pool hall, the street—where he regularly appears. His private life is lived offstage, and may be astonishingly ordered and characterized by the same theatricality.

In the world of players, the space where the action unfolds is explicitly conceived as a stage where men and women are defined as potential actors. Often, in order to avoid arrest, a prostitute may pretend to be part of the entertainment world. But in her own eyes and in her relation to the pimp, considered an impresario, she is really playing the part of an actress. Both the pimp and prostitute aim for the notoriety of stardom: they aspire to the prestige that the black community accords its entertainers. Their ambition pushes them toward show business; some take on the surnames of famous actors and imitate their eccentricities. They nurture their styles and cultivate their own fans and imitators. Theatricality is the very essence of their life.

Black drama constructs around these figures an ensemble of situations that represent the relations between men and women, and, implicitly, between white society and the world of the ghetto. It also builds a complex network of signs, which enriches the scenic aspect of performance. Added to the special language of the pimp are the activities that give him multiple functions. The character, often masked by an assumed identity—a nickname—is strictly coded; he is a typically "referential" figure[69] who is part of a specific sociohistorical reality as well as of legend and myth. The hustler-pimp is rooted in a cultural tradition; he finds his heroic counterpart in the trickster from black folklore. The theatricalization at the base of this character leads to a special kind of writing, a theatre within theatre, and serves as a metaphor of theatre itself.[70]

The theatre of experience gives multiple meanings to this figure, around whom a number of ethnic traits crystallize to make him one of its most representative heroes. As a popular hero, the hustler or pimp has a peculiar attitude about his blackness: he never uses it to explain his failures, but he includes it in his strategy as a trump card. In his game, the racial factor takes on an important dimension; at no moment does he want to forget that he is black. The pride he draws from his success increases his racial pride: he acquires the charisma that distinguishes the master pimp from the ordinary one and elevates him to the top ranks in the ghetto. However, he feels no obligation to his community or to the dominant society. He is accountable only to himself. He is supremely marginal because his triumph is not imposed, but earned; it brings a special privilege to this solitary hero who is respected all the more for being isolated from white power.

Yet whatever his prestige, the pimp is never totally out of danger. He knows that the slightest mistake can be costly, if not fatal. He must spend his time foiling possible traps, developing an astonishing versatility , outwitting the ruses of his rivals. The life he has chosen exposes him to everyone's scrutiny: constant paranoia is the ransom he pays.

Curiously enough, the principles of action that the theatre gives the pimp are similar to those of militant revolutionaries: discipline, aggression stemming from fear, calculated hardness, refusal to bend to authority. The image of success the pimp projects comes less from his material success than from the exemplary way he manages to survive. In his value system, hedonism leads to self-mastery. It is in this sense that he represents an authentic cultural hero. At the same time he offers a dynamic performance; he gives the impression of knowing how to master an environment that always inclines to change, as opposed to bourgeois stability. His improvisations that introduce an element of surprise suggest ways of struggling against determinism or resignation. The strategies for survival are defined as a *jeu*, meaning both a disruption that is introduced in the machinery of coercive institutions and the set of rules that must be followed. The more legal the game, the more one is aware of the rules and careful to observe them. This game is a metaphor for life itself; in the endless game played between pimps and tricks, or between the deceivers and the deceived, the politician and his voters, the boss and his employees, the white man and blacks, each is one and the other. The important thing is to be the pimp in most cases, to trick the other before he can trick you.

This hero is not, however, a potential revolutionary, for he works solely for himself and not for the good of the community. The goods he lusts after are those the dominant society presents as desirable: wealth, comfort, social success. As a member of an underprivileged group, he struggles against poverty without questioning the system; he knows only how to take advantage of it. Disavowed for good reasons by the revolutionary theatre, he is also rejected unexpectedly by nationalist theatre. Despite his authenticity, his extreme individualism threatens the integrity and cohesion of the group because he will not hesitate to exploit his brothers. Certain playwrights and critics have come to deplore the importance granted to this character.[71] However, his condemnation in the name of revolutionary or nationalist ethics has not kept the pimp from becoming a legitimate part of the repertory of black theatre. The ideological ambivalence of this kind of hero makes him an interesting dramatic figure. This ambivalence becomes an aspect of dramatic writing not only on the level of ideology but on the level of structures that build character and plot. The pimp is not always loyal or unconditionally attached to the environment that created him. The tough guy in the street dreams of returning to the family hearth — not to the home he left voluntarily because of mistreatment, but to the one he could create in order to exert his full authority as head of a household.

Ed Bullins' play *The Corner*[12] shows this character at a crossroads. At the height of his power, Cliff prepares to leave "the life" to marry one of his prostitutes and become a father. He wants to remake his life and abandons his partners, leaving them another prostitute and his pleasure-cruising automobile. The conversion of the pimp—the dramatic surprise of the plot—is sudden, and Cliff's departure leaves his friends totally at a loss. The coherent world he has created threatens to collapse. After him, who will prescribe roles and functions? Who will sanction wild behavior? Allusions to Slick, an adversary of Cliff, foreshadow an immediate successor.

Bullins' play occupies a key place in contemporary theatre, which arrives at an intersection of two types of drama: one that sees the family as the hero, the other the street. Although expository scenes show Cliff to be an uncontested hero of street theatre, the spectator (who is in the same position as Cliff's friends) should immediately revise this image according to another context: the dude is about to become a square. By rejoining the conventional world in this way, the protagonist risks losing his prestige. But to a certain extent, the play demythifies the image of the pimp as a cultural hero: when he says farewell to the corner, Cliff is expressing his scorn for this world, and his indictment retrospectively shatters the image he once embodied.

The conversion of the hero, however, is stamped with ambiguity. Will Cliff have as prestigious a role as head of the family as he had in the street? Is his departure a regression or a progression? He becomes a commonplace individual in a society he formerly defied, but the respectability he will obtain is enviable, for it will allow him to realize a dream that many ghetto inhabitants secretly cherish.

The Corner sets up a parallel between two types of heroes, rival and complementary, embodied by the same character: the man of the street, as procurer or gangleader, and the respectable citizen. Cliff's departure does not end his rivalry with other pimps. The pimp's rise in "the life" prefigures his rise in the family, and, by extension, in the black community. Being a successful pimp has prepared Cliff to assume the role of a respectable leader. In a sense the roles are the same: every pimp is a potential honorable citizen and each head of family remains, in spite of all, a pimp; each world reproduces the structures of the other. Bullins' play expresses an interesting dialectic between the home and the street, which are too often seen as simply antithetical.

The Trickster

The bad man, as hustler, pimp, drug dealer, or outlaw, finds a place in black theatre because he represents important values in the popular culture. He embodies ethnic traits that are formulated around several figures from folklore. His referential function involves not only the ghetto but an entire symbolic universe from which he draws new archetypal dimensions.

The archetype of the bad nigger is that of the trickster, the deceiver in African and Afro-American tales who appears in the United States as the well-known figures of the Signifying Monkey and Brer Rabbit. These tricksters choose subtle weapons of ruse and wit over direct confrontation or assult. Rituals of survival among blacks often refer back to this situation of pretense. Militant theatre also shows the deceiver as a hero: the astute burglar in *The Militant Preacher*, the maid in *Happy Ending*, the servant in *The Gentleman Caller* are all drawn from the same strategic model.

The trickster displays both physical and mental skills. Physically, he seems to appear everywhere at once, always on the lookout; like the skillful rabbit, he surfaces at the opportune moment and flees before he is caught. His mind is more lively than his gestures and enables him to size up a situation, recognize his opponent, gauge his weaknesses, and calculate his own chances. The trickster is also a good talker, able to sum up a problem in a few words, pretend to knowledge he does not really have, and force his adversary to take part in a verbal duel.

Dramatic structures in the theatre are organized around this same format. The hero knows how to set traps and avoid those set for him; ubiquity is one of his basic attributes. This type of character raises questions about the accuracy of the image of the black victim who is easily tricked and easily exploited. The weak now confronts the strong and with different weapons ends up the victor.

Animal references are used less frequently in the theatre than in folklore, but the hero is often indirectly seen as an animal. It is the theatre's task to show that the black man, considered a beast, has more intelligence than his adversaries, the white man and his ally the devil. Melvin Van Peebles' dramatic fable *Don't Play Us Cheap* changes humans into animals to show the triumph of ordinary people over that great deceiver, the devil. The initial schema is thus inverted; here the trickster is an adversary whose ruse is foiled.

Using themes from folklore, the theatre invents situations in which a weak figure overcomes an all-powerful adversary. On the symbolic level, the black man is thus proclaimed the winner, and the laughter that arises from the ruin of his adversary serves as a cathartic resolution of the conflict. Contrary to the good docile negro, who lacks imagination, the bad negro is lazy, a swindler and a robber. His "defects" actually represent strategies that protect him and allow him to defy all forms of authority. His behavior is subversive and thus worthy of admiration. His premier attribute is humor. The trickster's techniques provide theatre with a great many scenarios. Moreover, since the available stratagems are most often verbal ruses, black drama derives from these exchanges the very model of dialogue where a linguistic code can merge with a code of behavior, where a certain emulation is developed between protagonists, where verbal exchanges proliferate according to a rhythm that goes from soothing, nonchalant rapping to actual fights. It is on this level of language that conflicts surface and are absorbed. The ability to manipulate words attests to an ability to master situations; the victor is he who literally has the last word.

These forms of verbal attack, initially directed at whites, have become current practice among blacks. The relations within the group are marked by their historical relations to whites and a fear of being mastered by another; at the same time the culture values game, parody, mime, and the histrionic. Rituals created in this way oscillate between the serious and the grotesque, drama and comedy; the strategy of survival is sometimes confused with playful activity that allows one to laugh about the hardships of life. In the theatre of Ed Bullins, for example, the game becomes an important element of the drama both as a liberating sport and as simulated confrontation in which strategies are revealed. In certain sequences of dramatic argument, card games and checkers matches appear as the metonymy of the larger game of life. The game also constitutes a set of paradigms to which the modalities of characters are attached, including players of varying abilities, winners and losers.

In the *actantial* models, or functional oppositions within the text, created by the theatre, dissimulation is the rule. One must hide one's game while quickly identifying that of the opponent. As in the first shows created by blacks, the theatrical discourse develops a code. Taken up again in the theatre of experience, this game of dissimulation tests each person's knowledge of the cultural milieu in which he operates and evaluates his success.

If the hero is indeed the one who leads a verbal game in a sequence, who sets the tone and feeds the lines and whose role is modeled after the trickster, then we can say that the hero cultivates allusion and the indirect mode of double entendre: each person rarely shows who he is, but asks the other to discover his true nature through the signs he provides. Within the theatrical text, the hero's discourse is often addressed to two interlocutors. One in the role traditionally given to whites will from now on be played by a black person: he is ignorant of the code in which the people express themselves, apprehends only the manifest or literal meaning of the language, gives inappropriate responses, and is an easy target for the hero's attack. The second interlocutor knows the code being used and uses it with skill, often reaching the point of inverting the roles and leading the game. This speaker can also recognize the code and pretend not to understand it; he then acts out a comedy of ignorance and naiveté which becomes another possible defensive strategy. He may refuse to play altogether while clearly stating he is no fool and knows the kind of discourse being used. The decoding should be carried out simultaneously by the interlocutors on stage and by the spectator in the audience. The spectator thus becomes an interlocutor—it is he who is addressed in the first place.

To this entire discourse is added that of the author, the leader of the game, the eminent trickster who enjoys mixing the clues. He knows all the codes used by his intermediaries, the characters, but he does not know the degree of complicity of his real interlocutor, the audience. Thus, he will give this recipient all the possible roles. One can say that the diversified theatrical discourse that the author presents through several characters is his way of representing the various images he has of the spectator.

The nature of theatre leads him to reproduce a situation of basic communication similar to those defined by practice in actual life. Each subject is given a language, and each language a form of behavior. The many terms describing ghetto speech are evidence of the vitality of the modes of communication in practice. In theatre, the interplay between modes, the passage from one to the other, and the resulting tension constitute the turning point of the drama. In many sequences, nothing "happens" in the restricted meaning of the term. However, the right exchanges arouse emotions just as dramatic—that is, charged with action—as the real actions.

Verbal encounters in contemporary life have been labeled by the popular expressions of "rapping," "shucking," "jiving," "running it down," "gripping," "copping a plea," "sounding," and "signifying." Around each verbal action a specific actantial or oppositional model is constructed in theatre that places the subject in a position of superiority where he is free to manipulate his listener.

In rapping the exchange is a rambling yet rarely disinterested conversation. The discourse seeks to be persuasive, to charm the listener in order to coax him. The speaker studies his effects and tries to individualize his style. At times he unveils his intentions in order to extort money or some service.[73] Shucking or jiving involves more elaborate dissimulation and defines a type of behavior that the hero may adopt in the presence of a superior, an agent of authority, or a character to whom he provisionally gives this role. He dons a mask to feign submission, deference, innocence, or total foolishness. Often called "tomming" (after Uncle Tom), this behavior has historical origins and characterizes encounters with white southerners or their counterparts in the North: police, judges, teachers, social workers. Among blacks, this technique becomes a parody. He who is asked to play for mere fun must show that he is aware of the strategy; through comedy, he shows his appreciation of his opponent's art.

The most explicit manipulation is signifying. Through slanted verbal conduct or indirect gestural language, one participant seeks to provoke another. One repeats to a listener what a third party has said about him in order to arouse an immediate reaction of anger, hostility, or exasperation.

Sounding implies a more injurious intent. It is the very process used by the dozens to measure an opponent's resistance to insults and to test the control he can keep on his emotions. It involves, as we have seen, provoking anger by recalling the incompetence of an opponent's father, the promiscuity of his mother or sister, or any personal shortcoming. The ability to wield language and invent formulas, more than physical strength, arouses admiration. This activity is essentially creative, even artistic, and its theatricality is unarguable, as shown in Bullins' use of it in *In the Wine Time* or Paul Carter Harrison's in *The Great McDaddy*. The lines are concise, rapid, and generally rhymed. The search for rhyme gives a definite yet impersonal character to the formula because it is more percussive. Rhyme makes the line easier to deliver and indicates the phonetic pattern that must be filled. These games permit insults that would never be tolerated from outsiders and draw upon ethnic traits that whites usually distort or stereotype. The dozens is not played to establish or reveal a truth, but to stage a performance and a verbal competition. Unpleasant truths, when stated by a member of the group rather than by whites, assume a fictive and inoffensive character. The game simulates dangerous situations, and in rehearsing it the players are training for more violent conflicts.

If the hero is not always the victor in these verbal confrontations, he participates in such a ritualized manner that he avoids losing face. Gripping and copping a plea are terms for faulty behavior, born out of fear of a superior power that requires at least symbolic submission. They describe the mimicry of those who plead their error or guilt, who implore the mercy of the victor. But respect, fear, or contrition is faked in the hope of avoiding the worst.

Hyperbole also characterizes the verbal games and attests to theatrical discourse. By naming his troubles and by projecting them into dimensions that are larger than life, the hero frees himself from them. These games evoke conflicts and catharsis at the same time. They also emphasize the pride of succeeding in a performance, captivating a listener; they form, finally, the quintessence of popular wisdom that is most easily communicated in the form of play.[74]

Rituals of communication in the theatre underlie the entire dialogue and give particular singularity to plays by Bullins, Harrison, Gaines, and others. If these rituals leave much to improvisation and proliferation of language, they are responding, nonetheless, to specific conventions: a subject signifies his domination over another by the way he imposes rules of verbal exchange; it is he who chooses the ritual and decides to pursue it or bring it to an end. This quality designates the speaker as a hero, for his verbal mastery becomes the sign of mastery in other domains, particularly, as shown in Bullins's plays, in the realm of the emotions.

Verbal relations in this way determine actantial relations while remaining independent of them. The preexisting oppositions in dialogue can be changed, such as the initial dichotomy of dominator/dominated. Roles can be reversed in the course of one dialogue or a single scene: in *Clara's Ole Man*, Clara's presumptuous visitor is rapidly manipulated by the ghetto dwellers he tries to impress. In *Goin' a Buffalo*, the hero, a gang leader, is eliminated by the companion whom he taught the art of manipulation. And in a different way, Cliff in *In the Wine Time* remains the uncontested master of the situation and designates the role each person should play.

The theatre devoted to the man of the street lies at the center of the theatre of experience. It is a theatre of expression, not explication, of designation, not denunciation. It states the cultural grammar whose syntax is organized through words, idioms, proverbs, and fables that express basic activities (a struggle for survival or a simple reaction) and the wisdom of a people. It indicates the subjects of actions and categorizes them according to the cultural conduct manifested through language.

This theatre moves away from the didactic demonstration of the mechanisms of oppression and from social science discourse. As a theatre of recognition, it shows how the marginal in society live. It refutes the postulates of the theatre written by whites that shows blacks as simply comic or picturesque figures, passive and submissive victims or tragic and admirable heroes; it also refutes the theate written by those blacks who insist on portraying exploitation and rebellion. Its perspective is not neutral, but rather indulgent or satirical. Its characters well represent the affectionate humor that Langston Hughes saw in the "folk," those people who love and hate one another, who aid one another and tear one another apart, and who reach beyond the frustrations of Hughes's well-known character Jesse B. Simple to attain vitality and wisdom.

J. E. Gaines and Melvin Van Peebles: Humor and Play

Each play has its way of making the common man and the "wretched" folk of the ghetto into new dramatic heroes. And each playwright constructs characters according to different modalities and forms. J. E. Gaines attempts to record life exactly as it is and to show how "wisdom comes to black people in many disguises."[75] This wisdom, which is neither manifested nor recognized by community leaders, belongs to the little people who live an obscure life in what Gaines calls "basements," spaces below the street or at the end of courtyards and buildings, where he himself grew up. Popular wisdom, derived from long struggle, teaches how to survive in an inhumane environment. It appears in maxims, proverbs, and sayings, from which Gaines draws the title of one of his plays: "Sometimes a hard head makes a soft behind."

Gaines is most concerned about learning the experiences of blues people from within. What appears to the outsider as eccentricity is normal in Gaines's world. The people he depicts are exceptional, but their behavior is neither strange nor crazy; his purpose, however, is not to analyze them but to give them a chance to speak. Gaines chooses the mode of the blues, which is to say complaint or hope (heads or tails) as revealed in the song that explains his title, *What If It Had Turned up Heads*:

> I try for a while
> To give a smile
> To a friend or two
> But fate took a hand
> I lost my man
> And my child in her youth
> I was abused, and misused

So I'll find love where I can
And give to the bitter end
So lovers don't you wail
'Cause fate has turned up tails
Whwwwhat iffff itttt hadddd turned up heads![76]

Like the blues singer, Gaines's protagonists reckon with their unlucky life and still hope for a change of fortune. In the game of heads or tails one can at least hope to win someday.

The plot of *What If It Had Turned up Heads* concerns a man and a woman who meet, try to love each other, separate, and then come back together again. Jacob operates a small bar and clings to the memory of his glorious past as a pimp. Jennie is a former singer, with nothing left of her career but a shopping bag containing cheap beads and a red satin dress. The fallen star comes to the former pimp for a drink. He offers her a meal, then his bed and his house. She breaks away for a while, but returns to manage the bar and wait on customers: "Open a little business, take a trip, you name it and fate claims it." A jealous fate takes vengeance when two hoodlums beat up Jacob and rape Jennie, crushing lives already broken.

The metaphor of the game reminds us that life is a gamble with winners and losers, ups and downs. The alcoholic protagonists are united by their similar pasts and by memories that help them struggle against the mediocrity of their lives. Their hope for change allows them to imagine a better future. As in the blues, enumerating misfortune allows one to transcend it; giving voice to suffering ritualizes it and lessens self-pity. This recalls Ralph Ellison's classic definition of the blues: "an impulse to keep the painful details and episodes of a brutal experience alive in one's aching consciousness . . . to transcend it by drawing from it a near-comic, near-tragic lyricism."[77]   The blues offers a formula for survival that is based on group experience, and theatre objectifies this experience by stripping it of fatalism. The coming to awareness is accompanied by humor that keeps the traumatizing experiences at bay and thus transforms oppression or anguish into momentary catharsis. It orchestrates different moods that traditionally belong to the blues singer; it dramatizes the constant movement from laughter to tears, from reconciliation to anger. Desires, dreams, and pain are expressed and mastered. The hero's complaint, which is both individual and collective, gives voice to common experiences that the audience recognizes and sanctions. The therapeutic function attributed to theatre increases the feeling of sharing a common fate and of controlling destiny.

The richness and vitality of urban folklore find the most ambitious aesthetic expression in the plays of Melvin Van Peebles, whose prolific talent and taste for exploration have been shown in films as well as on stage. In a skillful scenic design that gives both a realistic and symbolic dimension to space, *Aint Supposed to Die a Natural Death*[18] orchestrates the many voices of blues people. Alternating sketches present well-known types from the world of "baaad people." Street people, prostitutes, addicts, lesbians, gay men, respectable citizens, and police pass through and confront one another, and voice their sorrows and hopes. Dominating the stage is an immense body topped by a grotesque white mask (like a marionette, it is attached to strings, which entrap those who bustle about the set). White power is thus signified as an absurd and fallen god. When a group of characters gather to move this inert puppet we see that it has life only through manipulation. The white presence is not an object of accusation, although a final song pronounces a ritual curse upon it. The play must not be seen in terms of this single imprecation; for more than an indictment against whites it is a verbal attack against the psychic and physical violence that occurs on stage when a black teenager and a black policeman in whiteface are killed. The song is the closing couplet of a lament that has been amplified throughout the production, emanating from each individual's attempt to find group expression in one last hymn. The old woman who casts the spell speaks for the community; she curses both the invisible power responsible for the deaths and the complicity of blacks, and at the same time she pays homage to the black spirit of independence.

The play is conceived as a succession of songs and separate challenges that echo one another. Each song is particularized, whether the solo of a lesbian in front of her lover's prison or the song of a wife who avenges her husband's infidelity. Insults fly, supplications become threats, and declarations of love turn into cries of hate. A policeman beats up a prostitute; a male transvestite states his desire for a lover; a prostitute swears her devotion to a pimp who mistreats her; a blind beggar searches for the woman of his dreams; drunks spew out obscenities; a postal worker becomes an assassin. It is the world of Saturday night in the ghetto, a feast for the senses that Van Peebles fashions into a celebration of meaning.

The play affirms that love, far from being the prerogative of the rich and beautiful of the world, is expressed everywhere and in many forms: a passion that is impure or profane, a fantasy, or a dream. Each figure pleads with a cruel lover, cries out his or her need for attention, and enumerates pleasures and torments. In the middle of these passionate declarations, gunshots are fired as if to remind us that violence overcomes tenderness and that love is perhaps unattainable in such a brutal world.

In such a theatre the blues finds its fullest expression. The song is first an expression of despair. It is also the expression of a people who by joining challenge with humor are able to laugh at themselves as well as defy an adversary and who proclaim their independence by making a principle out of their own chaos. Van Peebles explores social reality through the emotions it produces, and he conceives his play above all as a spectacle: dance, music, song, pantomime all give style and rhythm to the movements of the spirit as well as the body. Each sketch becomes a step in this gigantic ballet; each tableau centers on a character, a mood, a place, or a situation, as both distinct from and a part of a vast composition.

In *Ain't Supposed to Die* Van Peebles tries to renew the musical comedy tradition. To create the illusion of a busy and intense life and to show the theatricality of the street, he multiplies and superimposes characters and events. The scenic space is deliberately divided into several levels. The somewhat incoherent profusion of the street spectacle is not only transposed but recreated in a different semantic system, for the proliferation of signs does not detract from their rigorous orchestration into a complex polyphony. Arranged in alternating or simultaneous counterpoint, the scenes converge to produce a global effect as well as to make a statement about blues people and streetcorner society. Unlike a purely verbal message that remains linear, the theatrical message has both linguistic and visual depth. It makes performance into a semantic act that is "dense" and "extended" in the way Barthes uses those terms to contrast literary monody to theatricality.[79]

Van Peebles's use of music stems from musical comedy, but he takes up this tradition in a way that makes the work ambiguous. It becomes both a parody of the great shows of the twenties and a commercial and artistic exploitation of a popular genre. These shortcomings were not lost on some critics who saw the play as a purely Broadway product and who regretted that the black community was presented in stereotypes, as an exotic, marginal, and brutal world. It is noteworthy that the play had its greatest success with an integrated Broadway audience, where the black bourgeoisie and white theatregoers shared tastes and standards.

Even as a commercial show *Aint Supposed to Die* is an ambitious and original work, not only because it uses song and choreography but because it draws upon ethnic material. It seems to have been written with the same sensuality and freedom of improvisation as a jazz piece, which disconcerted those who favored a more traditional dramatic structure. Although the songs at times resemble those of an operetta, they still express the ironic and painful voice of the people, emphasizing emotions over ideas. In its own way, however, the theatre of Van Peebles constantly calls upon the intelligence of the spectator. When the play was first performed at the Henry Street Settlement in 1972, admirably directed by Gilbert Moses, it developed a complex structure of signs that had to be scrupulously deciphered. Van Peebles' audacity lay in giving significance to an existence that had been denied meaning.

Humor and sport dominate Van Peebles' *Don't Play Us Cheap*,[80] where the melancholy of the blues is held back only to be saved by laughter and mischievous pranks. "Sometimes it doesn't pay to get out of bed," says one of the characters; but when the time comes for a party, nothing can stop the revels of Harlem. The play explores an aspect of black experience that ensures group survival: the ability to have fun, to forget misfortune long enough to enjoy the illusion of being free and happy. Happiness and conviviality surge forth in every Saturday night party, which is a legitimate ritual of living. The party goes on until time and destiny can be cheated: "Real black laughter is more than just amusement. It is Amen to this, Amen to that! It is seeing the world like you want to, and especially it is freedom. It is the Parties of Saturday Night!"

Here again the plot is simple; it comes from a novella Van Peebles first published in France under the title *La Fête à Harlem*. Two agents of the devil, Trinity and David, dress up as roaches and set out to disrupt Miss Maybelle's party. It is a dangerous mission, one that has always failed. These people work all week and take their pleasure with such abandon that nothing can spoil their fun. The agents fail: one succumbs to the temptation to be human and falls in love with the hostess; the other is squashed as he tries to slip away. Instead of causing surprise by their intrusion, the devils themselves go from one surprise and failure to another. They break the records, but the music continues; they stir up trouble, but the women have enough skill with repartee to thwart them. When David thinks he has given wrong directions to three respectable guests, he learns that he has only kept party-poopers away from the fun.

The setting here, unlike that in *Ain't Supposed to Die*, is an intimate apartment where war is waged against boredom and melancholy, not poverty. In this evening devoted to fun, blacks experience a kind of metamorphosis or transfiguration in their joy. Van Peebles inverts the well-worn stereotype of the fun-loving, joyful black as insouciance and good humor lose all their negative connotations. The black man is not laughed at; it is he who mocks those who want to make him look ridiculous and destroy his fun. Through dramatic reversal (the trickster is tricked), Van Peebles parodies the tradition of the trickster tales. For once, the tricksters fail. The phonetical analogue between "imp" (demon) and "pimp" underscores the genies' attempt to use the strategies of the pimp, but those ruses fail outside their territory, and the genies are powerless. The devil here is the same popular figure whose pranks blacks always manage to foil. As for the genies, they are the real squares, mere amateurs who want to taste the pleasures of Harlem during the period celebrated in Carl Van Vechten's novel *Nigger Heaven*.[81] But the doors to Harlem are closed to them. The lesson is clear: black laughter returns to Harlem at the expense of the squares. The cotton fields and street corners have been hard schools for blacks; they have nothing more to learn from God or the devil.

Ed Bullins: The Language of the Blues

Next to LeRoi Jones, Ed Bullins is probably the most important black dramatist of the last twenty years. His numerous plays have been performed throughout the United States and abroad. Bullins has acknowledged his debt to Jones's early plays—*Dutchman*, *The Slave*, *The Toilet*—yet, after helping to establish revolutionary theatre according to Jones's directives and definitions, Bullins set out in his own direction and became a pioneer and innovator himself. No playwright better demonstrates how drama can alternate between political commitment and ethnic expression free from the constraints of ideology.

Bullins first collaborated with West Coast militants such as Huey Newton, Bobby Seale, Eldridge Cleaver, and others connected with the San Francicso Black House.[82] He used his talent as a playwright to serve the cause of the Black Panthers. But the Black House did not survive the schism in 1977 between those who wanted to use theatre to disseminate political ideas and those who gave priority to the cultural revolution and theatrical action. In discussing this period, Bullins has deplored the sacrifice of art to other aims.[83] While he wrote agitprop plays in line with the Movement's requirements (see chapter 2), he continued to pursue more independent projects in the theatre.[84]

Caught between ideological struggles and the provincialism of bourgeois art, Bullins accepted an invitation from Robert Macbeth in 1967 to help start the New Lafayette Theatre in Harlem. Bullins' decision was no doubt in part practical: when his plays were not produced in

San Francisco he tried his luck in the capital of American theatre. His choice was also an artistic one; his plays *Clara's Ole man*, *Goin' a Buffalo*, and *In the Wine Time*, drawn from his experiences in the Philadelphia ghetto, were more ambitious undertakings than those of most of his contemporaries. While he recognized the importance of revolutionary groups, he also understood that theatre must find its material and autonomy apart from their concerns. The path which led him from San Francisco to the New Lafayette is just as important as the road Jones followed from Greenwich Village to Newark. Bullins' approach to drama comes from a sincere conviction that black theatre should first speak to the common man, in whom he finds authentic inspiration. His journey is also a return home.[85]

Bullins is more interested in promoting an authentic popular theatre than in creating drama inspired by contemporary events. The blues people are not only his preferred audience, they figure at the very heart of his drama. For Bullins, a product of the city, street people create and animate black culture; they best reveal the dynamic quality of experience. His drama is thus preoccupied with creating an ethnic theatre. Bullins disdains the values and tastes of the dominant society and deplores the prejudices most critics bring to black theatre; nor does he spare blacks who subscribe to the canons of bourgeois aesthetics.[86] He attacks the aspirations of the black middle class who reject identification with the disadvantaged, and he warns them about their hostility toward popular theatre: the man in the street should not be a stranger to them, and white racism does not spare the black elite. By refusing to see reality, the bourgeoisie cuts itself off from its roots and falls into the trap of integration that binds it hand and foot to the aesthetic imperatives of whites.

In Bullins' theatre the love of black people comes with anger against the bourgeoisie. His drama seeks to debunk the comfortable world that the middle class believes to be a refuge; it dismantles this fragile edifice by revealing the inanity of the ideas and language on which it rests. At the same time, it restores the world of the common people, scorned by traditional drama. While it uses burlesque and satire to describe the bourgeoisie, it rejects any easy systematization in its depiction of the people; nor does it give in to the temptation of romanticism, exoticism, or ideological distortion.

One of the objectives of the new black drama is the indictment of the middle class. Whether it is Jones's Clay or Bullins' "electronic nigger," the so-called elite is not spared. In this respect the theatre joins Harold Cruse in criticizing the black intellectual. It must be noted that in theatre, debunking occurs through caricature and the systematic subversion of each gesture or word. Unlike Ben Caldwell, Bullins is not concerned about showing that the robot-character is really a traitor; rather, he makes the puppet a ridiculous anti-hero. As the protagonist of several plays, this robot also appears regularly in the background of works devoted to more authentic actors of black experience.

How Do You Do[87] dramatizes how stereotyped characters are created and manipulated by an invisible hand. Their respect for conventions dictates their actions and words. Their relationships in the world can be summed up in the polite greeting "How do you do?"; there is little real communication between them. Their speech is filled with unrelenting verbiage, inept or pretentious platitudes that reflect their life. They are what they say. On a second level, the play is a parody of assimilated blacks who avoid naturalness and become inauthentic characters through artificial speech. Bullins' "precious" ones—the seductive Dora and the refined Roger—do not know how ridiculous they are. Clichés and hyperbole ("How ecstatic!") and rare expressions mark a dialogue in which naturalness surfaces unexpectedly: "Did you fart?" Roger asks Dora. In a stream of formal words, these truths escape inadvertently and reveal the contradiction between pompous social discourse and precarious economic conditions. Polite formula changes imperceptibly into a blues song introducing concession, humiliation, and the misery of their life. In an outburst of violence and obscenity, language tries to free itself. The metamorphosis of robots into humans works thanks to the intervention of Paul, whose lucid and combative language reveals their artificiality and exhorts them to accept their blackness without shame and to use the weapons the oppressor has left them. What was once servile imitation should become skillful simulation. The couple should exploit the caricatural role given them, continue to speak absurdly until the day they learn violence well enough to satisfy their vengeance. This transformation was emphasized in the music and lighting of the production directed by Ed Besman at the Black Arts West Theatre in 1966. The blinking of lights and the dissonance of a harmonica evoked a world about to explode. The polite formula "How do you do?" becomes a demonstration of the "right way" to change the world. The metamorphosis is anticipated through the illogic and the violence of a new language made concrete in the staging. The subtitle Bullins gives the play, "A Nonsense Drama," is significant. It denotes an intention to show, in the mode of burlesque, stereotypes in action as well as absurd and tragic realities. But the play is also a song. Paul, the musician-poet, orchestrates the "precious" couple's inept words and composes a hymn that destroys the nonsense, breaks the yokes, and sets them free.

The Electronic Nigger is a farce that pushes caricature to the extreme.[88] Bullins' satire here has a double target: Mr. Jones, an honest teacher of creative writing, and Carpentier, a student who attends his class one day. The intellectual pretensions of the neophyte end up dumbfounding the instructor. This robot, who has been brainwashed for a long time, in turn subjugates the class by his pompous use of jargon. His meaningless talk and grandiloquence are more pleasing than the emotionless rigor of the shy professor. If Mr. Jones is an honest but ineffective intellectual who tries to justify his existence in a world where intelligence and art bring some privileges, then Mr. Carpentier is a dangerous specimen, controlled by an infallible mechanism. Bullins is less concerned with social types (the two versions of assimilated blacks) than with the linguistic process that defines them. His target is beyond the electronic nigger, that technical apparatus whites use to destroy the black soul. In spite of the professor's warning to his "lost brother," the play ends with the carping of the students as they leave the classroom behind their new master, Carpentier. The voice of the poet of the electronic age resembles the cawing of a raven, foreshadowing the death of a culture.

Bullins' theatre does not merely demonstrate the blindness and pretensions of those who have adopted white values. Apart from satire and burlesque, his drama explores the complexity of black life. Certainly the treason and corruption of the elite are part of this experience; however, to those who are waylaid by the illusion of assimilation, Bullins prefers the black man who confronts life without artifice and assumes his share of its joys and sorrows.

In a series of plays, some of which are part of what he calls the "twentieth century cycle," Bullins describes the lifestyles and strategies of the ghetto and explores the soul of the blues people. His goal is to present a whole experience with hardly any interference from white society, where an entire community searches for survival and happiness that they define on their own terms. It is no longer a matter of demonstrating the causes of oppression of these character-victims, or of judging the strategies available to them. Bullins simply shows how people live in the ghetto. He forgets the historical frame of the tumultuous years from the Civil Rights Movement to Black Power and focuses on daily life; his drama develops a complex answer to the question "How do you do?" His characters challenge, encounter, visit one another, and walk the long arduous road together; they exchange ideas and joys, failures and difficulties; they support or betray each other. And life goes on, for better or worse, with only distant references to ideological or political struggles.

Each play is situated in an American space and time: under the brilliant sun of California as in *The Fabulous Miss Marie*, or in the intoxication of summer and wine as in *In the Wine Time*, or in the fanatasy of a New England winter in *Goin' a Buffalo*. These geographical and seasonal contexts are given both realistic and metaphorical connotation. Space and time have a complex influence on the destiny of the characters who pass through them distractedly or with obstinate calculation.

A visit (*Clara's Ole Man*), a return home (*A Son Come Home*), a party (*The Fabulous Miss Marie*), a gathering of friends to plan an escape or a crime (*Goin' a Buffalo*) are for Bullins occasions to examine behavior and habits of living. In *Clara's Ole Man*,[89] Jack, a young intellectual who left the ghetto for the army, comes back to see his girlfriend Clara. During his visit he is the butt of sarcastic remarks by Clara's friend Big Girl, who calls him "Mr. Smart and Proper." Jack is later beaten up by three punks. Far from being an occasion to show off his superiority, Jack's return to the ghetto becomes a rude test, a distressing confrontation with a world that now sees him as an intruder.

Jack is surprised to learn that his education has cut him off from real life. Suspecting another man in Clara's life, he discovers too late that his rival is none other than Big Girl; he is no match for this opponent who has already exposed his weaknesses. By leaving the ghetto, Jack has lost every hold on reality; trying to remember some slang when he is caught by the hoodlums who beat him, he fails to establish communication. His new values are no help in the poor neighborhoods of Philadelphia. Jack's path is irreversible: in denying his origins he has betrayed himself. Through him, Bullins reiterates his accusation of the black bourgeoisie who never completely entered the dominant society, who were seduced only to be rejected, and who yet failed to recover their lost identity.

Clara can neither follow Jack nor get him back; her life is in the hands of Big Girl. Big Girl is the kind of matronly figure who fills the role of mother and provider. As both responsible parent and attentive lover, she protects Clara from the advances of vulgar suitors, corrects the education given by her overly religious parents, and gives her a home shared by a retarded sister, Baby Girl, and an invalid, alcoholic aunt. Big Girl also ensures the survival of the ghetto youth who seek refuge when police are on their trail. Occasionally their accomplice, she knows how to get their respect and protect her privacy. Initiator, educator, she teaches others the lessons of life, points out the rules to follow to make the best of things. Without pity for the young ambitious Jack who presumes to supplant her, Big Girl does not intervene to spare him the roughing up he gets from his former peers, and thus shows that she places more hope in the young hoodlums than in this member of the so-called black intelligentsia.

In Big Girl, Bullins creates one of the most important female figures in black theatre. The violence she uses to maintain order around her has neither the perversity nor the gratuitousness of some of her sisters in drama, like the matron in *Ladies in Waiting*. Her essentially verbal violence helps Big Girl control people and things. She handles language with cruel dexterity, but she is not destructive. Much to the contrary, she harmonizes life; she intervenes to restore people to their right roles, to minimize risks and trouble. She is able to order the chaos she sees, to offer refuge to those fleeing oppression or lies. She gives a merciless analysis of the failures of psychology in the insane asylum of the white world, symbolized by the hospital where she works. Big Girl teaches not only survival but how to live well: to have fun at the expense of others and oneself, to drink merrily and not to repress sensuality, to speak plainly and openly. She organizes her life around several rituals, which she controls with discretion. For her, if life is cruel, then it should not be boring; destiny must be distracted and, if need be, defied. One must laugh not insouciantly but out of a willingness to confront reality.

Bullins' drama brings together banal and simple situations, such as the mortification of Jack by Big Girl and his defeat by the hoodlums. Yet Bullins' main interest lies in a dialogue stamped with humor and tenderness that combines all the modes of popular speech, from banter to defiance, from teasing to provocation. The narrative mode plays an important part in the characters' use of language: it serves to give necessary information but especially to indicate the personality of the speaker. Thus, when Big Girl tells how she sheltered and raised Clara, her tale informs us of the past of the two women and especially reveals her own amazing character. When the three rogues describe their latest holdup, they mime their escapade and their craftiness according to the best rules of the genre of "running it down," increasing the credibility of the unreasonable through embellishment. They must convince Big Girl that the robbery happened perfectly and dissuade her from reclaiming her cut of the loot. Thus the episode is transformed through narration into an implicit celebration that makes an art out of strategies for living in the ghetto.

Appropriately, the "tragi-fantasy" *Goin' a Buffalo* was first staged in

1972 by Hugh Griffens at the Players Art Theatre in Buffalo.[90] The action takes place in Los Angeles during the early sixties. A group of friends plan a holdup that will allow them to escape the ghetto. They choose to go east (inverting the myth of the west) to set up a little business in Buffalo, "a good little hustling town." Money, the main concern in their lives, is needed to buy a car, maintain women, pay bail, or bribe a judge. Without money there is no freedom or respect. The paradox is that in order to buy their freedom they must resort to illegal acts that endanger the very liberty they seek. The characters are thus always in provisional freedom, if not always under surveillance. What they really want is an autonomous space. They have the skill and the know-how of the trickster, and they can fuse pragmatic realism with their dreams. If they cannot live in the best of all worlds, they can at least live in a better world. Bullins' play has a double dimension: his characters alternately confront sordid and often tragic life and drift toward an imaginary and unrestricted universe.

The dramatic movement in Bullins' plays thus oscillates between real and imaginary worlds and constantly shifts from despair to hope, from submission to anger, but also from revolt to inaction, from tenderness to violence. Stage directions emphasize this pendular motion by dividing the stage into superimposed levels and by using subdued or glaring light or colors that go from the opposition of black and white to that of warm and violent tones. Music is also used to suggest different moods. Bullins retains the antinomic modalities of satire and lyricism, of comedy and tragedy, to evoke the complexity of registers in a polyphonic drama.

In *Goin' a Buffalo*, a small box containing an aphrodisiac serves as a magical instrument of metamorphosis. The box belongs to the dancer Pandora. At the request of her friends, Pandora opens her treasure and passes it around; the lights modulate and soften the atmosphere, which becomes airy and erotic; each person is carried off to a private world of myth and fantasy. The place in reality that is most propitious to this kind of hallucination is the "habitat of whores" where one can totally let go. The magic lasts until it is interrupted by the imperious ringing of the telephone. Once the charm is broken, the interrupted activities and forgotten cares resume. Bullins does not seek to explain why ghetto residents take drugs; rather, he conveys the quality of that experience and evokes in the spectator a state similar to that of his characters. The situation is not analyzed, it is felt. One must listen to Bullins' plays as one listens to music and be drawn into the movement of broken rhythms, dramatic breaks, repeats, and lyrical crescendoes. The play unfolds like a musical score: each sequence has its own key and modality, each character a voice and register.

The hallucinatory scenes are always interrupted by the intrusion of reality. At the end of the second act a fight breaks out in the cabaret where Pandora works. The police come and make arrests. Money must be found for bail; the drugs that turned the dreams into life preservers have brought danger and the vigilance of the police; the camaraderie that has held Pandora's friends together crumbles. The selfish and calculating Art can succeed in his plan to escape to Buffalo only if he eliminates those the police point out as guilty. He does not hesitate to lie in order to get rid of his "brothers" and to have Pandora and her white prostitute friend all to himself in the snow of New England. He takes the two women away and leaves his companions, including Curt, his friend and Pandora's lover, to the icy walls of prison.

The traitor here is depicted differently than in revolutionary theatre. Art, who unscrupulously gathers up the loot and his friend's mistress, is not condemned. In the law of the jungle plans can go awry and friendships break up at any moment. The will to survive is so strong that it leads to any sacrifice for self-preservation. Art does not have to answer to anyone. Next to the traitor, however, are other characters who struggle to defend their integrity. The cabaret artists rebel against the industry that places them in the hands of bosses, and the women resent the exploitation they must endure. However, Pandora is blind and ready to let Art seduce her. She leaves for Buffalo unaware that her new lover has betrayed his associates and is planning to exploit her talent and charm without giving her love in return.

Paradoxically, it is Art who is the scoundrel. He remains too distant from the group to accept the moral code they all follow. But his final betrayal perhaps appears more as an initiation than an infraction: having eliminated rivals and companions, he will now be the only pimp and leader of the gang. At first a docile spectator and shrewd figurehead, he now becomes a full-fledged actor. And the roles are exchanged: Art takes over from Curt who has otherwise seen him as a worthy successor. "Man, you're like a little brother to me . . . Man, we're a new breed, ya know. Renegades. Rebels. There's no rules for us . . . We make them as we break them" (pp. 68–69). In defining the game dominated by arbitrariness and profit, Curt justifies a priori the way Art will apply his principles. Like a good initiator, he offers Art a reflection of the outlaw's destiny, and like a good disciple, Art beats him at the game. The hustle, scheme, or double game is thus set up as a model for living. These activities in the play structure the relations the characters maintain among themselves and with the world. The hierarchy of the dominant society is repeated among these marginal types, in which each person exploits the other or is exploited. The victory of tricksters like Curt and Art consists in duping society, in owing nothing, and in taking as much as one can. Art proclaims, "I am not a giver. I am a taker." The marginal figure also possesses a trump card superior to any title or diploma, one that cannot be taken from him: his wit, which is the source of his fortune and good luck.

Bullins' theatre is not limited to showing certain cultural types; he integrates their modes of action into dramatic structures. He develops a dramatic language starting from the discourse his characters themselves maintain with the real world. It is not the logic of reality that is important, but that which the characters provide. In relation to observed reality—the marginal world of the ghetto—Bullins' theatre affirms the same autonomy his characters claim in relation to their world.

In the structure of *Goin' a Buffalo*, game-playing assumes an important role. It defines the ordinary occupation of the characters as gamblers who risk life and money, but it especially structures their relations, orders their behavior and the deals they plan—the attacks and repartee, the advances and retreats. The game of chess that opposes Curt to his friend Rich furnishes a key to the entire play. The black and white pawns also suggest racial groups. The chess game is a dress rehearsal for the action. Each match sends out signs that let us know if the venture will end happily. Premonitions, predictions, foreshadowings abound, and in this game one of the players is immediately identified as the white adversary.

The chess game also represents a ritual that allows us to establish the hierarchy within the group. Curt, the leader, never loses. But even if the victor is known in advance, the match is still interesting because one must know *how*, by what ruse and in how long a time, the other will be put in check. Playing the game is more important than its outcome. The game thus offers a discourse on drama: what counts is not the end—since it is foreseeable by different indices throughout the play—but the strategy that leads to it. This game goes on routinely—Rich losing and Curt winning, until Art joins just as the black pieces are about to be put in check by the white; by moving a single piece, the black king, Art saves the situation. The spoken lines that accompany the game have double meaning: as commentary of the players about the match and as commentary about the drama, prefiguring the reversal that will follow. It is important that Art does not know which side to choose. His remark "Its according to which side I'm on," also reveals the ambivalence of a role that seems to occur by chance. By moving Rich's pieces, Art puts Curt in check; at this stage his decision still seems to come arbitrarily. Yet his remarks during the game — "Most kings need a queen to be most powerful, but others do the best they can"; "When you play the game you look for any break you can make" — predict his behavior in the next scene when he takes Pandora away. When Curt, who is Art's equal match, asks him to play, Art accepts the challenge. Now Curt's rival, he becomes the black king who will not be checked and who will hold onto both queens.

First performed in 1968 at the New Lafayette, *In the Wine Time*[91] presents a family and neighbors as they drink, have fun, and quarrel. Their daily life in the ghetto offers little but love shared in silence, and this precarious tranquillity is sometimes ruptured by violence. Three characters share the action of the play. Cliff Dawson has deserted the navy and is growing old too fast; he enjoys philosophizing as he sips cheap wine. He observes and comments on the family life on Derby Street and criticizes those who waste their time. He is a spectator but also part of the community, and the criticism he levies against others turns back upon him. His wife Lou shares his distress and the small pleasures he gets from wine while she tries to salvage their relationship. Through the two of them, their nephew Ray experiences the difficult transition from youth to maturity. He is initiated into the pleasures of drinking and the violence of the street. The aging couple tell the young man about their thwarted ambitions, and Ray awaits the day when he can break the cycle that inflicts the same failures on his generation.

The play opens with a brief lyrical prologue that relates the different seasons in Ray's life — similar to the long monologue in Sonia Sanchez's *Sister Son/ji*. From a succession of hot days, expectant twilights, inebriated nights emerges that long ago summer when Ray saw each day at the street corner a woman whose image still haunts him. His life has its routines: working the streets for money to buy wine, overhearing gossip from the door of the beauty parlor, sleeping off the wine in the mornings or hot afternoons and the shared nights that follow, exchanging secrets in the vapors of alcohol. The young woman is associated with summer, the summer of life constantly referred to in the play, that season of the year when the street and the neighborhood come fully alive. Days ripe for love and the ever-flowing wine and summers "in the wine time" scan his life. The summer becomes a succession of rites. It ends with a last encounter when the haunting woman speaks to Ray for the first time: "I must go now . . . out in the world. Remember, when you're ready all you have to do is leave this place and come to me. I'll be waiting. All you'll need to do is search" (p. 105). Both a declaration of love and an announcement of departure, this sad farewell marks the end of the summer and the beginning of a long quest.

The action of the three acts that follow occurs during the fifties. Summer is announced by a voice on the radio: "And here we are folks, on a black, juicy, jammin' n' groovin' hot August night." Like an additional character, the radio speaks in the ghetto idiom, giving advertisements and rambling news. Summer draws people into the street, makes private lives public. No one has secrets any longer; household scenes spill into the street and malicious gossip quickens its pace; drinking leads to arguments. The spectacle of another's misery reminds each person of his own and starts new quarrels.

Dialogue modeled after the dozens brings constant variation to the dramatic tension. At times one character provokes another, but a moderator usually interrupts them, like Lou who comes between Cliff and his nephew. When the opponent refuses to play, obscene joking can loosen up the atmosphere. A large part of the action consists of passing from one mode of language to another. Unleashed with malice but not viciousness, the verbal games stir up antagonism. Through sarcasm, Cliff incites Ray's friends to go against him; an expert stage director, he manipulates the teenagers and then enjoys the ritual of reciprocal aggression.

Cliffs life among the fauna of Derby Street is presented through the neighbors' gossip and in dialogue animated with accusations and insults. Cliff even tries the dozens on his wife:

CLIFF: That beak nose of yours comes from that shanty
Irishman who screwed your grandmammy down on the plantation.

. . . . .

LOU: Watch your mouth, Cliff.

. . . . .

CLIFF: Watch my mouth? Well, take a look at yours. Yours
comes from that Ubangi great grandaddy on your father's
side.   (P. 122.)

The fight ceases when each confesses guilt. Cliff enjoys parodying all the idioms he knows, from the dialect of a poor fool to the jargon of an intellectual. The spoken sequences introduce numerous variations on jive talk, parody, blasphemy, provocation (from Cliff), and anger, tenderness, and confession (from Lou). Cliff makes perfidious allusions to Lou's mother and the miserable life to which her daughter is condemned. Lou tries to stop the game that brings back a cruel past. Here we find the moment of breakup that is so familiar in Bullins' plays. As one of the protagonists gives up, the verbal game ends abruptly. Each person pursues his own thoughts separately. Lou brings up Ray's adoption. Cliff curses God for the fate He inflicts on blacks. Lou's tenderness fuses with Cliff's sarcasm; in simultaneous monologues her blues blend with his curses.

The past is constantly recalled; miserable as it is, one can always take some pride in it. Cliff remembers his life as a sailor. For the inhabitants of the ghetto, the sea signifies escape and security, open space and a job in the navy. For this reason no one wants to alter the glorious image Cliff has of his years at sea:

> CLIFF: I'll have you know that just because I spent one third of my navy time in various brigs . . . I was still one of the saltiest salt water sailors in the fleet . . . on dry land, in the fleet, or in some fuckin' marine brig!
>
> LOU: You wasn't shit, Cliff . . . You know that, don't you? (P. 132)

Even if he did spend so much time in the brig, Cliff will no more admit he was a failure as a sailor than that he is like the dumb black jackasses that swarm around Derby Street. He thinks he is a "bad nigger," part of the family of Stagolee or the Great MacDaddy, the hard men of folklore and legend. He even appropriates in his speech the words used by Mac-Daddy; "I dont fear nothin' . . . not God nor death . . .I got a tombstone mind and a graveyard disposition . . . I'm a bad motherfucker and I don't mind dyin" (p. 132).

Cliff takes on aspects of a "tall man," especially the bad nigger's ability to transform the events of his life into exploits. The transfiguration of reality occurs through language. Cliff is perhaps only a good-for-nothing who drinks and runs around. But he gives body and soul to this life of "nothing." In the eyes of his wife and neighbors, who represent the popular ethic, his time in the navy was a failure, just like his life in the ghetto. However, from the standpoint of the popular culture that Cliff constantly refers to, he is no poor fool, but a hero by virtue of his audacity, braggadocio, and high talk. Are not his defects then incomparable gifts? He certainly enjoys playing the party-pooper. He wants to be the bad boy outside the control of any law. "I am not a beast . . .an animal to be used for the plows of the world. But if I am, then I'll act like one. I'll be one and turn the fuckin' world of dreams and lies and fairy tales into a jungle or a desert" (p. 139).

Everyone knows that Cliff does nothing but talk. But his incessant verbal activity represents more than a preoccupation or a diversion. It constitutes his mode of interaction with others, the manifestation of his social being; it is especially a creative act that invents reality, arouses reactions, upsets habits of thought, turns situations around. And his character contributes much to Bullins' dramatic plan. References to the cultural heritage — in the sense that all aspects of black experience can be found in the folklore — gives a new dimension to Cliff's character as one who dreams of a life of defiance and victory and who finds his place in the pantheon of heroes.

The couple's teasing play follows a familiar ritual in which each knows which roles to assume, what tone to adopt, when to respond, and how far to go. Hardly secret, the ritual invites participation. The privileged spectator here is Ray. He thus learns that love is expressed by more than good intentions; as old sparring partners, Lou and Cliff have their own way of knowing they will never leave each other. Ray's friends and neighbors also join the ritual, either to share Cliff's drunkenness or to mirror the central couple by pursuing similar rituals.

The spectator in the audience thus watches a plurality of parallel and overlapping mini-rituals as they end and start again. He follows the amorous adventures and misadventures of the couples that form and separate in the wine-filled August heat. The party begun in drunkenness ends with violence: Ray gets angry when one of his friends, Red, steals his girlfriend. They settle up with fists in an alley, and Cliff joins the fighters just as the police arrive on the scene. Red is stabbed to death. Hoping to save his nephew, who has "his whole life ahead of him," Cliff takes the blame: "It's your world, Ray . . . It's yours boy . . . Go on out there and claim it." Cliff's farewell confers upon Ray the mission of pursuing the dreams Cliff had renounced. Ray's initiation is achieved at the cost of Red's death and Cliff's prison term. The murder Ray committed makes him lose forever his innocence, and with it goes the vision of the woman glimpsed one summer long ago. The time for drinking has ended. Yet Cliff's sacrifice suddenly places him in another category of hero and he joins the admirable characters of legend. Now he merits the title of spiritual father. As in *Goin' a Buffalo*, a character's double takes over from an initiator and assumes his role. By paying for his nephew's mistake, Cliff makes their fates inseparable. His sacrifice allows Ray to seek the freedom they both secretly cherish. His initiative also appears as another ruse of the trickster who dupes the police and finds a way out of a situation that jeopardizes his plans. What seems to be surrender is actually a victory.

In New England Winter[92] follows immediately after *Wine Time* in Bullins' "twentieth century cycle." The almost tragic end to a romantic summer here gives way to a winter that brings on other tests. Cliff reappears, older, a bit more resigned. He has finished paying for Ray's crime. Lou has left him with their child and has since had another by a different man. Cliff and his half-brother Steve, the play's protagonists, plan a bank robbery together. As in *Wine Time*, the meaning of the title is revealed in a prologue that echoes the earlier play; it also concerns love, but this time it is evoked through the troubled mind of a schizophrenic woman, Liz. Cold weather suggests the impossibility of love, the destructive roles each person plays for the others, the unleashing of catastrophies that extend from a small but uncontrollable event, and finally, the fear that a passionate love may lead nowhere. In her schizophrenia, Liz fears that her child will become like the New England winter, the image of the white world that freezes the ghetto inhabitants in ice.

The levels of meaning that *Wine Time* draws from folklore or culture do not appear here, and the symbolism of snow seems gratuitous; there is no evidence that it means a sense of fate; the episodes — memories, predictions, anticipation — remain simple procedures. The play's sole anchor is in what the preceding plays give it by foreshadowing certain roles and resolutions. Just as before, the scheme imprisons the protagonists in a cycle that cannot be broken. From one generation to the other the same conflicts, rivalries, unions and breakups appear, in which white society is never directly involved. The police remain in the background looking out for a victim, but they do not intervene until an offense is committed. A member of the family or community acts the role of fate and the banality of daily life takes a sudden turn for the worse.

In Bullins' plays it is not the mode of tragedy that predominates, but that of melodrama, which appears often in black theatre. The most popular plays in Harlem around the late nineteenth and early twentieth centuries had strong elements of melodrama, as did the vaudeville and the "serious theatre" black writers created between 1900 and 1910. It seems to have been a response to certain taste of black audiences and a search for a different kind of catharsis from what traditional tragedy offered. It should be seen as a rejection of the tragic vision — a vision of destiny that inspires fear and pity and over which men can exert no power at all.

Bullins abandons melodrama altogether in *The Duplex: A Black Love Fable in Four Movements*[93] in order to continue variations on his major theme: the cycle of love. The action takes place in California during the sixties. The title *The Duplex* indicates a specific space, but also states that the action unfolds on two levels. The set is suggestive, not realistic; two superimposed stages are each divided into several playing areas. Each room, belonging to a character or a couple, is both an autonomous private space where dramas and secret loves occur and a space penetrated by the outer world in the constant flow of visitors, friends, and troublemakers. Doors and stairways offer passage from one unit to the next and the possibility of many interactions. In these shadowy areas one hears approaching footsteps or waits with anxiety. Yet each person must face his guilt alone.

The complex stage directions suggest a world enclosed and cluttered with objects; the colors are garish; the overwhelming decorations give the impression of baroque unreality, as if they had come from "the more imaginative inmates of an institution for the insane." This set suggests an atmosphere of mystery and voluptuousness. The spatial organization of the set is part of the play's text. The entire action will unfold within these walls, and the street appears indirectly. The complexity of this space structures both the relations among the characters and the action. On one floor live the tenants, Steve and Marco; on the other, Velma, the beautiful landlady whose rowdy husband makes his presence known by noisy entrances and exits. Velma is attracted to Steve, and their affair risks being discovered at any moment by the unexpected return of the terrifying husband. The duplex is the space in which the two characters search for each other and fear getting caught, a space invested with dramatic value, for each movement creates suspense.

Bullins' description of this space serves both practical and poetic purposes. At times it gives precise directions for the performance, at times it helps to create the imaginary. It evokes a black neighborhood somewhere in the southwest around 1960. It also stands for the spatial relations and underlying conflicts in society. Finally it is a playing area or an autonomous space "where something happens on its own terms."[94] The game is Velma's seduction of Steve. The landlady can move about with more ease than her tenant; she is bolder than the young man who fears reprisals and often hides to escape Velma's attentions. The upstairs area is like an observation post from which Velma seems to direct a situation in which emotions are acted out.

The spectator occupies a privileged position, for he can see all levels and units at once. he knows who is going up or down the stairs and who is keeping watch on whom. He guesses before the protagonists can what will happen, and his surprise comes before theirs. The dramatic interest thus constantly rebounds, for the action plays upon the difference between the spectator's perspective and that of the characters separated by doors and walls.

The Duplex begins with a dual game: a card game around a table, and a theatrical game in which each character adopts a posture or dialect and feigns innocence or anger. To explain their game to Steve, who has just arrived, the cardplayers improvise a scenario in which each statement, each mime designates the winner, the loser, and the cheater. As quickly as the cards can be dealt, repartee and jokes begin; each partner enjoys accusing the other of losing to a third; each tells his neighbor what was said about him. Thus begins the playful round that will characterize the action. The game changes when Velma arrives; the jokes start alluding to sex in which each man is a seducer. Velma handles their advances with good humor, but loses no time in taking Steve away. Then a duo begins with Velma's complaints and anger about being a lonely, unloved wife and with Steve's procrastination. This scene informs the spectator about Velma's life: her children who are being raised by a grandmother in Tennessee, her husband, O.D., who carouses in the streets. It is not unlikely that the romantic Steve will one day become a tyrannical O.D. (whose initials allude to overdose). During the first days of her marriage Velma was happy. But now that O.D. has taken to the street, she tries to bring Steve into her domain, the duplex. But O.D.'s frequent intrusions threaten the peaceful haven, and it is Velma who must seek Steve's protection. Like Art in *Goin' a Buffalo*, Steve plays the knight who comes to the aid of a mistreated woman, but his eagerness makes O.D. suspicious and creates another danger. Velma, who thinks she is strong and independent, is really a fragile woman who fears solitude and needs her vulgar and rough husband's love as much as Steve's tenderness. She continues to drift between the two men, and the sways of her heart follow those of her body from one floor to the other. The gun she and Steve agree to buy one day does not help resolve the conflict: when the confrontation occurs, physical force wins, and O.D. takes possession of his wife. The verbal exchanges that went with the card game are repeated in the more brutal game in which the adversaries lay hold of each other. The last scene makes the threat concrete: in Velma's world the force of love should be shown in the strength of fists.

As in Bullins' other plays, the neighbors play an important role. Their visits punctuate the plot, and even when they are not on stage they are always ready to intervene. They keep watch and lend Velma a helping hand. When it is time for a party they rush in to dance and drink wine.

And they participate in the two-step between Velma and Steve. They also hope to seduce someone. Their hopes and dreams mingle with those of the main trio. Their discourse complements that of the protagonists.

This chorus of neighbors does not come out of nowhere. The spectator is supposed to recognize them from other plays. The elderly couple, Pops and Momma, resemble an older Cliff and Lou. And when his name is revealed, we learn that Pops Dawson, whose first name really is Cliff, is the father of the hero of the other plays. From play to play, the characters in this enlarged human comedy seem to depart and reappear. O.D., for example, is accompanied by a bodyguard, Crooks, who, like the Crooks in *New England Winter* surprises Steve when he arrives to settle accounts. Like Cliff in *Wine Time*, Montgomery, the father of one of Steve's friends, is an inveterate cardplayer who serves as a father figure for the young man. At one moment Steve, who likes books, reads the prologue from *Wine Time* to Velma, thus borrowing Ray's voice to round out his sweet talk.

Bullins encourages us to find parallels between characters and situations in his various plays. He also constantly inserts references within the body of his work, thus presenting the "twentieth century cycle" as a single text whose different episodes become mutually clarified. The different plays are variations on the same arguments and explorations. The later plays refer back to the earlier ones. Steve's monologue in *Duplex* responds to Ray's long narrative in *Wine Time*. And by picking up Ray's tale, Steve suddenly finds his own voice:

> You don't know me . . .Nobody knows me . . . what's in my mind and guts . . .Nobody knows the love and beauty I finds in holding my woman . . . nor will anybody know that she'll never know me . . . this black man . . . they'll never understand . . . these eyes that see the flames of the hell we all live in . . . live our black lives in here . . . in our cool dark little lives . . . getting ready to become something we isn't now nor will ever be . . . really. (Pp. 120–122)

Steve's speech is not simply that of Velma's lover but that of any "nigger," whether he is called Ray, Cliff, or Steve. The reference is no longer to the autonomous universe of each play or to the ensemble, but to the condition of blacks in America. Breaking away from the incident and anecdote where he seems to belong, each character has a destiny that becomes exemplary and metaphorical. Steve's discourse goes from the cry of a blues song, voicing his solitude and his love, to the rhetorical questions and exhortations of a preacher. Thus the distress of the black condition is expressed through individual voices and through that of the entire community.

The dramatic artifice of isolating a character and having him give a speech that clashes with his usual language indicates an important function of the theatre. When Steve pronounces his tirade, he is drunk and responding to his friends who try to persuade him to leave Velma; he refuses to use the mode of witty verbal game. In fact, he does not answer them at all; he talks to himself, trying to express his confusion which no other person seems to understand. He thus speaks to the spectator more than to the other characters. The communication he cannot have with them he establishes with the audience through the artifice of monologue. In this way the theatre allows a form of interaction that is impossible in real life. A message that goes beyond the perplexity of the characters must reach the spectator. In the labyrinth of the duplex, the playwright invites us to see a well-designed structure whose meaning eludes the characters who develop within it but not the spectator, who has a more privileged perspective.

The Fabulous Miss Marie[95] extends the cycle further. The play satirizes the superficial and sterile milieu of the black bourgeoisie of Los Angeles: "Maybe we're dying off, maybe we're a vanishing breed." A woman of "fabuluous" magnetism, Miss Marie makes herself the center of gaiety that dissipates daily concerns as well as the monotony of political struggles; there is always a party at her house. Outside, militants lead a campaign for civil rights and organize demonstrations. Presented on a screen to Miss Marie's invited guests, these actions arouse sarcasm and skepticism: "I don't need no raggedy-ass nigger beggin' and moanin' and gettin' their behinds whipped for my freedom." A sententious spectator tries in vain to remind them of their duty to the cause. But for Marie and her friends, the revolution is just another game, and a dangerous one at that. Better to be happy with the liberty each can get for himself without running up against the white world.

Bullins is courageous in showing characters who are indifferent or critical about revolutionary commitment. It cannot be denied that even in the most difficult period in the civil rights struggle, many blacks, and not only the bourgeoisie, felt no concern whatsoever. But in showing this on the stage Bullins has left himself open to sharp criticism.

For Miss Marie, the real struggles are those of everyday life. The occupations and obligations of her world are banal and fascinating, undertermined yet urgent and precise, enumerated like a litany ("I got places to go , things to do, people to see and myself to be, yeah!") in a kind of blues where each person sings about his own misfortunes and the difficulties and joys of the group. The "I" of character is a camouflaged "we," for it is very much a matter of common destiny. The choice is quickly made between service to the cause and the more lucrative prostitution to a career. However, love and good fortune are shown to be capricious toward all. Abandoned, deserted, or simply unhappily married, the unloved can only choose between the restrictions of an imperfect union and the solitude of an unwanted freedom. They must constantly guard and protect themselves from the society they reject. Plans are made and broken; love affairs bring on the same stray impulses and ups and downs. People leave school, a lover, a wife, or a profession with relative ease. Yet liberty cannot be found in futile promises, but in the right each person claims to be no longer controlled by the dominant society. The individual provides what he can for his own well-being, and this hedonism is unencumbered by metaphysical considerations; "I say the world is the world. It'll take care of itself, like we takin' care of ourselves."

Bullins does not set out to judge this bourgeoisie whose behavior shares something with the pragmatic philosophy of the ghetto. He contests it by giving it a voice. Implicitly, Bullins refutes the accusation of pathology and passivity so frequently leveled against blacks, and with the same stroke he accuses his own theatre, thought to delight in painting negative pictures of humanity. He gives his characters positive traits, emphatically underscored, as in the strong epithet given Miss Marie in the play's title.

Miss Marie is a strong woman who has only herself to thank for her freedom. Through Marie, the black woman appears as a lively force of the community. Marie has known her share of misery; her good-for-nothing husband, Bill, made her life hard and she refused to take it. When Bill joined up with a white woman, whom he beat shamelessly in public, Marie took lovers. Yet their union survived these infidelities. Marie did not have an easy childhood: born of an unknown father and a mother who died in childbirth, she was raised by a grandmother. The grandmother was one of the first black women to get an education, but she never used her acquired knowledge and she took to drinking with the complicity of her granddaughter. Marie refused to go to school, and led a campaign for her own civil rights. She became a free and happy woman who knew how to get respect.

This flattering portrait is given by Marie herself. Frequently in black theatre a character introduces himself, often in hyperbolic discourse that proclaims an exceptional destiny. Here we find the tradition of the "toasts" that recount the exploits of folklore heroes. This reference to legend confers an epic dimension upon a character and allows him to transcend everyday life and become an exemplary figure. In sum, it theatricalizes the character. Although women are rarely present in black folklore, Bullins creates strong female characters in his own mythology. Big Girl and the fabulous Miss Marie are rare examples of women who embody qualities most often attributed to male heroes; their physical power is celebrated as much as their fierce autonomy. In a sense Marie comes closer to the authentic MacDaddy of legend than does Cliff in *Wine Time*. She tempers her strength with qualities of love that "bad men" rarely possess. Considerable distance separates this female figure from other heroines in black theatre, such as the mother in *A Medal for Willie*. Even when women in nationalist theatre evoke their role in the community, they use more often the mode of complaint or of lyricism than that of the popular epic.

The play also gives considerable importance to scenic design and to staging. The text is scored with music and dance, and the lighting resembles Christmas decorations. The staging suggests the atmosphere of a party, indeed jubilation. The stage directions are as precise as choreography. Characters enter from different playing areas like dancers emerging from the shadows only to melt back into them. They dance a few steps from earlier periods— the twist, the soft shoe, buck 'n wing, the black bottom — and new steps as well. Interludes of erotic dance emphasize the fragility of the couples that form haphazardly and separate again. Pantomime repeats the action, which is further multiplied by the use of screens. Bullins creates a complex game of mirrors between the character's actions and different screens (television and movie screens, and scrims behind which characters mime in jest). The images confront and compose one another. The actors create on stage certain tableaux which the projected images respond to or contradict. When the broadcaster delivers the news, the actors mime it from behind another screen. The sudden transformations of actors into moving shadows also suggests a metaphor of the theatre: the characters present through their game an entire discourse on theatrical activity. The importance of the image is also stated. The passage from one scene to another—the changing of images as one would change television channels—defines the dramatic structure as a chain of images proceeding capriciously or arbitrarily. Moreover, the projector's beam cuts the stage into areas of shadow and light; its movement emphasizes the passage from one sequence to another, while its concentration gives intensity to the lighted stage. The projections meanwhile divide the space by multiplying the screens that limit and enclose the image. The concrete use of these techniques to create a total spectacle thus also offers an occasion for meditation on the nature of theatrical art.

With *Street Sounds*[96] Bullins proceeds further in his experimentation. The forty-odd vignettes of this play are intended to make up an almost exhaustive mosaic of the black community. Here there are no arguments between characters, but isolated subjects who appear and disappear, talking about themselves. The subtitle, "Dialogues with Black Experience," emphasizes the fact that there is no real monologue in theatre: those who speak always have a listener; if not on stage, the listener is implicitly present. Also, by definition, theatre always establishes a dialogue; the message communicated through the intermediary of a character passes from the writer-sender to the spectator-receiver.

The author's work is to find the right words to convey an aspect of black experience—made concrete through the fictional character. The theatrical discourse thus becomes an interrogation on the status of speech. The spectator's task is to identify both the speaker and the interlocutor, for dialogue exists between these voices as well as with the author or the spectator. In *Street Sounds* discourses are opposed, linked together, and reciprocally answered as in a call and response pattern: the addressee of one speech becomes the speaker of another. A woman sings her despair at being abandoned; another waits impatiently for pleasure. Here one character gets angry at the hypocrisy of most blacks without recognizing his own: there an explanatory speech from another figure reveals to him the sincerity of those he has misjudged. Here a writer abandons his creative project for a more ordered life; there a robber soon steals a neighbor's typewriter. Here a publisher congratulates himself on his successful business, there a nationalist critic gets angry about a writer's negative images of his race.

The interlocutor is at times a friend to confide in, a skeptic, an accuser before whom one justifies oneself, or an opponent who must be faced. At times he is all these at once: a dope peddler refuses to see his activity as immoral; an anguished man tells a friend his wife beats him, then suspects his confidant of being the shrew's accomplice; another refuses to be treated like a bad boy and locked up. Elsewhere, the characters are labeled by their function, occupation, or profession (Revolutionary Artist, Woman, Poet), the role they play in the discourse (The Doubter, The Explainer), or again, the function of receiver and passive object of an action (Seduced and Abandoned, Reconciled). Often the designation is ironic: thus the Liar announces he has decided to lie because the truth brings him only trouble. Or it is metaphorical: the errand boy becomes a messenger between the past and the present.

Each speaker, in his way, states a truth about black experience by discussing either his job, his political engagement, or his love life or sex life. Whatever business he is in or revolutionary slogans he pronounces, he always has some bit of wisdom to impart. Bullins orchestrates this polyphony as a single uproar rising from the street, alternately plaintive, boastful, supplicant, and accusatory. Each voice has the right to be heard, even those of Bullins' detractors who speak through the nationalist critic. Bullins thus proclaims a theatre where protagonists are placed in a position to speak, where different kinds of discourse are opposed and reconciled. He responds in this way to the voice of the audience and engages in dialogue with it through all his fictional intermediaries.

The different experiments Bullins pursues in his theatre have one essential goal: to show the dialectical relations within the black community. By listening to the blues people, Bullins places in bold relief their gestures, acts, and speech that have for too long remained invisible and hidden. The vision he offers does not make blacks any less uneasy. He has been reproached for showing only negative images, for revealing internal quarrels, for showing the ugliness of the black community, for insisting on vices rather than virtues. These criticisms come as no surprise to Bullins, who incorporates them into *Street Sounds* through one character whose words echo these accusations (p. 168). Bullins uses his theatre to answer his critics. The contradictory reactions that inspire his theatre are part of the dialectic he transcribes so meticulously. He rejects a suspect realism as well as the paternalistic attitudes of some people toward the lower classes. He is not concerned about making the spectator love or hate his characters, but about giving them an undeniable presence on stage. Only then will the problems they raise be taken hold of by the audience. Although his theatre offers no resolution, Bullins compels us to see and hear.

Edgar White: The Odyssey of the Picaro

Edgar White's modes of expression—allegory, fable, tale—have rarely been used in black theatre, although they hold a prominent place in the oral traditions of Africa and black America. With White, narration takes charge on stage. His plays follow a story line that develops an argument, recounts what has happened between two scenes, and furnishes insights that are often difficult to render in drama.

White usually adds to his regular cast of characters a narrator, who does not merely introduce other characters but presents an additional dimension of conflict himself: his commentary can arouse approval or hostility. White's use of the narrator establishes an intriguing set of relations between the stage and the house. Observing the events that happen on the set, the narrator presents one version from which the characters, who usually play directly to the spectators, draw part of the message they signify, but at which they also get angry when their words or actions are distorted. Their intervention and their legitimate reclaiming of autonomous discourse encourage the audience to reach a decision about the different versions of an event. A dialectic is thus born out of a doubling of the dramatic action through the behavior of the characters and through the narrative discourse. In an incomplete and biased manner, the narrator reflects both a character and the perception of it. The confusion leads one to question the traditional roles of the narrator and of the spectator as a passive receiver, and the conventions of drama expressed unilaterally for the audience. The inclusion of the narrative mode in a play shows the different points of view to be relative and allows White to offer new ideas about the nature of theatre.

The Burghers of Calais (see Chapter 2) well illustrates this interaction between stage and audience, and offers certain propositions for the new drama. The play picks up the history of the Scottsboro case. The accused act out their own roles before an audience of prison visitors who are first interested, then exasperated, and who walk out of the show one by one. A narrator situates the action and introduces characters; he also sheds light on the sociocultural norms that define certain roles and on the theatrical code that indicates the scenic game. He emphasizes the historicity and the ideological nature of the argument. Part of the dramatic action consists of the way the characters reject the proposed code and subvert this level of written theatre.

The Author appears as a character who sits in the audience of prison visitors. He intervenes to regulate the performance and becomes angry at the protagonists' lack of discipline. They in turn protest the situation that limits them to interpreting roles written by others and that forbids improvisation. The roles are both imposed by authoritative white dramatists in the theatre and meted out by society. Represented by an all-powerful author, this society can declare innocence or guilt without recourse to law. Once again the theatrical metaphor represents the situation of blacks and, conversely, a concrete historical event alludes to the world of theatre.

In *Burghers* the Author is a half-crazy drug addict who assumes the prerogatives of a lucid creator. In fact he is incapable of expressing himself; his characters have the coherence and eloquence he lacks. His dark glasses hide him from the real colors of the world. He combines the traits of a ringmaster who wants to entertain in the tradition of the black showman with those of a conciliator who pleads causes with cynicism or humor pierced with histrionics. The insignificant details that he lavishes not only on the circumstances of the alleged rape but on the physique and health of the judge and prisoners respond to the audience's desire for anecdotes in place of the truth. Yet these are the same details that filled the newspapers of the period, addressing the most superficial curiosity. When a character wants to make up for the lack of pertinent information, the Author promptly cuts off his lines.

The spectator witnesses the unrest in the production and the conflicts among characters, Author, narrator, and visitors; he hears all the voices. A basic question is raised about the reactions of the visitors who leave the performance. Do they disapprove of the farcical aspect of the trial? Or do they refuse to hear uncomfortable truths? It is significant that each hasty exit occurs just when a prisoner is about to take the floor. White's play shows a grotesque scenario in which the only authentic witnesses are rejected by the audience. It thus questions the traditional division of labor among author, narrator, character and theatregoer.

The real event, the Scottsboro trial, serves as a pretext for a symbolic representation of black experience, whose central metaphor in White's repertory is marginality, expressed through the antithetical themes of imprisonment and odyssey. Characters in *The Burghers of Calais* are condemned to spend their lives in prison; in *The Wonderfull Yeare*[97] they remain wandering captives of the streets or of funeral parlors that they never manage to leave. And the canvases of the artists in *The Wonderfull Yeare* show a society full of confusion and incongruity: one paints what hurts him, another paints what amuses him. The last painting is a blank canvas carried in a funeral procession behind a coffin and a baby carriage, which absurdly contain neither corpse nor baby.

White's heroes are not only blacks of the United States, but their companions in misfortune from Puerto Rico, the Caribbean, and Latin America. Marginality, for White, is not limited to any one race, and his stage extends beyond the borders of one continent. His characters flee an America that crucifies them (the metaphor in *The Crucificado*) or incarcerates them (*Burghers*) only to encounter on the same road other miserable people in exile, other pilgrims searching for an identity or a job. They inscribe their visions and impressions of the world they pass through in poems and paintings, without ever finding a home. As

romantics, they continue to believe in human solidarity; as sensitive beings, they give voice to suffering; as philosophers, they claim wisdom in
humility; as prophets, they announce the end of an abominable world
and the coming of an era of joy. Contrary to the world of cursed artists,
their experience helps create a brotherhood of men who find salvation
through humor and wisdom, through their amused observation of the
spectacle of mankind.

White's plays are inspired by traditional genres. *The Wonderfull
Yeare* borrows its exuberance and improvisations, its jibes, situations,
and characters from *commedia dell'arte*. From Greek comedy White
borrows the concept of the *agon*; the dramatic technique in *Fun in
Lethe* comes from Chinese theatre. Everything is at once sordid, poetic,
obscene, and tragic; as unpredictable as it is inescapable, as
preposterous as it is pathetic. White brings the best-known types from
traditional repertory—sorcerers, machiavellian merchants, Don Quix-
ote–like gentlemen, prostitutes, outlaws—together with characters from
his ethnic universe, endowing them with larger life. These references
also allow enough distance from the contemporary event to give it
another dimension: "The play—and the issues it concerns—must have
nothing to do with the temporal 1970's; it has to do with always." The
allusion in his plays to the N.A.A.C.P. as a "persuasive unit in the
American business world," to the Negro Business Guild, or to the actions of militants who want to understand the enigma of their people's
condition thus take on a perfidious character: the black struggle
becomes somewhat ridiculous when placed in the jumble of situations
where nothing has changed for centuries. White does not set out to
denigrate militancy. But in opposition to revolutionary theatre he offers
a more detached view. Humor becomes his instrument to enrich experience rather than let it grow rigid with authoritarian prescriptions or
Manichean analyses. His heroes are neither good nor evil, loyal nor
deceitful, but truculent people full of exuberance or melancholy, great
improvisers of roles and challenges, tirelessly drawn from one adventure
to another. They adapt with ease to changing circumstances and willingly intervene to alter the course of events. The picaresque mode,
which plunges the characters into a multiplicity of actions, suggests a
metaphor for the black condition, while borrowings from *commedia
dell'arte* lend effervescence to the stage. White's theatre records the
dynamism of a life that seeks to be victorious in spite of obstacles; he
celebrates the spirit and vitality of a people on the move. The
simultaneity of places and periods becomes a condition for freedom
because it multiplies the perspectives. The central metaphor in White's

theatre is organized between two poles: an odyssey that appears as either a constraint or a liberating conquest versus the immobility of a static and confining world.

White does not neglect reality as a reference; he simply transfigures it. The sordid way the characters evolve does not keep "the sad walls from falling in love with the sky." Indeed, in *The Wonderfull Yeare* "the tenement houses are making love to the skies and the city is putting on colors" (p. 16). Misserimus, the poet-painter in the play, paints the world from a baroque palette, symbolically spreading a protective salt around him. Every event has both a serious and an incongruous quality. The vermin invade the city without weighing heavily upon the people. Young Salvador is brutally killed after a chase with the police when he trips on some dog excrement. The juxtaposition of the two facts of unequal weight takes the trauma out of the event. Salvador's friends mourn his death. The funeral director, however, rejoices in having so much work and charts his success in the business world. The father of Misserimus and Salvador, a janitor in the municipal hospital, is gathering material for his autobiography, and like a blues singer he evokes the joys and sorrows of his life. He ends up stating that from now on he will no longer feel anything:

> DON HERNANDO: It's nothing that I feel . . . nothing, a space between happy and sad, a space which all the days and all the years and all the streets and all the hospitals fill up.
> SECOND ATTENDANT: Is it death that you mean?
> DON HERNANDO: No, it is the thing other than life that I mean.
> (P. 201)

Little by little, Misserimus' canvases also empty. However, a form of life goes on to which the poet dedicates his work; cradle and grave are filled. While some people know fame and fortune (Misserimus himself is recognized and promoted to be a professor), the world continues to be reborn and to suffer.

In *Fun in Lethe (or the Feast of Misrule)*[98] a West Indian poet, Harmatia, travels to Great Britain—the mother country of the founders of America. In a succession of real and imaginary scenes he encounters many characters: a bum; the son of a butcher, who keeps dead mice in a birdcage; an editor, Pennfeather; a troubador; Pakistanis; a West Indian writer recently fired from the BBC for airing truth about his island home; an Irish poet; and several real Anglo-Saxons.

In the mode of tragicomedy, this epic presents the adventures of His Majesty's bastard in a racist society. Like the Puerto Rican in America in

The Wonderfull Yeare, Harmatia cannot forget his color for one minute. As a British subject, he is also regarded as a "topic for discussion and commentary" in a land where he is taken to be either an African or just a "plain nigger." He discovers that his identity is both vague and well defined. The perspective he brings to this pseudo-game is unindulgent but not without humor. When he encounters an honorable Briton who has traveled throughout the Dark Continent, he takes ironic note of the double movement of "Fowler's sons," armed with "Christendom and cricket," embarking for distant lands, and of the disinherited children of a crumbling Commonwealth returning to England.

Harmatia has written a play whose theme also serves as a metaphor for the situation of the unwelcomed traveler: a student and a professor, both white, and a West Indian clockmaker fall one by one into a sewer and land on a garbage heap. In this place of no exit, the presence of the black man soon becomes intolerable to the others. After harassing his companions with his rhetoric, the professor bludgeons them to death. The humor here denounces the imperialism of the strongest, but this fable also suggests the anguish whites feel in the presence of blacks.

Harmatia's destiny is clarified by Samuel, an Irish poet he meets in a pub. Weary of life, Samuel wanders about dreaming of the house of death to which no one can direct him. A stranger to himself as well as to his country, he awaits death by meditating on the tendency of humans and rats to kill their own species. Death comes not from God but from man.

In the last scene, as if in a nightmare, Harmatia is traveling day and night on a train through sinister and ephemeral cities. Passengers get on and off but he perceives only their shadows and changing voices. He remains a solitary traveler without goal or destination. This last image returns us to the theme of the eternal wandering of the Flying Dutchman or of the phantom subway.

The hero of *The Mummer's Play*[99] posesses all the qualities of White's other characters—tenderness, courtesy, humor—and like them he has the misfortune of being black: "Demosthenes Bellysong Jones . . . would have been a success in this world instead of just a massive phenomenon were he not . . . so unmistakably Negro and moreover poor" (p. 125). At the morning hour when most Harlemites are just waking up, Bellysong returns home after a night of wandering. He takes up his favorite pastime, reading the obituary columns of the newspaper for the death of his landlord. He also imagines an announcement of his wife's death. The plot of the play follows the peregrinations of this retired sculptor through Harlem during one whole day: several visits, encounters, exchanges of words, but no real action. It seems as if speech is the only activity remaining in an incomplete and morose world that even the Creator has abandoned out of boredom.

Yet the characters use language with verve and vitality that triumphs over the long wait and the overwhelming silence. Bellysong and the poet Pariah, who is just back from a fruitless trip to Europe, discuss life and the United States, that "large unflushed toilet." According to Pariah, movement and action are illusions: "No one's moving anywhere. We're just looking at each other through frosted glass . . . We're standing perfectly still" (p. 135). No occupation or escape is possible for those who are neither Anglo-Saxon, Jewish, nor part of the black middle class, and Pariah indulges none of his friends who take themselves too seriously. He tries to unite with Jews by courting the daughter of a liberal lawyer who gets all his clients, whether innocent or guilty, off the hook. Pariah has no scruples about taking money from this lawyer-protector who has harmed so many others. Of all the roles society has to offer—artist, public entertainer, petty bourgeois—that of parasite attracts him most. That way, he says humorously, he can help ease the white man's burden and divert the embarrassment caused by his presence.

Pariah decides to leave this world. Accompanied by Bellysong, he arrives at the gates of heaven, only to discover that he is not expected there either:

> ONE OF THE ANGELS: I say, there must be some mistake, there was no one expected here today.
> PARIAH: Mistake? I am Pariah Anon, the formless son of a discarded race, who, after much sea change and tumult, am here to see the Lord, your God. (P.164)

God, the painter of an unfinished canvas, remains aloof from this scene; St. Peter is his absurd representative. At the doors of paradise, St. Peter sees that the dead keep their appointed hour and has only nice words and candy to offer the men who arrive prematurely.

White's most ambitious play to date is *The Crucificado*,[100] in which he further explores marginality and wandering by orchestrating them through brief but dramatic sequences and through characters whose presence or actions constantly change the protagonist's situation. In the Black Mecca, Morose is no ordinary pilgrim. Although he joins the chorus in praying for bread and for peace in the world, he is aware that a talented young black man can stagnate. He believes he is both chosen and cursed, not because of his artistic talent as an architect-writer but because he knows "the implications of [his] history." This history constitutes the argument of the play as it is discovered and lived by the protagonist.

In the eyes of his friends, Morose is a jobless man who takes drugs, chases women, and runs from life. But White gives this too-widespread stereotype poetic and tragic as well as grotesque dimensions; the use of irony allows him to revivify clichés about the black condition. If he has nothing new to reveal, he can at least proclaim in a new way the truths that have been dulled and watered down.

White sees strong similarities between dream and wakefulness. In an early sequence Morose loiters about the square of a church, where a beautiful Puerto Rican woman sells him dope and says he is looking for death. Thanks to the drug, which allows him to forget the nightmare of his life, Morose hopes to escape the destiny of the cursed poet Gongora, who has lost his eyesight from seeing too sharply. Drugs are not Morose's only vice. When his father reproaches him for choosing art as a career when things are going so badly, he answers: "It seemed the most graceful form of suicide."

Morose's destiny is both ordinary and exceptional. His adventures lead him to his estranged father, El Cid, and this encounter confronts him with a world he has known only piecemeal. The father, who has made his fortune as a drug dealer passing as a manufacturer of toilet paper, decides to help his son get on the right track; he offers him a trip around the world as an education before taking him into the business. The return of the prodigal father questions the choice made by the artist son and leads to a brutal ending. When his entry into the business world seems most sure, Morose kills his father who has taught him only the value of money: Isaac sacrifices Abraham.

Here White seems to be playing with all legends. The procreator who is uninterested in his descendant evokes the image of God in the other plays as a deity who left his creation unfinished. The paternal image also evokes the authoritative white man who dictates behavior and demands respectful gratitude. Morose's action is his break with history: he refuses to contract the debt that continues to enslave son to father, blacks to a white master, the artist to society.

The fellow travelers who surround Morose are extensions of him. Each embodies one of his traits; thus they dramatize the conflicts that tear him apart. Morose is also in love with two women. One, Celestina, a creature of the night, is the prototype of the bitter black woman who judges her lover to be weak. She expresses the black woman's reproach to the black man throughout time. The "conscience" of the black man, for a time embodied in theatre by a white woman (such as Lula), is now presented in the figure of the black woman. Celestina thinks Morose is crazy for refusing his father's offer of money and security; the way she forces him to deal with reality pushes him to take charge. But if he seeks to defend the cause of black men, he also refuses to enter into battle with his black sister who, like him, has been made violent by whites. All the while accepting the protection of Celestina, he prefers the sweet companionship of Soledada. A third woman, Melibea, occasionally comes to Morose's aid: effective and vigilant, she is finally unable to convert him to the world of business.

Pedro, one of Morose's companions, is the male double of Celestina. A realist, he knows the cost of Morose's scorn of the rules, and he harbors no illusions about whites. In an imaginary dialogue with Morose, he opposes the naive obstinacy of the artist who believes in his art (against the sadism of whites who exploit it):

MOROSE: What is it you want of me, world?

PEDRO: We want you to labor, nigger.

M: Labor at what?

P: It does not matter as long as you don't enjoy it.

M: But what about my art?

P: You are black, aren't you?

M: Yes.

P: Black people aren't allowed art.

M: Oh, damn, I forgot. (P. 83)

Whites expect blacks to be brute laborers. Being the strongest is the only thing that counts, as Pedro shows the blind poet Gongora by fighting him. "I'm standing on your chest. Write me a poem to make me get off . . . Go on artist, use words tender enough to move my heart . . . If I had raped your woman or your mother, and had put chains on you, what could you create that would move me enough to repent?" (p. 122). Gongora, however, knows he is stronger and attributes Pedro's brutal reaction to fear. Gongora conquers his own fear, and when he tells the white man unwelcome truths he is gagged for his audacity. This scene as acted by the characters mirrors the relations of blacks to American society.

Pedro and Gongora thus represent two sides of Morose. Just like Celestina, Pedro denounces Morose's idealism which refuses a fortune in the name of an unattainable spirituality. Gongora, however, embodies faith in the artist's mission at the cost of a more total destitution. He knows the torment of the poet: "He does not curse God for bringing him into the world too late for he thinks it would have been harder for him were he born before. Likewise he does not curse God for being born too early for he knows that the next generation will be more desperate . . . He says that he curses God for being born *at all*" (p. 105). Gongora congratulates himself for not having children. By denying himself descendants he can stop the course of history.

Added to Pedro's lucid violence and to Gongora's fervor and disenchantment is the image of Randolph, who taught Morose architecture and opened his eyes: "Taught me colors, space. Cause he said a canvas was a sheet, and, see, people are trapped inside. Love hard enough you free them . . . So my eyes are open now. Start noticing walls where sky should be" (p. 115). White often illustrates the black condition through the metaphor of the plastic arts, but here the spatial image prevails. In the buildings he erects, the architect sees the walls of a prison constructed around men; his ruler and T-square are the very instruments of power. The relations of domination are expressed by perpendicularity: one part of humanity is kept down by those who crush it with a mighty verticality.

Morose's voyage occurs within this spatial metaphor. He flees the streets of Harlem where people are reduced to pairs of feet hurrying to a catacomb; he flees the creaking city where people are hungry and sleepy, where buildings shriek with all their lights; he moves toward serene mountains. The world is a succession of gray dawns that spill frightened, starving people into the streets to rob and kill. At the end of the voyage is his father's house awaiting him like a tomb. Refusing to be buried under this edifice, Morose kills his father in a liberating ecstasy.

Musical background all through the play ("Father, Sun and Holy Ghost" by Coltrane, "Mysterioso" by Thelonius Monk, and "Deux pensées devant trois" by Erik Satie) and lighting effects orchestrate the movements that make the characters oscillate from the confines of dream to reality, from "campos verdurados" to streets torn up with cries of pain. In search of an impossible identity, White's protagonists are haunted by fears that often transform their days into nightmares. Only they can save themselves, by some courageous act that exorcises terror and fantasy, since God the Creator has abandoned them.

The mode that dominates Edgar White's theatre is undoubtedly the grotesque, which allows a constant interplay between the fantastic and the ordinary and reveals the absurdity of the world. White is one of the few black writers to create a theatre of the absurd; he emphasizes contradictions and offers no resolutions other than parody. Finally, he stages a play of incompatibles and brings an interesting dimension to the new drama.

It is not surprising that the grotesque should appear in new black theatre. What is astonishing is that it happens so rarely, except perhaps in the fiction of Jean Toomer or Ralph Ellison. Its resurgence can be seen during periods of change and insecurity. This mode leaves the artist the choice between an attempt to raise issues of social reform in order to remedy an absurd situation, and the decision to accept the absurd by taking a distance from it through the use of paradox. White chooses the latter course. He uses the grotesque to show an existential situation and to try to escape that situation's inherent tragedy. With an inexhaustible and perverse virtuosity, this playwright attests to the incompatibility between the condition of the artist or the black man and the surrounding society. Pariahs because of vocation and color, White's heroes find themselves in many baroque and incongruous situations; they discover salvation through marginality and reject the destructive integration of their talents or their ethnic identity.

White accomplishes this through several means: he shows the comedy of the irrational by breaking the relation of cause and effect; he fuses tragedy and comedy, the fantastic and the realistic; he offers no juxtaposition but an association of genres, one running over into the other without major changes in their respective characteristics. His grotesques make the absurd concrete.[101] In a dynamic process, White underscores the paradoxes and incompatibilities in his subjects and submits them to constant change. The eternal play between the two domains, whose polarity is emphatically affirmed, provokes exchanges and leads to transformations which can only be shown in the theatre. The stage is animated, and the transformation occurs in full view of the audience.

White toys with space by multiplying the characters' playing areas, by moving them from one place to another, by giving them the gift of ubiquity in order to arouse incongruity or to create a distancing effect. The character is where he should not be, or he never arrives when expected. An accurate perception of things, a dizziness before their opacity or transparence, a visionary power are the qualities that make White's hero a singular witness.

White also plays with temporality by projecting his heroes into the destiny of lived experience in the past or the present or a timeless world. On stage the most unexpected thoughts materialize, the metaphors come alive, the images fit. Language assumes a life of its own, continuously proliferating and inventing. The playwright thus projects a universe of dream, which does not end with a return to reality but overflows into it or changes it into a nightmare. The grotesque affirms the presence of obscure, worrisome, demonic forces without explaining them. It is content to state the inability of the characters to find their way in an alienated world or to transcend their bitterness. The grotesque, however, develops less from fear of the unknown or a desire for the impossible than from a need to confront the rich incongruity of reality in order to master the chaos of experience. White thus aims more toward unification than toward disjunction.

Paul Carter Harrison: For a Neo-African Theatre

Neo-African Philosophy and Poetics

Periodically, black Americans have been invited to reflect upon their African ancestry and to evaluate their experiences in relation to a time before slavery. The concept of a black nation has developed around this African background, which offers a source of identity to members of the community and acts as a cultural matrix for many artists. But the relation of blacks to the African continent differs profoundly from the ties other immigrants have kept with their countries of origin; brutally exiled, isolated, deprived of their culture, and dispersed throughout the New World, blacks had little contact with Africa other than that provided by new arrivals on the slave ships. For more than a century slavery broke all ties with Africa: the continent became for most of its descendants a land more mythical than real. The only institutions that maintained a kind of tribal membership among free blacks and slaves in the cities were local organizations called "nations," headed by "kings." These spontaneous associations grew according to divisions and rivalries within the community, and were occasions for some members to practice African rituals in secret. When these "nations" disappeared with the end of the slave trade and slavery, ethnic differences among blacks were more or less erased. No longer defined according to geographic or ethnic origin, and forced to give up their names, blacks became "negroes," forever exiled. If ethnologists today can prove the predominance of particular African cultures in certain regions of the United States (Fanti and Ashanti culture on the "Gullah" islands in Virginia, Dahomean and Bantu culture in New Orleans), they also show that this predominance has no correlation with the numerical majority of one ethnic group or another.[102] Generally, ethnic origins are eclipsed by a broader Pan-African culture in opposition to the Americanism of the surrounding culture.

For blacks in exile, Africa is a memory anchored in the collective consciousness more than in actual reality. Although this memory was transmitted from generation to generation, black Americans were under pressure to construct a cultural form made up of different behaviors and customs. Black culture in America is not African but Afro-American, developed in response to the requirements of a new environment.

One of the first anthropologists to examine the presence of Africanisms in black American cultures was Melville Herskovits. His *The Myth of the Negro Past* created a stir among ethnologists because of his arguments against those who saw black culture as disorganized. He affirmed the existence of an undeniable African heritage and the continuity between the former homeland and the new continent. He maintained that the cultural situation of blacks led them to defend their African heritage even more. The scientific validity of historical continuity and heritage on the one hand and of retention and survival on the other has been questioned, most notably by Bronislaw Malinowski and Roger Bastide. Both argue that a culture cannot consist of survivals that may become anachronisms and lose all function in the surrounding culture; a survival is perpetuated only if it acquires a new function. The concept of survival prevents black culture from being seen as an organic living whole and makes it merely the sum of fragments—retentions, reinterpretations, or syncretisms of other cultures. "We must not attribute such phenomena to impossible 'survivals,'" says Bastide, "but see them as genuine and original, produced in response to new conditions of life." According to Bastide, studies of Afro-Americans have focused on the peak points of the culture, especially religious or folkloric practices, which offer more of the exotic and the picturesque than the more routine aspects of life. And it is precisely in these peak points that ties with Africa are preserved: "It is possible that the 'peak points' of an Afroamerican society may always be African in origin, whereas the same Negro who subscribes to it belongs (as far as his day-to-day life is concerned) to a culture which is not African but Negro—something very different."[103]

The plays and theories of Paul Carter Harrison participate in this debate on blackness and Africanness. For Harrison the theatre is an arena where the destiny of blacks can be staged; it is a privileged environment where art can save the ethos of a people and restore these peak points to Afro-American culture.

Many black dramatists have defined their theatre as non-Western and have stressed the importance of turning away from Euro-American traditions which impose their Judaeo-Christian world view, aristotelian principles, and rationalist structures on dramatic arts. Harrison's originality goes beyond this rhetoric: he has developed—in his own plays and in those he has directed—a theory of drama that rejects Western aesthetics, and he has articulated principles for organizing theatre activity.

Harrison may appear to be an unlikely writer to champion a neo-African or Africanist theatre. He is one of the few contemporary black dramatists to have been thoroughly exposed to European influences, through his university study as well as his long stays in Europe. Interested in philosophy, particularly phenomenology, Harrison rigorously pursued ideas about Western art and thought. For several years he studied the craft of European theatre, trying to reconcile the very different ideas of Artaud and Brecht. He joined with artists in Holland to create a total theatre, making his debut just when the black movement was growing in the United States and revolutionary experiments were happening on the American stage. His first plays, written between 1961 and 1965, included *The Pestclarks*, *Pavane for a Dead Minstrel*, *Top Hat*, *The Experimental Theatre*, and *Pawns*. They were written for the European stage and some had to be rewritten for production in America. This was the case with *Pavane*, first staged in Amsterdam and later at the Actor's Studio in 1963, then in Buffalo at the university in 1965 under the playwright's own direction. Expatriation had placed Harrison in a privileged and ambiguous situation. No doubt he saw more clearly from Europe the risks of a black theatre, but his exile threatened to cut him off from the vital forces of the community and to compromise his aesthetic project. His homecoming was even more radical than those of other artists of his generation.

Harrison attributes the uniqueness of black experience to the fact that Afro-Americans are former Africans. For him, their art would have little authenticity outside of revitalizing African aesthetic sensibility and expression. In opposition to historians and sociologists who maintain that original black culture was destroyed by socioeconomic conditions, Harrison asserts that culture involves all levels of experience, language and idiom, behavior and thought processes, strategies for survival, narrative and popular legends, even the characteristics the collective imagination gives to certain men and heroes of the community. African distinctiveness appears most strongly in religious life and in music and dance. Harrison sees expressions of African experience in popular culture through Song, sacred or profane; Dance, all African rhythms; Drum, music symbolized by that eminently African instrument. These are the components of a black sensibility and a cultural heritage which the artist must renew. The role of theatre is to revalidate the spirituality of black America, to revive the collective race memory by retaining remembrance of slavery, and to reinstate an African vision of the world. Harrison thus rejects both the model of American dramaturgy and the requirements of a sociological theatre aimed at denouncing oppression. He refuses Western theatre because it restricts free expression of black creativity, and he rejects the theatre of oppressed victims because its use of social realism shows only one side of human relations:

> Social realism is at the heart of the problem: it deters the fullest excavation of hidden meanings by locking images into fixed relationships with the surfaces of social life. The mode becomes static . . . Characters most often are designed to explicate the most overt reactions to an oppressed social modality; and they usually arrive at individualized resolutions.[104]

The theatre cannot ignore social problems, but it should consider them only as indices of a larger field of forces that must be explored. According to Harrison, too many artists have limited themselves to expressing the most obvious reactions to oppression. The dominant society is thus perceived as the most dreaded force, as a macrocosm to which one must constantly refer. In place of this single relationship—the oppressive white society versus the oppressed black community—the new theatre substitutes a more complex system of references which endows the black community with autonomy and renewable strength. This energy comes not only from the universe of the surrounding society but from creation itself: far from being reducible to social dimensions alone, black experience is part of the cosmos, and it is precisely in this fundamental relationship, indeed complicity, with the cosmos that blacks must find weapons for their resistance. Their intuitive knowledge of the world will help them confront elements that threaten group cohesion and universal harmony.

Harrison proposes a drama that takes its organizing principles from African philosophy. That philosophy has been the object of different studies and interpretations, from those by Karl Jaspers and Bronislaw Malinowski to the work of Janheinz Jahn, *Muntu* (1958), which is Harrison's basic reference.[105] Africa appears successively as a world deprived of civilization and historicity (Jaspers), as the place of an acculturation process engendering forms that belong neither to an indigenous tradition nor to European civilization (Malinowski), or as a continent possessing a specific culture drawn from a world view that organizes the cultures and the histories of various nations and ethnic groups (Jahn).

Muntu was one of the first studies to attest to the richness of African philosophy and to the complexity of a so-called primitive culture. Jahn sheds light on the fundamental characteristics of Pan-African culture beyond regional variations, and illuminates the development of a modern culture. His analysis also permits an important parallel to be drawn between African and Afro-American nationalism. Many black Americans, reclaiming their cultural autonomy, see themselves as the African intellectual whom Jahn describes as "wanting to integrate into modern life only what seems valuable from the past."[106]

For Harrison, the essential goal of theatre is to offer a representation of cultural tradition that establishes indissoluble ties between Afro-American theatre and the component in all black cultures which is Africa itself. The theatre must give a semantic content to ethnic membership which, although difficult for the black American to define, still remains a point of reference.

In his book *The Drama of Nommo* and in his introduction to *Kuntu Drama* Harrison offers one definition of the new black theatre, taking the terms *nommo* and *kuntu* from African philosophy. Man and things are forces from one of the cardinal categories: *muntu* (human beings), *kintu* (inanimate objects), *hantu* (space and time), and *kuntu* (modality). The cohesion among these forces is embodied semantically in the suffix *ntu*, the cosmic universal force of existence and being. While *ntu* designates the existence of forces, *nommo* (the word) designates the power that activates them. Harrison draws the principles of his drama from these concepts as defined by Jahn in his chapter "NTU": the concept of force—a force that is exerted in a specific field and that produces events—and that of modality or mode. Man is considered a force capable of mastering the nommo. Other subordinate forces are in a frozen state and await the injunction of a muntu, a man whose intelligence activates them.[107]

One can see the consequences such a conception would have for the definition of dramatic character. Seeing the world as a play of forces embodied in human beings eliminates psychology and challenges the basic tenets of Western drama. No plot as such develops; rather, events unfold through episodes which lend rhythm to the action like the beats of a drum (Harrison calls these moments "beats"). The characters are propelled within a space and time that are both historical and concrete, mythic and imaginary. The world is depicted as a place of flux where forces often give rise to unpredictable events.

The art of drama can be defined as one of the manifestations of the modal force kuntu, through which the world expresses itself with laughter and with beauty. The term *nommo*, related to similar concepts in other African cultures, comes from a Dogon creation myth: "Amma, the only God, created the earth as a woman, and then married her. His seed, Nommo, is water and fire and blood and *word*. Nommo is the physical-spiritual life force which awakens all 'sleeping' forces and gives physical and spiritual life."[108] The theatre of nommo seals the alliance of different elements and the two orders of flesh and spirit. The Word, as charm and evocation, praise and curse, reigns in this theatre of magic where man brings order to chaos. As a principle of transformation, it commands births and continuous reproduction: the act of naming creates the named one. Speech activates the life of things.

This conception of a reality always in process, of the responsibility given to speech, and of the capacity to transform the world through the word has major implications for dramatic structures and character. The character will affect the world through the gesture, the act, and the supreme word. He is both subject and object of transformations that hold our attention and interest. The force of change postulated by the metaphor of creation and transformation inspires the spectator to take part and in turn to become a creator. The theatre is the place where this incitement leads to real commitment. The action of theatre can also be defined as a great shout, which, according to Aimé Césaire, "the black man should utter so forcefully that the very pillars of the world will be shaken."[109]

As the same principle of negritude, nommo designates the function that the artist echoes: a magician in the African sense of the term, he calls things into being from the great All; he finds in the cosmic harmony the image of the world he seeks to create.

Nommo, the word, creates images upon images and transforms them and the poet with them. For he himself never approaches things unchanging; since he too is in nature a force among forces, he changes with them and from them. The "things" are of his kind and he of theirs. He, too, therefore is subject to the same magic of constant transformation.[110]

The artist thus expresses himself in the name of his community and his people. His imperative and prophetic voice raises up images that have concrete presence in real life. Art states the laws and puts the forces to work. Naming, evoking, invoking, incanting, become the major "modes" of his art, which is revolutionary in developing the certainty that everything can be changed by the power of the word. The chains of injustice are broken by the particular utterances of laughter or madness which are shouts for vengeance. Everything is triggered toward the creation of the future. Subordinated to continuous change, commanded according to a precise goal, propelled by the imminent force of images, the present is continually modeled upon the future, which arises to confer meaning. The past is projected into the future that is born, but it also proposes a model where the ancestral wisdom and knowledge of the world are stated and which helps to clarify that future. Present, future, and past are the material of kintu, which should be under the control of the dynamism of active forces. This vision of the world forbids any belief in an inescapable doom. In all respects this poetic principle is incompatible with models of aristotelian aesthetics.

As an essential component of kuntu, rhythm is inseparable from nommo; as the procreative dimension of rhythmic utterance, it creates and completes the world. The first rhythms in African societies were those of percussive instruments that speak the language of the drum; the principles governing their combining served as basic structures for all modes of expression. Using beats to punctuate the action, varying the combination of its sequences as percussion varies its meters and distributes its accents, the drama can be modeled on the polymetric and polyrhythmic voices of drums.[111] Other forms similar to African musical meters can be found in drama: superpositions, repetitions, encounters, oppositions.

Rhythm thus becomes, for Harrison, an important element of drama. Unity is created out of the repetition of gestures, actions, songs, words, or phonemes. There are also secondary verbal rhythms and new figures, variations of which are introduced in the sweep of dramatic action and its significance. They articulate meaning. The oral literature of storytellers and griots had recourse to the same devices to captivate the listener and to reinforce the significance of their tales. Harrison is well aware of the ability of rhythm to transport meaning and to propel the narrative.

> Repetition is a device of most black narratives—as it is in music—which is used to reaffirm the dramatic pulse of the statement. The repeated phrases may issue from words or gestures; in either case, the incremental effect introduces new information while advancing the dramatic imagery. The image is also given a unity through the progression of repeated phrases, and the variations induced to the mode. Repetition tends to revitalize rhythms, thus adding to the intensity of the word's force.[112]

More and more attentive to the beats of a distant drum, the theatre artist revives nommo.

The drum, for Harrison, is also the symbol of African culture. As a language, a form of acoustical writing, the sound of drums has played a role in Africa more important than writing in other cultures. Drum language is also a natural, instant translation for tonal languages whose phonemes are not easily transcribed alphabetically. Harrison has perceived the value of such a language in the theatre where the heard word (not the read word) plays a predominant role. By dint of this important function the drummer becomes, in the neo-African aesthetics, the symbol of the artist. The modern dramatist should use him as a model: like the drummer, the dramatist must have a profound knowledge of traditions and legends and know how to revive past epics. In return, he should enjoy the right, conferred on the drummer, to be free from censure.

As a heightened mode of expression, the drum is a cultural matrix through which all messages pass. It is not surprising that this vehicle of a common language among Africans of different linguistic backgrounds was forbidden in the New World. Contemporary Afro-American art reclaims the drum as a basic model. By bringing the drum into drama, Harrison gives a larger range of expression to theatre, a harmonic and tonal system, a repertory of accents that increases the power of language tenfold and renews a unique form of sensibility. Every artist becomes a "different drummer"[113] who sounds the rallying call, mixes his distinctive voice with others that echo him, modulates the rhythms and the sounds that compose the hymn of the black community, and creates a free song, different from what the whites like to hear.

African Myths, Afro-American Folklore

The theories of Jahn and of Harrison allow us to isolate several basic principles of traditional African art and contemporary neo-African aesthetics. It remains to be seen how these components can be worked into the development of Afro-American drama. An examination of Harrison's play *The Great MacDaddy*,[114] staged in 1974, can help trace his use of African nommo.

The play is inspired by *The Palm Wine Drinkard* (1952) by Nigerian author Amos Tutuola, the first African novel in English to gain an international audience. Tutuola's work offers the playwright not only a narrative full of dramatic episodes but also a "kuntu" style of accumulating comic textures, strong images, and frequent transformations of character. Harrison draws from it a daimonic inspiration, a humor colored with magic that the author shares with his characters.

While Harrison does not hide the African influence of his play, neither does he pretend to recreate an African work. The title and setting immediately place this epic drama in the culture of black Americans during the era of Prohibition. MacDaddy comes directly out of Afro-American folklore, which depicts him as a fortune-hunter of the twenties. Tutuola's protagonist and Harrison's, however, belong to the same family of mythic heroes and both embody the same basic spirit.

The Great MacDaddy presents a ritualized event that shows the confrontation between mean creatures, such as the character Scag in his many guises, and beneficent, regenerative spirits as embodied in Song, Dance, and Drum. MacDaddy, the hero, encounters personifications of these forces, which approach him under various disguises: each proffers an enigma that he must solve, and he must identify the interlocutors in order to know whether they are friend or foe as events constantly threaten him with death. The narative of his adventures is measured by the beats of a drum: Harrison separates the episodes into "primal rhythm," "beats," "transitional beats," and "terminal rhythm." The dramatic structure orchestrates these different rhythms, and song and dance are intimately connected. The set design also becomes part of the organic whole, adapting to many changes and magical transformations. The spectator is taken to task and is not allowed to abstract himself from the performance.

The spatio-temporal environments of the action are signs of the gestures and events about to unfold; they prepare the way for apparitions to emerge upon the scene and, not unlike characters, they transform themselves and shift between mythic and real boundaries. Each place marks a stage in the peregrinations of the hero and a step in his initiation. On the set the dead and the living play hide and seek: some characters are reborn while others prolong their dying. The dead come to torment the hero, then leave him maliciously, only to lure him to a new form and a new place. They then trap him at the border of a funereal world where it is impossible for the living to remember those departed from life.

In the first scene MacDaddy buries his celebrated father, Big Mac, who has bequeathed him a prosperous business and a prestigious name: "The Great MacDaddy, son of Big Daddy, who is dead, making you the greatest Daddy of all the MacDaddies, who can do anything in this world" (p. 262). Destined to be great in everything—" as a lover, patriarch, and hustler"—the hero conducts his father's funeral with a mixture of sadness and pride. Impatient to realize his future, he wants to exert a power that he has acquired without effort. He wants to continue the family's prosperity by making a great palm wine, but he has no inkling of the dangers that await him; he fails to heed the warnings of Deacon Jones, who reminds him of the existence of the Man: "You know the ways of the Man . . . It's the law of the land. And on this land, the fruits of the land must pass through his hands" (p. 263). Although MacDaddy measures himself with impunity against the Man, the proverbial "father" of black people, he never escapes his hold. The shadow of the Man appears behind the scenes as the very architect of Prohibition.

McDaddy pays no heed. Instead of the wisdom of the old Deacon, he prefers the enthusiastic toast of one admirer whose verbal exuberance confers upon him unearned titles: "Big bear hugger, Momma plugger . . . the maker of crumb snatchers, the smasher of crummy crackers . . . carved the world out of wooden nickel and called it the Bucket of Blood . . . my main stem under a lady's hem and a gangster's brim, MacDaddy!" (p. 264).

Around the tribute paid to the illustrious deceased and the easy assumption of power by his son, one can see the triumph of nommo, which revels in words and associations of sounds, producing unexpected meaning out of deliberate nonsense. The apostrophe in ghetto jive culminates in the magical power that creates and recreates rhymes and transforms them continuously. MacDaddy at once possesses and is possessed by this ability; apparitions loom before him and he cannot tell whether they are his own or those of an invisible force that challenges him.

Even before MacDaddy leaves the funeral parlor to go conquer the world, his mission is in jeopardy. Wine, the father's companion and sole holder of the formula of the magic potion, dies after being beaten up by agents of the Man. Without Wine, whose generous blood brought the people's spirit into contact with the ancestors, the future suddenly dims for MacDaddy and the community. MacDaddy's adventures begin at this grave moment when his survival and that of the community are threatened. Yet Wine has barely given up the ghost when his body disappears. His death then becomes suspect, and the magic associated with Wine brings on new enigmas and new revelations: Does the spirit of Wine still live? Can MacDaddy retrieve the formula? The young hero takes heart and, like Tutola's protagonist in search of his "tapster," sets out to find Wine.

From this point on the play unfolds on another level. In search of Wine, MacDaddy unknowingly embarks on an initiatory journey sanctioned by the community that designates him as its leader: he must search for the Wine of life in order to save the spirit of his people. The humor of the play lies not only in the accumulation of mishaps but also in the incongruity between the tasks the hero must accomplish and the choices he makes. MacDaddy is naive, and does not know how to behave; he is equipped neither to succeed in business nor to keep up with the spirits. The play, conceived as a parable, reveals a lesson; the hero learns through his tribulations that the secret of wisdom does not come through a magic formula but through renewed contact with the spirit and culture of one's people. Throughout his journey, MacDaddy encounters cultural heroes who offer him wisdom. He also encounters the menacing Scag, whose disguises play upon his innocence.

The first apparition, Shine, comes in the middle of the Nevada desert. Professionally, Shine is a humble bootblack who tries to polish shoes as well as brighten up the day for his clients. Physically, he is the black man whose skin is so black that it shines. Culturally, he is the folklore hero who owes his fame to the sinking of the Titanic.

According to legend, Shine who is forced to do the worst job in the ship's boiler room becomes the sole survivor of the disaster thanks to his strength and common sense. Conscious of the danger that threatens the ship, Shine alerts the captain, who ignores his warnings. Determined to save his own skin, Shine jumps overboard and swims away as the boat starts to sink. The victims implore his aid: the captain, a banker, and young women who promise him pleasures of mountain and sky. Shine resists their pleas, saying "Get your ass in the water and swim like me." The intrepid Shine escapes sharks and whales, refusing to be swallowed like Jonah. Then, turning up his nose at riches and condemning the values of w ite society, this devil of a man, invincible on land and sea, becomes master of his destiny.

Many versions of this legend have been widely circulated.[115] Harrison here offers a variant in which Shine escapes a fire in a mill factory and is solicited by the captain and his daughter. Shine tells his own story: "That's how I lived to tell the story that wasn't told," he concludes like a second Ishmael. He is the sole witness and from now on the only teller of the tale. The dramatic presentation of the legend by the shoe shiner who proclaims himself a hero and the insertion of a rhymed narrative allow Harrison to revive the legend in the play. The incredulous Mac-

Daddy, who does not recognize his interlocutor, sees Shine only as a desert bootblack without any clients:

MACDADDY: Now Blood that's sho nuff simple-minded. Ain't nobody gettin' no shine in the desert.

SHINE: You gettin' one right now suh. (P. 270)

MacDaddy, who doubles here as actor and spectator, hears for the first time a story that seems to be created just for him. But MacDaddy is less aware of Shine than is the black spectator who knows the legend. The spectator's interest is drawn simultaneously to the character of Shine and to MacDaddy, who reacts with annoyance. The spectator enjoys seeing someone so mystified who has just presented himself as being greater than anyone else. The hero becomes a poor figure next to those who challenge his self-image. Interestingly, Shine places MacDaddy in the role usually reserved for whites in black popular lore. MacDaddy, who thinks himself so mean, is held in check by witty and enigmatic repartees.

Shine hardly shows himself to be the Shine of the legend he unfolds. He says that his real name, in fact, is John Henry, the steel-driving man. He thus throws another curve ball to MacDaddy and to the spectator. And Harrison takes us back to the epic of the superhuman carver of tunnels.

Unlike Shine, John Henry really existed. His legend appeared at the end of the last century in popular ballads commemorating the building of a railway across West Virginia around 1870. In showing the victory of manual labor over a steam engine, the ballad denounces mechanization and attests to the hero's prodigious strength, invincibility, and humanity. John Henry is a hero not only because of his prowess but because he was always conscious of his singular fate and the death that awaited him. Unlike the trickster, he preferred to confront the adversary head on, refusing to die without a hammer in his hand.[116]

Shine and John Henry are part of the same pantheon of modern heroes and belong to the same archetype of African folklore. John Henry's fate is also more exemplary and more tragic: human power is crushed by mechanical force. Merging these two figures into one allows Harrison to point out that they are only masks worn by Wine, temporary embodiments of the qualities of the black community. The many figures of folklore are thus singular, interchangeable, complementary.

After this enigmatic encounter with Shine, MacDaddy spies an elderly couple, Old Grandad and Momma, whose presence in the desert is also incongruous. The sequence follows the same pattern: the hero questions these ancestors in order to identify them; they answer him in phrases with double meanings and aphorisms. The spectator perceives a multitude of signs that allow him to decode the metaphors thus suggested. The old people, who flee the white world which like a cloud of locusts devours them, symbolize the continuous journey and the eternal search of blacks for the promised land. MacDaddy impresses them not at all: "He bees a pretty lil' nigga . . . but his shoes aint shined" (p. 274). They become indignant about his inexperience and his lack of respect; yet they confide in him their hope to find Diddy-Wah-Diddy where food, joy, and spirit are generously shared.

Their words bring ancestral wisdom to the hero in the maxim "Folks on rich bottom stop braggin' when the river rises," which serves as a metaphor for the black condition and evokes in a more general way Shine's narrative. "Wine is hard to find in stormy weather" alludes to the evasiveness of Wine and to the difficulties MacDaddy will encounter in his quest. From his angle, too, the hero pronounces sayings, but their full meaning escapes him: "Talking to you old folks is like getting blood out of a stone." The image expresses his discouragement with his interlocutors, but also reveals their true identity: from this stone will flow blood, wine, and truth. The two old people, like the other figures, are incarnations of the elusive Wine.

The old couple tell the hero about a creature greater than he—Scaggarag, who lives on the other side of the moon, commands weather and men, and wields a fearful power. While Wine represents the beneficent potion, Scag figures as the white, destructive drug. This personification of evil and death reverses the qualities that make black heroes. The terms "meanness and badness" revert to their conventional meaning, suggesting evil when applied to Scag. But like other characters, Scag proclaims his identity with verve and vigor: "I'll make your liver quiver, your body sag like a rag." The words become nets that trap his victims. MacDaddy dances and brandishes his cane to conjure away the evil power. He captures his enemy and brings him before the old people, but Scag, as unseizeable as death, escapes, happy now to be among the living. The spectator recognizes him as a familiar character in the new theatre, similar to the evil Beast of *A Black Mass* who is introduced on earth by the unsuspecting black magician. Like Yacoub, MacDaddy is responsible for the return of evil among men.

All of MacDaddy's encounters are characterized by precise forms of verbal exchange, from the boasts of Shine to the jiving of Old Grandad. Each sequence reproduces an aspect of black speech. The hero's ability improves with each verbal contest. On the dramatic level these transformations of language accompanying each apparition and change in character allow Harrison to integrate various aspects of black experience as manifested through words or images. The dialogue adapts to the tonality and to the atmosphere of each encounter, thus offering a variety of modes.

Strangely, all the characters MacDaddy encounters along the way have tried to isolate themselves from the world. And each offers his own description of the land they are searching for. Their quest enriches Mac-Daddy's. His narrative will be ramified and enlarged from all the narratives offered by his new acquaintances.

As sequences are repeated in scene after scene, the hero alternately initiates an interrogation and submits to one. In the verbal contest he has to be as quick and as skillful as his adversary in order to identify the kind of discourse used, adapt to it, surpass it. This mode of exchange is close to the dozens. The character must also accomplish some feat in order to prove his worth. MacDaddy is thus placed in the position of blacks who are always under attack and in exile. But this situation of the wanderer is also that of the epic hero in popular narratives who must resolve enigmas and go through many trials.[117]

MacDaddy's adventures lead him from desert refuges to city jungles where people prostitute themselves in order to get rich. As he pursues his voyage he becomes, imperceptibly, an incarnation of Wine, the beneficent spirit that brings life and energy. More agile now, he can go anywhere, and he can better foil the stratagems of other characters. He brings hope back to an old war veteran by freeing his daughter, the beautiful Leionah, from the world of gambling and false glamour. He tries to control Signifying Baby, the naughty child of Leionah's love affairs, and to calm the community outraged by the newborn baby's insults. At a dog race in Arizona, he disguises himself as a dealer to fool buyers into paying more for their pleasure than they receive. He pretends to put Leionah up for auction in a parody of the slave market where, as a good con man, he avenges the humiliations suffered by his brothers. He fools a border patrolman and easily passes to "the other side of the tracks," thumbing his nose at the white world which seeks to restrict his territory. In the west he confronts the sheriffs and the heroes of white culture, the cowboys and Jesse James, and frees Niggertoe from dancing for their pleasure. He makes Niggertoe stop his servile pantomime and use dance as a weapon. He defies Scarecrow and American Eagle who keep blacks from entering suburban Heavensville. And he opposes the perfidious weapons of Scag with the more powerful ones of nommo, the magic of words, music, and dance. Meeting up with Stagolee in St. Louis, he plays a round of cards with the mean outlaw, but wins with the wisdom of an older card player, "a trump card can bust anybody in the rump." In Louisiana, MacDaddy finds voodoo to be not only a survival of African wisdom but a way of life drawn from African and Caribbean customs.

Finally MacDaddy discovers Wine on an ash-covered island off the coast of South Carolina. The joyful companion of yesterday has become resigned to exile, giving up all trade with men and wine. The only formula he has to offer MacDaddy is the enigmatic maxim "Pie are round, cornbread are squared." When the hero returns to the community he finds the people frozen in the same positions they had before. Having failed to bring the dead back to the land of the living, he now tries to bring hope to those still alive. He sings and dances in order to reactivate their inert bodies and spirits: "I got the cornbread/ square out the ground;/ my woman's got the pie,/ round as a world/ kissed by the sky" (p. 350). This new magic formula revives the ritual of a mythic creation of the world by the first couple. Once a pretender to the throne, Mac-Daddy is now the legitimate heir. His encounters with all aspects of black culture and history have in effect transformed the adolescent. As a member of a community of legendary heroes, badmen and tricksters, wise old men and uncontrolled youth, MacDaddy takes knowledge from each. The Great MacDaddy of the legend was only an arch scoundrel; his son becomes a hero. Harrison gives him the words that, according to tradition, the elder MacDaddy might have said before dying: "I got a graveyard disposition and a tombstone mind . . . I'm a bad mother-fucker but I don't mind dying." Yet Harrison maintains the right to offer a more positive interpretation of the hero's function in black popular culture.

The relation in the play between the character and the narrative that constantly transforms him must also be examined. As morpheme almost without content (the hero defines himself tautologically by his name and his ascendancy), the Great MacDaddy builds up multiple meanings. The meaning of his character is constructed by repetition or accumulation of detail, and by his relation to other characters (in modes of similarity and difference, opposition and complementarity), which changes from sequence to sequence. Barely developed at the start—he is identifiable only by reference to a cultural code that comes from legend— MacDaddy finds his complexity in reference to the internal system of the work; his signification develops on the level of narrative; the characterization begins with scattered elements which are reorganized. The figures he encounters are assigned functions that often correspond to categories outlined by analysts of folktales: Scag, alias Skull (in Tutuola) is the mean one, the aggressor, the opponent. Stagolee is the false hero. The community can be the helper, arbitrator, hero, beneficiary, or receiver. Wine is the object of the quest, but so is Mac-Daddy, who searches for his own identity. The nature of the quest has changed; first oriented toward selfish ends, it soon aims to liberate the community and to eliminate Scag. The beneficiary of all the hero's deeds first is the hero himself, then the isolated individuals whom he aids, and finally the community he regenerates.

The cast of characters and their functions in relation to the central figure, the ubiquity of this figure, and the structural organization of the play all create the hero. MacDaddy becomes exemplary not because of an innate virtue or courage or knowledge, but through his situation in relation to figures of black folklore. At the end of the play his name becomes a sign: MacDaddy, spiritual father of a community which, thanks to him, recovers the wine of life. The hero, as a composite of many descriptive features, thus helps the spectator decode the fundamental elements of black sensibility. Harrison finds these elements in Afro-American culture, and the sensibility he recovers is African.

These characteristics of nommo in theatre call to mind the qualities of a dionysian theatre, and more particularly, of a voodoo theatre. Harrison conceives the dramatic creation as an integrative, holistic experience in which all aspects of black consciousness once isolated by reality and all the figurative representations from myths and folklore converge. It is a journey into the collective imagination and a return to the cultural matrix; in a sense Harrison is right to speak about a "ritualized event."

The Great MacDaddy takes up the project of creating drama from Afro-American experience and from the specific cultural heritage of the community freed as much as possible from models in Euro-American culture. Renewed in this way, the theatre finds its ethnicity, its *raison d' être*, and its autonomy.

Theatre and Culture

 IN ORDER TO DEVELOP the artistic and ideological basis for a new drama, black theatre establishes strong ties with Afro-American culture. Art brings together the different cultural experiences it helped to create and which, in turn, gave art its form and substance. Combining the three principles of drum, song, and dance (or music, voice, and body), theatre associates textual with scenic writing and performs functions that were once held separate in the other arts.

Any study of the relations between theatre and culture raises both ideological and artistic questions. From the Harlem Renaissance to the sixties, theoreticians of black art have always placed culture at the heart of this debate. As an instrument for reflection and analysis, theatre is viewed as a continuous means to rediscover, recapture, and reinvent the cultural heritage.

Of Time and History

As a space where people can be confronted by their history, theatre reshapes and energizes the past. It brings back ancestral myths, defuses painful experiences, heals certain wounds, and revives racial pride and solidarity. In dramatic discourse, the past becomes a syntagmatic element of the total history of Afro-Americans, which is decoded, recognized, and separated into smaller units. The theatre shows blacks as a people and a nation. It records a broad spectrum of events in which rhythms, pauses, breaks, and continuities are discovered. Once the different acts of the past have been shown, the future can be foretold and new roles assigned. Theatre thus bears both a historical and a mythical relation to time.

Although most dramatists are preoccupied with rediscovering history, they do not follow the same path. Many plays accommodate the traditional deterministic structure of drama that confers a passive role on blacks. Others question this representation of "the destiny of blacks" and reexamine the various roles and identities blacks have assumed.

Also revealing is the choice of genre: in the repertory of black American theatre there is no tragedy similar to, say, *La Tragedie du Roi Christophe* by Aimé Césaire. Tragedy is best expressed through more subversive modes that do not excite fear and pity. Whatever crying over the fate of blacks there is should be done in the mode of the blues. And if fear must be considered an appropriate reaction to drama, it will be the fear that whites and their accomplices experience at the exact moment of their destruction.

Each sign communicated by the text harks back to the culture that produced it. Anchored in this manner, the text can be identified in all its composite elements, in the continuity and the diversity of its signifiers. The image of the black community is thus reconstructed by the same signified throughout history. The act of reading or of performance controls this image and interpretation. The dramatic work appeals to the symbolic consciousness where a fundamental mythic content present in the whole culture can be reached. Each referent assumes several dimensions—the realistic, the symbolic, the mythic—and a plurality of meaning that can surround a single sign. Such a reading, carried out on several levels, reveals the ideology that supports the work and that promotes a different image of blacks by unmasking the mechanisms of previous characterizations. Afro-American drama is often constructed around the double perspective of destroying the foreign code imposed by the dominant ideology and of developing its own more relevant system.

This double movement occurs inside the work where various scenarios expose the hegemony of white culture and extol the triumph of the oppressed. One dialectic, for example, tries to make oppression a thing of the past, an irrefutable state of existence but one that must be overcome, and to show how certain moments in history were characterized by a desire for liberation that foretold the current renewal.

In recording symbolic time, theatre situates itself at the dramatic moment when confrontation reaches a climax. The reign of the oppressor is broken and a new era begins, reviving the time "before history," before the appearance of the White Beast and destroyer, symbol of an authoritarian cultural system. Thus theatre does not just point out the values in black culture, but shows them in opposition to the forces that have imperiled them. Time plays a crucial role in the ideology of a work and in its structural organization. The present moment intervenes in history. "The time is *now*." And the dialectic of "before" and "after" shifts to accommodate this moment of rupture and transition, sometimes confusing it with other phases of time: chronological or psychological time (individual or collective), mythical or ceremonial times of origin, biblical times of resurrection and apocalypse.

The plays offer a metaphorical reflection on contemporary events. The theatre, which is inspired by these acts, reconceives them through different signifieds. The new drama challenges irreversibility and instead of linearity, which places too much emphasis on uncontrolled enslavement, offers discontinuous or fragmented rhythms: the break between the sequences that Harrison calls "beats" indicates that certain things should not be taken for granted. Oppression is explained by different mechanisms whose processes are brought to light. What is true for liberation is true for revelation: neither occurs without force or an act of will. Black theatre shows a preference for epic times of action over tragic moments of resignation. The rhetoric of change, no doubt more evident in militant theatre, is also present in the theatre of experience: the latter affirms the oppression of a people, which is perpetuated by many rituals, and if the protagonists appear more preoccupied with living in the world than with changing it, they nevertheless continue to assert their autonomy.

Cultural Identity

As the main signified principle in black drama, cultural identity is represented as a difficult conquest, not as something granted. It receives the attributes of a protagonist; alternately threatened or scorned, defended or sought after, it is sometimes hidden under ambiguous masks. The theatre points out the error of seeing cultural identity where it does not exist or failing to recognize it when encountered. Hence the use of fable or allegory, the use of masks (white masks to designate the identity proposed by white culture) and rituals of exorcism against demons in the alienated black consciousness. To varying degrees the mulatto of Adrienne Kennedy, the coons like Court Royal and apostates like Jacoub of Jones, the robots like Bullins' electronic nigger, all embody the drama of cultural disintegration while other characters heal and revitalize the black psyche. The playwright acts as a magician and the theatre becomes the collective consciousness, shedding all alienating and suicidal white masks.

This state of development in the drama reaffirms the existence of a scorned culture and corresponds to Fanon's analysis: discovering the futility of his alienation, the individual who is considered inferior returns to his original state of being. His once abandoned and rejected culture now becomes an object of passionate attachment.[1] The recapturing of cultural consciousness is at the core not only of black ideology but of all serious art. Models for forging a new theatrical language are sought within that very culture which, long scorned or destroyed, is rediscovered, legitimized, and reinvented. Certain elements, borrowed from the oral, musical, or religious traditions or from rituals of daily life, are integrated into the drama as a morphology, a structure, or a sign-system; they codify its aesthetics and create a new art form which no longer finds its basic principles in the dictates of Western dramaturgy.

The Oral Tradition

The oral tradition holds a prominent place in Afro-American culture. For slaves (who were often forbidden to learn to write) it was the safest means of communication. It provided basic contact with Africa as a homeland and a source of folklore, a contract also between ethnic groups unified under a common symbolic heritage, between generations, and finally, between the speaker and his audience.

In the theater oral expression, which encourages exchange and immediate response, serves as a model for patterns of participation and involvement. The dramatic mode derives most of its forms from the art of storytelling and in many ways stems from an analogous situation: the storyteller addresses an audience, and organizes his story to elicit certain responses or to stir emotions.[2] This staging and manipulation are not unlike the effects author, director, actor, and character all strive to achieve. One is also reminded of Brecht's statement on the "street scene" as an archetypal model for his epic theatre.

There are further similarities between the dramatic and narrative arts: both rely on improvisation, on the ability to create and captivate an audience, and on the modulation of speech patterns. Just as a tale can be presented in many different versions and remain, as it were, "open," dramatic performances are likewise never identical. Variations are constantly being introduced, bringing new meaning and significance. In both arts language, mime, voice, and gesture receive particular emphasis, a quality that accounts for what has been called the enunciative and illocutionary force of dramatic speech, and a signifying whole is built up through mediation with the audience.

Because the oral tradition has long remained a living practice in Afro-American culture, the dramatic artist has been tempted to emulate not only the art and techniques of the storyteller, but also his prestigious social function—that of recording and reformulating experience, of shaping and transmitting values, opinions, and attitudes, and of expressing a certain collective wisdom.

The storytelling situation itself is often represented in the dramatic text, either through the presence of a narrator who comments upon the protagonists' deeds (as in White's or Harrison's plays), or through characters who have a propensity for narration and are inclined to tell their own stories in accordance with the toast tradition (as often happens in Bullins' drama), or through whole narrative sequences that sum up the action and offer comments or interpretations with which the subject-hero may disagree (the argument between narrator and protagonist enhances the dramatic action of White's *The Burghers of Calais*) and which the spectator is free to accept or reject. The use of the narrative mode delays or diversifies plot development, multiplies subplots, perspectives, and counterpoints, and creates suspense or relief. The action is not only seen and acted out but also told and often presented as a fable from which a moral or message should be drawn: each recorded event is turned into an image. This syntagmatic structure suggests a certain reading of the plays (as syntagma). And like the concluding section of a tale, theatre makes frequent use of aphorisms, proverbs, and popular sayings.

The oral tradition also provides a repertory of situations and figures, enunciating certain strategies of survival through which the weak but witty can overthrow the strong, the mentally alert can overcome brutal authority. Many folklore heroes—Slave John or the trickster fighting against hypocrisy and power, the bad man who fears neither God nor the Devil—serve as archetypes for theatre protagonists and question the validity of stereotypes of blacks, while demonstrating the oppressed people's refusal to become victims and their ability to triumph. Finally, the hero is often a teller who builds up his own character and transforms his companions into listeners. Thus at the core of its structure, the theatre recreates the narrative situation.

The Musical Tradition

Black music also contributes to this creative process. As a domain which offers the best example of cultural independence and artistic autonomy, it is also the most authentic expression of Afro-American life. From its first appearance on the American continent, black music reproduced the African structure of call and response, a structure that has influenced every cultural form. From early on the message, which even the revolutionary ideology of the sixties could not fail to hear, was that through music black people affirm their ability to control chaos, to confer meaning on absurdity, to restore spirituality to the universe. Spirituality or soul, the governing principle of this music, is both a strategy and an aspect of character, a conscious and active step in bringing about change, turning (in Jones's words) "old liabilities into new assets":

It is an attempt to place upon a "meaningless" social order an order which would give value to terms of existence that were considered not only valueless but shameful . . . It is an attempt to reverse social roles . . . by redefining the canons of value . . . "soul brother" means to recast the social order in his own image.[3]

This music is as fundamental a rite as life itself ("a kind of ethno-historical rite as basic as blood") where the most fundamental ethnic traits can be found.

Music has always been connected with various activities in the everyday life of blacks, and this ensures its functionality. As such it represents a model for every form of art that seeks a social role. Its subversive character has often been emphasized; it is a call for action, for solidarity.

The call and response model adopted by the majority of songs thus provides the theatre with the pattern of interaction it seeks to establish with the community. A dialogue can take place between the group and the individual. Work songs made the call of the leader alternate with the response of the group; and even the blues continues the pattern of those first songs, for the solitary singer often answers his own voice. Moreover, the polyphonic structure of black music adapts well to dramatization and to dialogue. It is no accident that, from 1909 on, blues singers regularly appeared on stage at the Lincoln Theatre: the music was considered to be a show, the musician a "performer," an actor.

Similarly, the characters created by Bullins and Van Peebles can be seen as blues singers; they create a climate of confidence which renders their sentiments immediately perceptible. They also become interpreters of collective experience; their individual situation reminds blacks of their isolation in the ghetto, and the song becomes one of anger as much as of nostalgia. The theatre amplifies the contrast between solo and chorus; with individual voices it can compose a collective song, as in Bullins' *Street Sounds*. The structure of call and response reappears, certainly, in jazz, where one musician conducts the ensemble then listens to the others who by turns express themselves. The movement in drama goes simultaneously from the playwright, who listens to his characters and orchestrates their voices, to the director, who listens to the actors in order to harmonize their interaction, and ultimately to the actor, who cannot ignore those around him. They all turn toward the audience, the concrete representation of the collectivity, which must be enlightened and invited to participate.

Theatrical dialogue analogous to the vocal part in music recreates the call and response pattern. The frequent use of a chorus allows the structure to change. The call is given to the solo and the response to the chorus; but this schema can be altered so that the chorus intones the call; it is then the hero who responds, as in *The Burghers of Calais*.

The dramatist also borrows freely from the repertory of black songs, often juxtaposing them irregularly. Like the blues singer, they draw from cultural heritage, giving earlier works a new expression. This process establishes a historical continuity and a kind of fluidity among different genres: oral tradition, musical theatre, song, liturgy.

Thus theatre is a collective art with an open structure. Like popular tales which have neither beginning nor end, or music where one song takes up where another left off, black theatre freely sketches out a motif, develops it, leaves it, and takes it up again. The theatre of Ed Bullins, for example, is organized around this principle; each play achieves full significance only in relation to the others. The analogy with musical structures leads to a broader reading of the work or of an entire repertory. Black theatre is not a theatre of authors: even works as important as those by Jones or Bullins are only moments in a larger discourse which others are invited to pursue. Clearly Jones has played the role of conductor, pointing out the multiple motifs that can inspire numerous variations.

Even a private reading of a work must involve a broader reading, linked not only to other works but to the cultural context. The antiphony or dialogue of one author with the elements of cultural heritage that were his first motivations are the composite parts of an art that sees itself as collective. This principle of intertextuality conflicts with the aesthetics of the dominant culture, in which art is first an individual creation by a particular author. When many black dramatists adopt such a fluid structure, they also oppose rigid prescriptions and dogma. Openness of form rejects the need to find one expression of the black condition, which is itself fluid and open-ended.

The analogy between music and dramatic structure has often been pushed quite far. Paul Carter Harrison, as we have seen, uses "beats" to establish dramatic rhythm and to accent the divisions and transitions from one "session" to another. This percussive rhythm of drama and structure of dialogue joins two principles: the periodic reiteration of the theme and the movements of characters entering and leaving the stage as they speak or remain silent. Both occur like measures in music, and other musical devices are used: different meters come together, rhythms are crossed and combined, different parts of the same measure are accented by syncopation and counterpoint. The underlying principle of this construction is unity in diversity, one of the main tenets of black aesthetics.

The analogy between music and theatre has multiple implications. Although rhythm has been used to stereotype and denigrate identity, it appears here as an organizing force. The precise use of repetitions and their variations on every level must be studied, including language where alliteration, paranomas and anaphora use similar phonemes. For Harrison, dramatic narrative combines the rhythms of music and those of oral literature. The repetitions extend the dramatic sweep and underscore the significance of the event. Rhythm propels action and conveys meaning simultaneously: rhythm and meaning are inseparable.

The narrative is also punctuated with the reactions of the listeners. The clapping of hands, tapping of feet, the hoots, cries, and whistles can come from a real audience or from a listener who figures within the play. To these rhythmic elements are added the melodic variations sometimes indicated by *didascalies*: categories of modified sounds, intonations, volume, and timbre of voice.

The theatre of experience, generally speaking, is more concerned than the militant theatre with modeling itself around music. However, both are theatres of the blues, in the generic sense of the term. Each utterance takes the form of a song, even in the most discursive dialogue. Thus in *Dutchman*, as Clay's consciousness is raised he rediscovers this quality of the blues singer who does not *talk* about revolt, but shouts and sings it. Explanation, which appears so frequently in protest or militant theatre, disappears in the theatre of experience for the sake of expression itself. But the song is everywhere present: the lament lodges a complaint and becomes as much a plea as an indictment. Joys and pains, resignation and anger are part of the song.

Far from interpreting the blues as music of patient suffering, revolutionary theater infuses it with all the anger it first had. The blues not only reflects emotions but generates them. Dramatists who study the true nature of the blues rediscover the primary function of the theatre: to encourage confrontation with real experience. The song becomes a challenge. And thus the heroes in the theatre of experience affirm their desire for autonomy. If the theatre of experience turns toward expression and militant theatre toward action, each gives the same symbolic virtue to gesture and words. They express aggression and a need for recognition.

Theatre seeks to take the exemplary role that music has traditionally played for blacks. It confers meaning on an existence that seems chaotic, changes the psychic state when the material situation cannot improve. It also perpetuates the traditions and values of the group; it reaffirms the will to resist and the possibility of recovering a spirituality that endeavors to be African. Lastly, it brings aesthetic pleasure. Simultaneously raising emotional (a call to feelings), mental (a call to revolt), and aesthetic states, music becomes a supreme model for a theatre that aims to reach multiple levels of consciousness.

Very few plays exist for which stage directions do not suggest musical accompaniment, the use of a song or a refrain. These elements are not introduced simply as background to create an atmosphere. Rather, they fix or amplify a meaning. Instead of illustrating a text, music can contradict it, sketching out a truth different from the one the words indicate.

One must ask what concrete musical elements are to be used in the text and on stage, what choice is proposed by the drama (Why John Contrane here, or Sun Ra and Charlie Parker there? Why rhythm and blues or bebop elsewhere?), and what initiatives directors can take to incorporate music not already indicated in the text. One must also notice at which moments in the action the music appears and what function it serves for the characters who perceive or produce it; finally, what role it plays in the development and reception of the theatrical message for the audience.

The Religious Tradition

The influence of music on black theatre can also be seen in forms of religious worship. An entire body of music, from the early spirituals to gospel songs, grew out of the black church. Sacred music influenced secular music; both use the basic structures, rhythmic arrangements, and polyphonic organization of African music, and both merge in the theatre. Whether in the church or in daily life, black music expressed the same message of a people's desire to be reborn in a better world and their will to be free.

Religious music, although appearing to express resignation, actually communicated the will of blacks to change the world. Biblical figures became models for building the destiny of a people. The devil, whose cruelty seemed indomitable, appeared frequently as a force to be overthrown: "The devil is mad and I am glad/ He missed the soul he thought he had."[4] This image of evil will be used to represent whites, who lose their humanity by victimizing blacks and who bear the sins of the world. The devil is linked with figures from popular legend who are as malevolent, and who are vanquished just the same.[5]

Theatre finds in religion the spiritual inspiration and support for struggle and a mythology that alters time and space in relation to the black man's place in the universe. Major biblical events suggest a direction for Afro-American history and proclaim a world that has transcended limitations. Just as scenes in oral literature show the triumph of the trickster over a more powerful adversary, those of religious mythology depict a similar trial and liberation. Church services also provide theatre with a structure for drama, an ensemble of symbolic rites, and a form of group performance.

One must keep in mind that during slavery theatre, like religious worship, occurred clandestinely. Secrecy added a subversive and distinctively black characteristic to the action. Far from the surveillance of whites, a ritual could be created that legitimized free expression and revived African beliefs. Each person could participate in the ceremony. From the very beginning theatre and religious ritual have shared common features; the atmosphere of intense emotion in modern drama seeks to recreate the same conditions of ritual.[6]

Many descriptions of church services, particularly those in Baptist and Pentecostal sects, attest to the theatricalized character of worship with its mix of improvisation and order, call and response, its predominance of rhythm and music, and its alternation of individual and group voices.[7] These variations and their passage from the pulpit to the stage become both a model and a challenge for the theatre.

Harrison's chapter "Nommo and the Black Messiah"[8] shows how the worship service can be a model for the theatre by its spiritual force, by the power of the Word, and by the moments of revelation created. In renewing ties with religious sources the theatre recovers its sacred and magical characteristics. The director becomes a kind of preacher who manipulates and organizes the forces in his congregation:

> The opening hymn from a soloist . . . paves the way. The groundwork has now been laid for the preacher who steps in to take advantage of his first piece of stage direction, having signalled the soloist to be seated. He now begins slowly to test the power of the spirit, carefully selecting the words of compounded utterances that have the force of words which transport the congregation through serenity into the necessary turbulence that unlocks the truth and restores harmony to the inner being.

Harrison's description shows the theatricality inherent in ritual and the dramatic effects of spontaneous acts. Both the preacher's power of language and the energy released by the congregation bring forth nommo. For Harrison, religious rhetoric provides the curses and commands that usually appear in drama, particularly the sermon whose illocutionary force determines the modalities of reception (injunction, promise, assertion). The preacher holds his audience's attention with such phrases as "I am talking to you" and "Do you hear me?" and provokes a response. His words combine invective, invocation, incantation, recitation, and litany. Relying upon eloquent gestures, they set in motion a biblical imagery and a cosmology filled with as many African as Christian elements.

The rhetoric of religion which has so inspired political discourse is thus easily introduced into theatre, where several characters may officiate. In Bullins' *Death List*, for example, the revolutionary hero, like the finger of God, designates which victims are to be sacrificed. Imprecation is often used for parody, as in the improvised and grandiloquent summation in Caldwell's *The Militant Preacher*. In theatre, rhetoric is no less effective; rather, it prostrates listeners and sows sacred terror. It recreates the occasion of the sermon: characters become preachers and the audience a terrified congregation. Theatre language regains its primary function, which in black culture is to bear witness.

Ritual

Ritual is most often considered to be a pretheatrical form. The priest/sacrificer plays the role of actor/director, and the sect members or initiates are the spectators. Without taking up the controversy among ethnologists about the spontaneous nature of possession that occurs in ritual, it must be noted that ritual prefigures a theatrical situation and offers a way of understanding drama.[9] Every rite is by definition a situation that is acted out. In playwriting and directing, Afro-American artists have paid close attention to African ritual, particularly the *djego* initiation ceremony of Gabon and the *egun* ancestor worship of Nigeria.[10] Ritual helps people to understand the mysterious and hostile forces around them. It urges them to act by stimulating their imagination in order to restore harmony between man and the universe. As Franck Fouché has found in voodoo, ritual can mobilize people "to take charge of themselves."[11]

Furthermore, the collective character of ritual makes it an instrument for cementing the unity of the group and for integrating individuals. Dance and song express the people's joy and pain, their aspirations, resistance, and deliverance from hysteria. The core of the ritual is the group, and it takes possession of space and enlarges it to express communion. Dance creates a specific area where gestural language can reveal secret human aspects and the point of contact between man and the hidden god. As a language, movement exists before song; vocal and instrumental music amplify the rhythm that becomes supreme. Within the ceremony itself, sacrificial rites are used to appease anger and to restore peace.

Myth is essential to ritual, for it postulates a meaning, a past, and a memory that organizes and identifies the world. Both historical and metaphysical, it acts out the image of a group in relation to its past and to the outer world. The connection between these two systems — the group and the world — is clearly stated. As in all myths, it is "paradise lost and found," and speech violated and restored, that "account for man's behavior."[12]

Aspects of ritual can easily be seen in theatre, not only because drama and scenic design borrow from it so freely, but also because theatre in modern society assumes the functions ritual did in traditional societies. Free from aristotelian formulas, theatre recovers its dark and dionysian function. The propitiary sacrifices are kept (especially in revolutionary theatre), and the ritual murder that used to take place in African ceremony is feigned or staged and valued as an example that engenders both fear and exaltation.

Ritual is progressively secularized by its theatricalization; increasing importance is given to the figurative aspects of dance and song and to gestural and physical intuition; and a movement takes place from the religious to the aesthetic, an aesthetic that merges into the religious. The most remarkable example of theatricalization can be found in Yoruba theatre in the entertainments that developed from *egun* during the period of the Oyo empire. Initiates were replaced by professional actors, but the elements of the original ceremony remained intact (song, dance, symbolic action in which the song became praise and the dance acrobatic). The drama is improvised and mimed by the actor. The mask gains meaning from its color and material. And the play is divided into tableaux and episodes with interludes of mime and drum. (This kind of drama, incidentally, is similar to Brecht's epic theatre.) In effect, forms of Yoruba theatre that emphasize fable over plot reappear in many Afro-American plays. The spectator is captivated but not held captive by a technique of narrative continuity or discontinuity: breaks in the story line permit digressions and ensure the autonomy of each sequence. Such theatre is most effective when it integrates familiar elements into different situations:

A work of art is believed to have aesthetic value to the extent that it communicates an intelligible message. This means that theatrical pleasure can be derived only when the essence of the total performance is meaningful. The creative arts combine with religion, politics, psychology and medical practice to construct a

complete system. It is the fusion of all these elements that forms
Yoruba aesthetic theory.[13]

Whereas Yoruba theatre reached the point of secularizing ritual,
Afro-American theatre has tried to preserve the sacred character of ritual
as shown in the very terms used to link theatre to religion, terms such as
communion and ecstasy. The artist is said to have a mission, not a craft.
Theatre aims to create a climactic moment that brings a new order into
being. Religion is reconverted into theatre, not only in the manifestation of a show, but in its ideology, which sustains a kind of layman's
religiosity. Revelation comes about through a phenomenon similar to
mystical ecstasy or trance which creates a contagious delirium and produces full exorcism. In this mystic conception of theatre the relation
between actor and director becomes that of initiator and initiatee.
Theatre thus becomes a magical and purifying art, intent upon restoring
the equilibrium that dogma used to provide.

In modern society, ritual drama thus takes on the functions that rites
alone used to serve in traditional society: it is a communal art, a unifying link, a mobilizer, a rallying point where commands for struggle are
transmitted. Finally, it serves a mythic and symbolic function. The
ritual expresses the cosmic harmony that society should recreate, for in
its microcosm harmony is always threatened. Ritual reaffirms that the
individual exists only through the community and that moral imperatives dictate good relations between them. Some productions in
black theatre have come close to being rituals and have aroused a quasi-
religious participation, around which a new mode of performance
developed. These shows create a montage out of autobiographical
documents, stories, poems, and pieces of music, whose effectiveness
depends on the spectator's familiarity. Thus contrasted familiar
elements are placed in a new light and given unexpected meaning, as in
the shows of Vinie Burrows.

Rituals have been performed by the Spirit House led by Jones/Baraka
in Newark and by the New Lafayette Theatre as collective creations in
which writers and directors participated. The National Black Theatre
under the direction of Barbara Ann Teer, Glenda Dickerson at Howard
University, and Robert Macbeth in New York have also developed
rituals.

The range of this cultural phenomenon of ritual can be seen in Glenda Dickerson's "The Unfinished Song: Reflexions in Black Voices,"
presented at Howard University in 1970. This ritual tried to show how
the function of music changed in the journey from Africa to the New

World. Songs that were first used to bring rain during periods of drought told of the experiences of a unified people exposed only to the caprices of nature. When missionaries arrived, songs attacked the foreign precepts that interfered with ancestral wisdom; during slavery in America cries of protest were raised up in the cane and cotton fiields. The lost music found its way back through the spirituals, gospel songs, and blues and regained its vigor with the reappearance of the drum.

Dickerson's ritual retraces the epic of a people by following the modulations of songs that expressed joy, tribulation, uprootedness, and evil. Music provides the structure for the rituals, gives it coherence, and leads the listener through a rite of passage. Each instrument (kalinka, luth, saxophone, drum) has its own function. Sequences of poetry are used to emphasize the narrative line and add the poet's voice to that of the people. Dance enters under the pulse of music and words; it modulates and creates its own motifs. The different elements of the performance are at once integrated and autonomous. The ritual also follows the rules of a ceremony structured according to a long measured movement until a rupture of the harmony occurs with menacing silence. The tension mounts as the song begins again in accelerated, syncopated rhythms. The intensity of the sound corresponds to the vigor of the recovered word. The frenzy of the dance expresses the joy of a victorious people.

The actors appear on stage, in the aisles, and on platforms. They merge with the audience. Their displacement disrupts the physical separation between the stage and the house; their movements match the cadence of the music and are punctuated with shouts of "That's Right!" and "Teach!" At the climactic moment, reality becomes myth, for the mass of spectators has joined the actors in one celebration. Listeners and officiants collaborate: the latter seem at first to direct the spectators, but the spectators by their spontaneous intervention give new force to the unfolding ritual. The performance stirs up emotions then channels them until the final burst of energy.

The ritual arises from a certain mythic model, that of a return to origins whose truths are presented intact.[14] The paradisiacal state that must be reconquered represents the ideal situation before the arrival of whites. An exuberant imagery stages the end of the world and the wait for a new world. But in the seventies blacks were no longer content to wait; the proliferation of rituals from 1970 to 1972, and the conviction of theatre artists that this was the only form capable of reaching audiences, proclaimed the beginning of a new era.

Ritual performs a double function. As theatre, it indicates the desire to break free from Western drama by integrating musical forms, narrative, and choreography specific to black culture. As church, theatre is a place of fellowship and communion. The collective memory reactivates history, whose symbolic reiteration confirms the uniqueness of an exemplary itinerary and the possibility of mastering a destiny more clearly perceived. The ritual is an initiation; it points out proper behavior; it responds to both moral aspirations and social imperatives; it expresses and codifies beliefs, safeguards principles and puts them to use.

The experience of ritual for Afro-Americans enriches contemporary reality. It also points to certain tasks and the way to accomplish them. The mode is often rich with cosmogonic symbolism in which the creative situation is rediscovered. From there, the ritual offers a solution to negative situations and restores the community's psychic well-being. Africa, the place of origins and of creation, appears as a motherland to be venerated, a lost paradise. Here eschatology comes into play: cataclysms, which play an important role in revolutionary theatre, are indispensable for any new beginning. A final decisive struggle assures the victory of the elect against the white demons. The ritual places the advent of black power or nationalist awakening in a cosmic universe. Messianic characteristics are attributed to a culture hero or an ancestor who will return among the living.

Narratives of mythic adventures, in which a hero penetrates the matrix of prenatal darkness, returns victorious, and acquires a new identity, serves as a model for rituals that follow the same sequence: original peace, introduction of evil, persecution/imprisonment, struggle, final liberation. The rituals of black theatre are also analogous to healing rites that bring a sick person back to health. The long subjugation of black people is compared to an illness, a plague that leads to despair. In the Yoruba myth the Supreme Being abandoned humanity to inferior gods that made it suffer; this schema is found in Jones's *A Black Mass* and continues to reappear. The rituals of the sixties, however, unlike the revolutionary theatre, placed less emphasis on the eschatological elements and more on the imminence of the future. The final sequences of the spectacle—explosion, ecstasy, communion—come in the image of a burst of life and fertility that reigns over the recreation of the world. The ritual helps to free the psychic energy and spirituality necessary for regeneration.

The return to ritual characterized the work of many groups after 1969. The New Lafayette Theatre devoted its entire 1969–70 season to different rituals, whose titles are significant: "To Bind Together and Strengthen Black People So That They Can Survive the Struggle That Is to Come," and "A Black Time for Black Folks: A Play Without Words." In May 1974 Buddy Butler directed a ritual by Norman Jordan called "In the Last Days.[15]

One criticism must be made about the use of ritual in black theatre: The New Lafayette Theatre's rituals were failures. The Harlem public often had negative reactions and expressed them in indignant remarks. The calls to righteousness and references to beliefs long ago discarded were not understood. In this way, the warning to "the participant" in the program for "To Raise the Dead" was troublesome: "Do not conjure the spirit unless you feel pure and righteous, for it is told that when this deity is summoned it never returns where it comes from without a soul, and if the caller is not righteous in the way of his people, then his dearest loved one will be taken back to the land of the dead to return never again."[16] Could such injunctions really move their audience? The rhetoric of the New Lafayette appears cut off from the realities of the ghetto. The rituals were often conceived as shows where the aesthetic search brought along other preoccupations that were foreign to the public. The failure of its rituals was no doubt also linked to the way the New Lafayette divorced itself from the community.

Barbara Ann Teer took this search much further. Her analysis of Nigerian ritual came closer to the life of the ghetto to recover the forgotten expression of Africanness. Teer made no compromise with the norms imposed by show business. For the National Black Theatre (NBT), ritual is a communal event organized and studied, refined and unambiguous. It aims not to bring African ritual into a different context, but to create a ritual that renews the ties among cultural elements alienated from one another: "There is no such thing as a stage, nor such a thing as an audience; only liberators and participants. And you try to remove that psychic distance, that nigger space that separates Black people from each other. In a ritual you mold, meet and merge into one. You feel, laugh, cry and experience life together."[17]

The ritual releases a psychic liberating energy; thus Teer calls the actors "liberators." The only theatrical model that NBT follows is that of the Apollo, the popular variety showplace in Harlem where the public always participates. Of all the directors, Teer has probably led the most systematic examination of the possible relations among different aspects of black culture and black theatre. She has put theatre in the service of the community and has defined the dialectical relationship between artists and the community as represented by the assembly. "The black artist must remember that it is the people that give him light and clarity of vision and who reinforce his sensibilities."

Dance

The role dance plays in contemporary culture[18] must be studied from the perspective of its early manifestations in religious worship. In Vodun and the Yoruba religions dance brings about possession. In Afro-American culture dance expresses the vital force embodied by the gods who, like the *orishas* of Brazil, are "the great ancestors" who used to be men. The prayer-dance recreates a world-view — confronting the forces of destruction and renewal — and establishes a constructive relationship with these forces. Some dances have been noted for their deliberately grotesque character as well as the acrobatic virtuosity required of the dancers. Mimed dances, developed from a precise choreography, are inspired from a well-developed symbolic aparatus and are often accompanied by a myth or parable: a story in song narrated and recreated by dance in mimed and rhythmic tableaux.

Dance served a cultural function in early Afro-American culture. It was quickly introduced in public performances around carnivals and festivals such as "Pinster day," an "African" celebration of Pentecost.[19] Masks were used for caricature and the dance for satire as slaves began to parody the ceremonies of whites.

Just as religious dance came to serve a secular function, secular dance preserved its ritualistic character. Dance (in Jahn's words) "manifests the life force."[20] In addition to movement, it has content, purpose, and meaning. Jahn has shown how black dance, in submitting to Western aesthetic norms, lost its symbolic power and was deprived of its meaning and importance. Black artists later recovered this meaning in contemporary theatre.

Afro-American dance is still a *spectacle*, but one that blurs the distinction between spectators and participants. This characteristic undoubtedly favored the incorporation of dance into drama: it was adopted both for its own qualities of theatricality, rhythm, visual effect, symbolic force, and concrete expression, and for the place it has always held in the cultural life of the community, in the worship of ancestors or the dead, in group activities surrounding marriages and births. In the narrative and poetic traditions dance accompanied the story, the music, or the chant. This ubiquity predisposes dance to theatrical use. "We are a people of dance," writes Léopold Sédar Senghor, "whose feet grow strong by beating upon the ground."[21] The phrase well translates the significance of dance: to express the people's strength, their desire for freedom, and their refusal to be enslaved.

The choreographic figure found in most dances is the circle, particularly the "ring shout," which appeared in the United States during the Great Awakening religious revivals of the eighteenth and nineteenth centuries. The circle plays an important role in dramatic ritual. Symbolically, the circle represents both a scenic design and the unity of the black nation. The space occupied by the dancers is the same as a stage formed by the circle of observers who offer rhythmic encouragement. Audience participation can enlarge or reduce the playing area; an observer can at any moment slip into the center and join the dancers. The circle is also the archetypal image of the community: it signifies both the relation of each member to the central nucleus and the ties among members. This morphology merges into a dynamic equilibrium the faculty of integration and the possibility of combining opposites. The motif of the circle is also used as a configuration of the production and as a scenic element, for the circle can control space and intensify emotions; it also breaks free of the constraints of the proscenium stage.

In drama, choreography can revive the principal moments in the history of the black nation: confrontation, ruptures, encounters, dispersal, resistance. And certain dance steps can signify different behaviors (*chicken* fearful, *Watusi* proud and jeering, *bougaloo* explosive and daring, *tightlip* reunifying.) The dramatic text itself may suggest a whole repertory of gestures. Mindful of the close ties with dance, theatre artists have frequently worked with choreographers like Arthur Mitchell, Eleo Pomare, and Pearl Primus to develop their productions and to restore the importance of movement. Scenic language is not only developed from a text, it is acted out. The importance of a gesture to express a situation, an attitude, or an action has often been attested to: "The gesture, unlike the actions and activities of people, has a definable beginning and end. This aspect, strictly and squarely restricted by each element of an attitude, however, appears as the main thing in a living flow, one of the basic dialectical phonemes of movement."[22]

The expressiveness of black gestural language, as observed in real life, is explored systematically in the theatre. On stage, the gesture is introduced with keen emphasis. This stylization is one of many effects produced for the spectator. In the theatre the body recovers its authoritative role. The emphasis on gesture becomes a reaction against psychological theatre and a struggle against the audience's lack of imagination. It reinstates the primary function of every production, which is to *show*.

Whether or not dance is integrated into the performance, it is present throughout the new black theatre. It inspires the work of many groups (particularly the Urban Arts Corps and the Afro-American Total Theatre) and the most noteworthy direction by Gilbert Moses in *Slave Ship* and in *Ain't Supposed to Die a Natural Death* as well as the dramatization of the poems by Ntozake Shange.

Dramatic Structures and Theatre Craft

The revolution in black theatre over the past few years has thus proceeded from cultural references different from those which previously determined the modes of performance. The theatre becomes an instrument for both discovering and analyzing these elements. It postulates the existence of a community of experiences and becomes a space where they can be represented, evaluated, actualized, and emotionally apprehended. It elaborates its own dramatic conventions from modes of representation, communication, and reception suggested by the narrator/storyteller, singer/musician, preacher/officiant, dancer/choreographer. Combining the singular mode of each "performance," it creates a ceremonial of its own in which the playwright finds new situations and characters, and the director and actor a model of theatre practice.

Many productions incorporate material from nonliterary sources (oral, musical, religious) in order to highlight nonverbal elements and to bring a degree of improvisation to the text itself. The text cannot be dissociated from the scenographic work involving voice and body that it suggests, implies, or dictates.

As for the dramatist, he is less inclined to fathom his characters' individual psychology than to define their place in an ontological system, to determine which roles should be rejected, assumed, or promoted, to offer a grammar through which behavior can be analyzed and decoded. The spatial metaphor—a place to be somebody—becomes all important, for it combines images of verticality, imprisonment, the "underground" world, and disjunction with images of harmony, fulfillment, and adjustment. Two fundamental conflictual and complementary relations come to light. The entire scenic space is organized around these shifting configurations of individuals and groups that precipitate outburst, rupture, and reunification. These configurations are defined by gestures, action, and the movements of actors; in other words, a precise collaboration between dancers, musicians, and choreographers.

The conception of theatre craft has been modified over the past years. Just as one can distinguish a piece of music from its execution, one can also distinguish textual writing from scenic composition although the two are closely tied. The joining of theatre with other arts has led to new ideas about the roles of artists and the various elements of the creative process. Theatre is conceived as a collective activity. The isolation of the dramatist ends, but at the same time his authority is called into question along with the relation between text and performance. The text is no longer thought of as an ensemble of signs meant for a single performance, but as a step toward the creation of a theatrical event. Often the performance no longer develops from a preexisting text, but from an outline given in the didascalies, the schema of possibilities for dramatic action. The "literary" texts often come from nontheatrical forms such as poems, sermons, or legends.

Curiously enough, the theatre revival, which was credited to such dramatists as Peterson and Hansberry in the fifties, is now most often attributed to directors. As the barriers between the arts are abolished, different creative activities fuse, and theatre becomes a space for synthesis and of unification (a musician like Archie Shepp, a painter like Oliver Jackson have been called upon to help with productions), the roles traditionally given to the director, author, and actor are also redistributed.

Yet the emphasis on the nonverbal and scenic material aimed at creating a total theatre represents only one trend among others. Certain companies still have their "writer in residence," and many still offer a repertory based on the production or the staging of a text. Yet when one considers the paths black theatre has taken, it seems as though a new era is arriving to erase the theatre of author and text. Total theatre also corresponds better to the tastes of black audiences eager for aural and visual images and to the vocation that theoreticians have ascribed to theatre, which is to integrate all aspects of the communal culture. A similar direction in theatre has occurred among the avant-garde. Using different cultural references, Andrei Serban, Meredith Monk, Richard Foreman, and Bob Wilson have given new importance to choreography and to visual and sonorous elements, and have broken with conventions that formerly defined dramatic text and the art of directing.[23]

To a certain extent the black dramatists started this trend, although it brings them very little return in the theatre today. It was they who first drew attention to the possible enrichment of drama by extending theatre signs beyond verbal discourse. The important minimalization of spoken text in such works as *Slave Ship* and *The Death of Malcolm X* are clear indications of this evolution. Dramatists such as Bullins, and especially Harrison and Edgar White, have proposed a new organization of the creative process and theatre practice.

Surprisingly, the writer's theatre that developed among blacks from 1950 to 1970 leaned toward ethnic theater and the kind of collective creation that is embraced today. The supremacy of the text coincided with widespread literacy and produced a substantial black readership. At a time when production was not forthcoming, publication of plays stimulated the writing and distribution of numerous texts. Publication also brought prestige and recognition to black theatre and challenged the cultural imperialism of whites by going beyond the "primitive state" usually associated with nonliterate societies.

Some contemporary artists are no longer interested in a theatre of texts and authors. The primacy of the word has been replaced by a drama created out of the spatial language of voice and body. Performance is no longer restricted to the acting out of scenes, but becomes a theatrical creation all its own. Yet it would be false to predict the disappearance of the text, for only in a few cases is the actual writing eliminated. The relations between text and performance have only been modified, with the text losing its primacy. Equally false are those theories which see the text as "a simple script to be read and theatre as something to be performed."[24]

Theatricality, in this light, can be seen as emerging through the text as well as through performance. If it is true that a performance builds up a plurality of meaning that extends beyond the limits of textual space, it is also true that no one performance or staging can realize all the possibilities offered by a text. Black playwrights have suggested new areas of exploration in religious worship, music, and dance for the actor and the director to use in redefining the theatrical event. These suggestions aim at questioning existing conventions (often dictated by white aesthetics), at rethinking the representation of character/situation/action and the relationship between stage and audience, and at exploring new fields wherein forms of black expression can be found that enrich and transform the dramatic medium.

Audience Awareness and Participation

One of the conventions that has been systematically reexamined is the role assigned to the audience in the creative process. The cultural references postulate a community of experiences. And part of the theatrical event relies on the spectator's familiarity with this material and calls for a *reconnaissance*, a cultural or ideological acknowledgment of the experience that is to be reactivated through collective memory and restructured on stage.

The problem of modes of reception is crucial, for it touches on the function that theatre has for the spectator. The reception of the theatrical message occurs according to certain general mechanisms, but also according to cultural behavior peculiar to the group. The construction of the work takes into account the effects it seeks to produce. The spectators come with their own determinations — tastes, preferences, habits, ways of thinking. By meeting or challenging these expectations the theatre creates new behavioral patterns in its audience.

The first stage of reception has been defined by Demarcy as the anxious wait for the end.[25] The spectator is drawn to the action and its shifts. He is spontaneously more interested in following a plot than in analyzing its progress or decoding its signs and indices. If this thread does not exist, he will invent one.

Identification serves to support this passive mode of reception, whose first inclination is to escape. The spectator projects himself into the action seeking compensation. He may identify with both the character and the actor. This phenomenon has often been analyzed according to the schema presented by Melanie Klein as identification/projection/projective identification. These mechanisms still operate on several levels. In black theatre, identification can lead the spectator to forget about his real condition and the theatre to renounce its primary function. The audience's captivation by the theatre would only prolong the captivity in which the audience is held in real life. If the theatre wants to play a part in the liberation of a people, it must break with this pattern of submission.

An entire movement in drama was developed to produce this rupture by questioning the idea of a hero as the central consciousness and by opposing the cathartic closure of dramatic structure. Purgation, in effect, expressed "the ideal of sublimation which gave art the unique function of making the aesthetic appear to satisfy legitimate instincts and needs.[26] Encouraging such identification, the performance of passion on stage steered the spectator away from the kind of alienation effect necessary for new action. Catharsis happens in the imagination, not in the real world. The spectator must be pulled out of his passive attitude. Identification together with alienation allows the spectator to reflect and to perceive the world as a reality that can be transformed and acted upon. The audience is no longer the consumer of an artistic product; it must participate in the creative process. The drama recovers its didactic function and teaches the spectator to identify the tasks necessary to effect his complete emancipation. If during the performance the onlooker learns to free himself from his traditional role, he may also be better equipped to understand the roles he has been assigned in real life.

The new drama calls for two readings: one is horizontal and follows the syntagmatic/narrative structure, the fable that captivates the spectator; the other is vertical and searches for paradigms, signs that convey the ultimate significance of the work. This deciphering of signs must proceed through a precise decoding. One is reminded here of certain characteristics of the dramatic medium: the signified is expressed in a multiplicity of languages—visual, auditory, gestural—and each sign must be efficient and immediately intelligible; theatre language is therefore often redundant. It constantly reassesses its theatricality; also, because of its intermediary position between several languages it is subject, more than any other art form, to the exigencies of symbolic thought. The real dimension of the sign is to be found within the work but also in its relation to the culture. The reading of the performance must be carried on simultaneously on three levels, syntagmatic, paradigmatic, and symbolic, according to Barthes' analysis of "the imagination of the sign."[27] Audience awareness can no longer be reduced to a merely psychological process, engaged in identification, sublimation, and release from inhibitions; it is also a social, cultural, and as such ideological consciousness.[28]

The task of restructuring this consciousness has to take into account certain characteristics of black audiences and move beyond stereotyped representation of naive, inordinately spontaneous, and unsophisticated spectators. In Afro-American life, most cultural manifestations assume the presence of an audience, a presence defined mainly through the call and response pattern. In this exchange the spectator is an active element in the communication of a message of which he or she is both the sender and the receiver. We have seen that oral, religious, and musical traditions are all articulated around this pattern of exchange and participation. These cultural practices predispose the black audience to the theatrical experience. Its active participation is a given, and does not have to be elicited through artificial devices such as those which some radical groups have developed.

The black audience is exuberant and shows its enthusiasm or disapproval straightforwardly. It cannot be easily duped or carried away. It has its say about the characters' behavior, challenging, encouraging, or becoming indignant. Its keen perception demands to be verbalized immediately; it preaches, forewarns, criticizes, participates. The shouts, gestures, hand clapping, and foot tapping punctuate the discourse in a ritual of participation that accompanies the performance.

This ritual of participation has been acknowledged by certain playwrights to the point that they have included it in the dramatic structure (Edgar White); occasionally two or three characters symbolize the presence of the audience, or this participation is further encouraged by multiplying addresses or by inserting elements that stimulate reactions. In some performances, as in ritual, the creation of the performance becomes the primary goal. Important factors such as the composition of the audience and the presence of whites determine the degree and nature of participation. Middle-class theatregoers tend to model their behavior according to tenets of respectability. Other blacks, long excluded from "legitimate" houses, transfer to theatre behavior practiced in other situations—worshiping in church, listening to music, attending sporting events. These reactions are manifested more spontaneously when there are no whites in the audience. The Apollo theatre in Harlem has been seen as one place where cultural behavior could be freely expressed. But as soon as the house was integrated the phenomenon of participation changed. White spectators reacted with hostility to every intervention of blacks in the polite reception of the performance. The frequency of mixed audiences and the acculturation of the black middle class threaten the future of participatory rituals. Participation remains, however, a lively practice, not, as is sometimes heard, a survival or an artificially recreated procedure. Many theatre artists have used participatory modes in order to combine pleasure, spontaneity and reflexion, understanding and imagination. The intervention of the audience is not left to chance. It is planned and closely controlled, as in the National Black Theatre, which invites audience participation. At an extreme, this encouragement may be seen as manipulation, but for the most part it involves putting to work a potential that has not been fully realized.

The theatre constantly reminds its spectators that it is not life or a mere reflection of life, but a reconstruction; thus it encourages symbolic activity. An interplay takes place among audience, stage, and outside world; participating in the development of a new consciousness that can help to build the world in which the group wishes to live, the theatre contributes to recreating a sense of community. Theatrical work, carried on collectively and with the presence of the artist-spectator, is never closed or totally finished. It is constantly in process, and it gets its fullest meaning by receiving new reactions, calls, and responses.

Conclusion

BEGINNING WITH an often radical assessment of the function and practice of dramatic art in the dominant society, contemporary Afro-American theatre has sought to modify the perceptions and the procedures of performance. The theatre has systematically criticized the images the black world had accepted and has examined the ideologies that produced them. First timidly, then violently, it has tried to break away from the kind of drama that imposed false images and inhibited freedom.

This theatre assumed a privileged role at the high point in the struggle for black liberation. As the place where controlling images could be forged, it was intimately associated with the task of rehabilitation and emancipation. It created a space parallel to the real historical scene where the situation could be understood through new perspectives and new dramatic structures. The systematic exploration of black culture allowed the theatre to uncover the principles of an ethos and the foundations of a drama. In militant theatre, the investigation of certain alienating aspects of the culture led to rupture; in the theatre of experience, a search for ethnic continuity legitimized the culture.

The fight against the oppression and alienation of blacks in American society caused militant theatre to take action against those responsible, to stage their trial: the white man appeared as the accused, and judgment was brought against his black accomplices. Different scenarios offered images of the various punishments awaiting the guilty parties. While some plays showed how institutions work to subjugate blacks and blind them to reality, others recalled the heroic resistance that has occurred since slavery. At times the theatre showed alienated and revolutionary moods simultaneously; at times it alternated between them. It also claimed the coming of a new era. Scenarios of the destruction of the white world led to those about the building of a strong and reunified black nation. Passionate denunciation turned into ardent celebration.

The theatre views temporality as a double dimension: it refers to the individual's moment of psychological commitment, and to the group's historical and mythical past. Some plays embrace the goal of restoring historical continuity; the liberation of black people is seen as the result of a deliberate and continuous struggle. Other plays see liberation as part of the natural order of things, placing history outside the realm of human will. The spectator is asked either to create history or simply to contemplate it.

Such is the very heart of the dialectical nature of the theatrical experience, which transforms the world into discourse and real life into a figure. As Anne Ubersfeld has said:

The theatrical experience is a reduced model that makes an economy of lived experience and exorcises it just as it makes one live by proxy . . . And pain and death are pain and death at a good distance away, indeed banalities: we are in the privileged domain of catharsis, where insoluble conflicts are given a dreamlike resolution, and we leave it happy, for they will be worked out without us.

This "reduced model" can also be an instrument of knowledge. In the discourse proposed by black theatre, elements of a semantics proper are sketched out:

To semantize the signs is to give or be given the power to understand the world before changing it; it is to understand the conditions of exercising speech in the world, the relations between speech and concrete situations; discourse and gestural language designate the unspoken that underlies discourse. The theatre, being a reduced model of relations of power and finally of production, appears as an exercise in mastering a smaller and easier to handle sample object.[1]

Black theatre oscillates between these two functions, which are not mutually exclusive. The drama traditionally written by whites requires catharsis, whereas the ideology of revolutionary theatre establishes more critical reflection. By refusing catharsis, black theatre does not renounce its emotive function, but adds exercise to exorcism. In the best performances, like those of *Slave Ship*, reflection stems from emotions and creates the effect of shock. Emotion is not an end in itself but a means to construct meaning.

If political theatre asks us to make sense of all of history, then the theatre of experience focuses no less ambitiously on everyday life. The combativeness of the drama is oriented toward the affirmation of ethnicity. Black people, who had been reduced to mere objects of domination, now become the subjects of art. Protest still exists in the theatre of experience, but it is part of the form rather than the content. The artist manifests his freedom through his independence from existing forms of expression. Content alone becomes less important than the ensemble of theatrical activity that is redirected and restructured. The white spectator cannot be involved to the same degree as the black audience, which benefits from an intimate knowledge of the material. The theatre thus helps to institutionalize a cultural code that is not recognized in the way blacks are portrayed in white theatre.

The relation of the artist to his work is also radically modified. The work is no longer the subjective expression of an individual artist's experiences. The artist is the representative of the group and speaks in its name. The manifestations of a single work matter less than the way it fits into the whole discourse that theatre develops about black experience.

Theatre practice thus opposes the concept of an individual genius who situates his creation in timelessness and universality. Rather, it expresses the way a particular consciousness reacts to the conditioning of the world. It is ephemeral by nature, since the work, which is made concrete only at the moment of performance, can disappear as quickly as it was created.

If Afro-American theatre is to restore the autonomy of art vis-à-vis the dominant ideology, certain basic conditions must be met. To examine the situation one must ask, first, what kind of autonomy black theatre enjoys within a system that discourages diversity and protest, and secondly, to what extent working in the dominant society threatens the principles of black theatre.

After opposing the emergence of ethnic cultures for so long, the informed American society today displays a less hostile but equally dangerous politics. Black theatre, because it was marginalized and nonprofessional, long escaped the laws of the system. Its relative success now makes this impossible. When art becomes integrated into the marketplace it is subjugated and culturally exploited. As Adorno and Marcuse have argued, art is neutralized by commercialization.[2] Adorno has emphasized the antinomic nature of art, which is both a description of our mutilated world and the evocation of a world that could be. Art is thus opposed to alienation. Its language becomes polemical in order to expose a reality that is obscured. Thus, Afro-American theatre contests black alienation in American society and promises liberation. The plays necessarily oppose domination by the system.

Marcuse discusses the negativity of art, its power of negation. It is in being differentiated from reality that art expresses another state than what exists, or what could exist in a society free from "barbarism." Art loses its *raison d'être* when it is transformed into a consumer good, a part of the culture industry. Rendered banal, it becomes inoffensive and inauthentic; its violence is denied, and it loses what Adorno calls its "truthful content." Just as society tends to deny the existence of antagonism within social reality, it denies everything that in a work of art, recalls these conflicts. Deprived of its challenging power, art loses all its characteristic praxis. It is relegated to the sphere of aesthetics by the official culture. The consumer takes it over in order to render it like himself rather than to be identified with it. The world of production is thus cut off from the consumer, the theatre artist from his audience.[3]

In an entirely different context from that suggested by Marcuse or Adorno, A. J. Greimas, in his analysis of the ethnosemiotic object, attests to the possible consequences the banal can have in ethnic theatre. According to him, the ethnosemiotic object transforms mythic phenomena into aesthetic ones, and group manifestations into individual ones. Greimas' analysis focuses on the three manifestations or "languages" whose presence is essential to theatre discourse — the poetic, the musical, and the gestural:

> A global mythic phenomenon, which is to say a semiotic object whose meaning is manifested by poetic, musical and gestural codes, in developed societies is at once dissolved and appears, in the end, as disjointed and autonomous discourse: poetry, music, dance. Instead of being viewed as diverse manifestations of the sacred, these different autonomous languages . . . assume ludic or aesthetic functions.
>
> Instead of being collective manifestations, the poetic, musical or gestural expressions derive, depending on their production and use, from individual stylistics. Instead of being productions of meaning from a group, the semantic objects generated by its languages become essentially objects for individual consumption.[4]

To a certain extent, this description applies to tranformations imposed on Afro-American theatre and sends us back to the different processes previously noted: secularization of theatre, reduction of its multiple functions to those of aesthetic entertainment, passage from group production to individual consumption. Such banalization affects not only the work's revolutionary form but also its ethnic character. As an attempt to reactivate poetic, musical, and gestural languages as systems of communication rising from a specific community, black theatre is a process of restructuring black cultural givens which are threatened.

The practitioners of black theatre have not always perceived the contradictions in which the official cultural politics have placed them. After reexamining the structure of the society and the function given to art, black theatre now seems to want to be integrated into the very system against which it was formed. Partly imposed by circumstance, this backward turn risks compromising the future of this theatre as the manifestation of a specific cultural community. The theatre must either take charge of its own aesthetic power or resign itself to a growing heteronomy. Every artistic endeavor is faced with this choice: to please and to gain a large audience, or to utter an often unpleasant truth. But this problem is posed in a particularly poignant way for black theatre if one takes into account its double vocation as revolutionary theatre (a total rejection of society) and as ethnic theatre (connected to the former because ethnicity can be affirmed only in opposition to the dominant culture).

Because the existence and rationale of black theatre have been promoted in racial terms, the true problems have always been obscured. It is not enough to say that black theatre should be written, acted, and managed by blacks, speak about them, and address them. Such a definition creates a false optimism about progress made since the twenties. Already black theatre includes a good many influential dramatists, famous actors, numerous companies, and productions known nationwide; moreover, it is now managed partly by blacks, and black criticism has developed. Yet such an evaluation remains purely statistical: it measures theatre in numerical terms and according to criteria (fame, audience, influence) which, though not negligible, reveal only the most superficial aspects. It also poses a *sine qua non* condition of the racial identity of the theatre artists and relegates other considerations to second place. Whatever his specific function within the world of show business, the artist of black theatre has earned the right to be seen as an artist and not simply as a public entertainer; and yet the problem of theatre practice still exists. Black theatre has seen in separation the necessary condition for the creation of ethnic theatre, and this strategy has been taken up by cultural nationalist ideology; yet total separation has proved unattainable. This is true because of the pressure exerted by the larger society and the temptations of a larger audience, but also because of the lack of a cultural politics with which to resist these pressures. Among blacks, the appearance of divergent ideologies caused a rupture at the heart of the theatrical endeavor.

Initially, black theatre owed its existence to subsidies received from white America. This aid was first provided as part of the antipoverty campaign through government arts councils and private foundations. Nationalist ideology was able to accommodate to this situation by arguing that the black community had a right to this aid; however, the financial support had strings attached and involved some control. By stressing cultural achievement, this kind of support directed revolutionary energies toward activities less politically dangerous.

Transformed into a commodity for profit, black theatre has had to contend with fluctuations in the theatre industry. Trends and fashions have a more radical effect on theatre than on any other cultural form because theatre depends so heavily on producers. Today the vogue has passed and most black theatres find themselves in disastrous financial straits. Some, like the New Lafayette in Harlem, ceased functioning once the grants were withdrawn. In effect, the programs for cultural assistance had envisioned several months or years of support in order to create structures that would make the theatre self-sufficient. These policies were a disservice because they encouraged institutionalization and because the criteria for receiving grants favored aesthetic experimentation and professionalism, thus modifying the whole practice of black theatre, since efforts had to be focused on presenting shows that conformed to the norms of the industry and on seeking commercial success.

As the official culture offered to distribute black creations through the most prestigious structures, black plays became part of the repertory of American theatre; all the large New York theatres have had posted at one time or another a work by a black playwright or company. Melvin Van Peebles' plays *Don't Play Us Cheap* and *Ain't Supposed to Die a Natural Death*, the Lincoln Center's production of Bullins' *Duplex*, *The River Niger* and *Bubbling Brown Sugar* on Broadway, all attest to the interest of the entertainment industry in black theatre and to the vitality black theatre has brought to the New York stage.

For producers of black theatre, Broadway and off-Broadway thus constitute a lifesaver. This success nevertheless poses serious problems for the future of Afro-American theatre and the pursuit of its original objectives. Integration works only after a selection has been made according to the criterion of profitability. Shows unable to appeal to a large audience are eliminated. By following the paths of American theatre production, black theatre is placed more than ever at the mercy of mainstream critics, although critics like Clayton Riley and Peter Bailey have tried to break the hegemony of this discourse.

Any play written to be performed before a black audience loses a vital element when produced outside the community. This raises a question about the danger a decline in segregation causes for black theatre. To a certain extent, ethnic theatre was created out of segregation, whether imposed or freely chosen. Discrimination sent artists back to their community, and cultural nationalists saw this separation as necessary for the development of black art. It seems now that many artists viewed this return to the black community as a limitation. Black artists have continually vacillated between the desire to serve their racial community and the temptation to seek recognition in the dominant society. After a return "home" during the Black Arts Movement, many have left for the Great White Way.

It is difficult to separate choice from necessity. Integration as a strategy of survival is perhaps freely chosen by the black artist. But it may also reflect a sense of failure: the theatre work undertaken in the black community did not attain the hoped-for results. Black theatre did not reach financial autonomy, a condition indispensable to its artistic autonomy. Not did it gain the audience it sought. The black middle class did not suport ethnic theatre. As the only holders of capital, they chose to invest it in other enterprises; and as an audience, they preferred the productions offered by the white American stage.

Curiously enough, black productions on Broadway sanctioned by the official theatre institution bring the black middle class back to a repertory it once scorned. The middle class constitutes an important part of the audience, for it alone can afford the high ticket prices of the major houses. But the middle class rarely ventures into community theatres. Having abandoned the ghetto as a place of residence, it is unlikely to return for an evening's entertainment. Its attitude toward black theatre is ambivalent; it does not forget that revolutionary drama placed it on trial, but it follows the fashion of ethnicity and sees theatre as a civilized pleasure.

Today black theatre is isolated from the audience on which it had basedits existence and vitality. First set up in places that were provisional and close to the everyday life of the community, theatre later assumed more permanent and rigid structures. After the renewal and dynamism that marked separatism, the reconciliation with the dominant society estranged black theatre from the black community.

Afro-American theatre, it seems, has reached a crossroads in its evolution, and a double hypothesis can be presented about its future. First, this future is in the hands of a system of cultural production that has eliminated some former prejudices and that, animated by liberal pluralism, is making some room for different ethnic theatres. This future is subject to changes in fashion but also to the fierce competition in the entertainment industry at a time when film and television threaten to supplant the theatre. Secondly, the future of black theatre is also in the hands of the black community as a whole and not just the artists. The theatre is not only the creation of authors, actors, and producers; it brings together the thinking and feelings of the community. If, as Peter Brook says, theatre is "an empty space to be filled," then this arena can become the place of lively dialogue only when all the elements that compose the theatre act are present. A truly ethnic theatre cannot survive

without the concerned attention of its audience. This is not to exclude
other audiences but to encourage the involvement of the black community. Moreover, black theatre will survive only if a dialogue with the
group is maintained and if the forms that support that dialogue are constantly renewed.

Notes

Introduction

1. Frantz Fanon, *The Wretched of the Earth*, trans. Constance Farrington (New York: Grove Press, 1966), p. 30.
2. Mikel Dufrenne, *Art et politique* (Paris: Christian Bourgois, Collection 10/18, 1974), p. 173. Unless otherwise indicated, all translations are by Melvin Dixon.

1. The Historical Precedent

1. European and American travelers of the period frequently alluded to these performances, the true meaning of which was often misunderstood. Several such accounts are quoted in Lawrence Levine's *Black Culture and Black Consciousness* (New York: Oxford University Press, 1977). References to festivals can also be found in local newspapers, such as the *South Carolina Gazette*, and in slave narratives. Consult the narratives of Solomon Northup, Henry Bibb, and William Wells Brown in *Puttin' On Ole Massa*, ed., Gilbert Osofsky (New York: Harper and Row, 1969). See also James B. Cade, "Out of the Mouths of Ex-Slaves," *Journal of Negro History* 22 (April 1935): 328–329.
2. William D. Piersen, "Putting Down Ole Massa," *Research in African Literature* 7 (Fall 1976): 166–180. Piersen shows that these parades were similar to demonstrations outside the United States, particularly in the "chaluska" of Haitian Mardi Gras, where participants would imitate the generals. Although the shows that accompanied the election of governors seem to have occurred only in the United States, their form can be found elsewhere.
3. See *From Slave Cabin to Pulpit: The Autobiography of Peter Randolph* (Boston, 1835), pp. 202–203.
4. For more on the minstrel show, see Hans Nathan, *Dan Emmett and the Rise of Early Negro Minstrelsy* (Norman: University of Oklahoma Press, 1962); Edward LeRoy Rice, *Monarchy of Minstrelsy: From Daddy Rice To-Date* (New York: Kenny Publications, 1911); Robert Toll, *Blacking Up: The Minstrel Show in Nineteenth Century America* (New York: Oxford University Press, 1974); Carl Wittke, *Tambo and Bones: A History of the Minstrel Stage* (Durham: Duke University Press, 1930).
5. The African Company, playing at the African Grove Theatre, brought together such celebrated actors as James Hewlett, who founded the first Afro-American troupe in 1821, Ira Aldridge, and an author known as Mr.Brown, thought to be the first black playwright. Mr. Brown's play *King Shotoway*, written around 1823, depicted a slave revolt. The author of the first black play actually performed in America, *Life in Limbo, Life in Love*, has not been identified, although Mr. Brown and sometimes James Hewlett are often credited with it. Victor Séjour, originally from New Orleans, is also mentioned among the dramatists of this period. Like

Aldridge, Séjour left the country: his plays, only one of which has black characters, were performed in Paris. See Thomas D. Pawley, "The First Black Playwright," *Black World* 31 April 1972, pp.16–24.

6. Brown's play *Escape; or A Leap for Freedom*, written one year after the Dred Scott Decision and one year before John Brown's raid, criticized corruption in the South, but it catered to the meoldramatic tastes of the day. William Wells Brown fought for emancipation, and his voice carried some weight. But he never managed to champion the cause of black playwrights in American theatre.

7. *A Trip to Coontown* by Bob Cole created a new genre in 1898. This show, written, produced, and acted by blacks, was doubly revolutionary. Two years later another black show, *Oriental America*, reached Broadway, and for the first time black actors could leave the mode of farce.

8. This collaboration is evidenced by *Clorindy*, written in 1898 by the poet Paul Laurence Dunbar with music by Will Marion Cook, and by Black Patti's Troubadors, which Bob Cole started with the singer Sissieretta Jones in 1896.

9. Robert Kimball and William Bolcom, "Reminiscing with Sissle and Blake: The Black Musical in America," *Yale/Theatre* 4, no. 3 (Summer 1973): 69–80. Loften Mitchell wrote a play about Williams and Walker and the black artist on the American stage. See *Star of the Morning*, in Woodie King and Ron Milner, eds., *Black Drama Anthology* (New York: New American Library, 1972), pp. 575–640. Hereafter this anthology will be cited as King and Milner.

10. With the prompting of Ford Dabney, James Reese Europe, Will Marion Cook, William Handy, and the Jubilee Singers, music came to hold a prominent place in theatre activity.

11. J. W. Jeliffe, "A Negro Community Theatre," *New Theatre and Film* (July 1935): 13; Terrence Tobin, "Karamu Theatre: 1915–1964," *Drama Critique* 7 (Spring 1964): 86–91.

    Of all the theatres founded during this period, only the Karamu is operating today. Others included the Pekin Theatre in Chicago, the Morgan College Players organized by Randolph Edmonds in Baltimore, and the Montgomery Players by Montgomery Gregory and Alain Locke at Howard University in 1921. Harlem also saw a proliferation of groups: the Renaissance Theatre, the Harlem Experimental Theatre, the Negro Art Theatre at Adam Clayton Powell's Abyssinian Baptist Church, the Harlem Community Theatre at St. Mark's Church. Finally, a company organized by W. E. B. DuBois, the Krigwa Players, performed in theatres nationwide.

12. Alain Locke and Montgomery Gregory eds., *Plays of Negro Life: A Sourcebook in Native American Drama* (New York: Harper, 1927). Other anthologies are Willis Richardson, ed., *Plays and Pageants from the Life of the Negro* (Washington, D.C.: Associated Publishers, 1930),

and Willis Richardson and May Miller, eds., *Negro History in Thirteen Plays* (Washington, D.C.: Associated Publishers, 1935).

13. In *Black Manhattan* (New York: Knopf, 1930), James Weldon Johnson chronicles the cultural life in Harlem.

14. Magazines like *Crisis*, organ of the NAACP and under the editorship of DuBois, and *Opportunity*, journal of the Urban League, tried to define directions and to encourage artistic production. But these are isolated examples. The most radical political wing, the socialists of Harlem, were not very concerned about the black renaissance. The various nationalist movements that started in Harlem between the wars were not able to develop a cultural politics sufficient to counteract the integrationist philosophy of the NAACP.

15. Black theatre of the FTP has been studied by E. Q. Craig, *Black Drama of the Federal Theatre Era* (Amherst: University of Massachusetts Press, 1980), and important documents have been collected at the Research Center for the FTP at George Mason University, Fairfax, Virginia.

    The locations of FTP centers included, in the East, New York, Newark, Philadelphia, Hartford, and Salem; in the South, Atlanta, New Orleans, Birmingham, Raleigh; in the West, San Francisco, Seattle, Los Angeles, Portland, and parts of Oklahoma. African expatriates from Ethiopia and Nigeria were also involved. The first "living newspaper," *Ethiopia*, was performed by Nigerians who also acted in *Bassa Moona*, directed by Momodu Johnson.

    On black theatre within the FTP see Frederick Bond, *The Negro and the Drama* (Washington, D.C.: Associated Publishers, 1940), pp. 165–174; Sterling Brown, "The Federal Theatre," in Lindsay Patterson, ed., *An Anthology of the American Negro in the Theatre* (New York: The Publishers Company, 1967), pp. 101–110; John Houseman, *Run Through* (New York: Curtis Books, 1972); Hallie Flanagan, *Arena* (New York: Duell, Sloan and Pierce, 1940); "The Role of the Federal Theatre, 1935–1939," *Journal of Negro History* 59 (January 1974): 38–50.

16. On this subject see Grace Overmeyer, *Government and the Arts* (New York: Norton, 1939). This campaign against racism was marked by incidents on which the WPA tried to take a firm stand: for example, when a company director attempted to separate black actors from white technicians during a tour in Texas and offered them transportation in a special train, he was immediately dismissed.

17. See John Silvera, "Still in Blackface," *Crisis* 46 (March 1939): 76. The production of *Come Seven* by Octavius Roy Cohen was severely criticized and accused of being only a farce in the style of "Amos 'n' Andy."

18. A scandal followed the performance of *Turpentine* by Agustus Smith and Peter Morell in June 1936. *The Naval Stores Review* and *The Norfolk Journal* attacked this protest play for presenting the struggle of black and white workers in Florida in a positive light. The affair was used two years

later by Senator Russell of Georgia before a Senate commission to withdraw subsidies; the seemingly subversive character of *Turpentine* became a good pretext for suspending grants to the FTP.

19. The show considered today as the most original production of the Harlem FTP is not a black play, but an adaptation of *Macbeth* by Orson Welles called *Voodoo Macbeth*. The action takes place in Haiti, evoking the deeds of black liberators and substituting voodoo priestesses for the witches. The cast included such well-known actors as Canada Lee and Maurice Ellis. This "black Macbeth" opened at the Lafayette, then played downtown at the Adelphi Theatre on 54th Street. Percy Hammond wrote in the *New York Times* on April 15, 1936: "The Negro Theatre, one of Uncle Sam's experimental philanthropies, gave us last night an exhibition of deluxe boondoggling."

20. Few sections had black directors; of particular note were Ralph Coleman in Boston and Clarence Muse in Los Angeles; in Harlem Agustus Smith and Carlton Moss took over from John Houseman when he left the Federal Theatre. Theodore Brown was an assistant director in Seattle. See the chapter on this company in Karen Taylor, *People's Theatre in America* (New York: Drama Book Specialists, 1972), pp. 186–190.

21. "The Negro Playwright's Company: Statement of Aims." Printed sheet, n.d., p. 2.

22. See Loften Mitchell's discussion of the play in *Black Drama* (New York: Hawthorn Books, 1967), pp. 170–179.

23. New York: Knopf, 1951.

24. See Allan Lewis, *American Plays and Playwrights of the Contemporary Theatre* (New York: Crown, 1965), p. 112.

25. See Harold Cruse, *The Crisis of the Negro Intellectual* (New York: Morrow, 1967), pp. 267–284.

26. *New York Times*, October 11, 1964, sec. 2, p. 3.

27. The FST was started in 1963 by three black students from the North, Gil Moses, John O'Neal, and Doris Derby, who came south to participate in the Civil Rights Movement. Their work is chronicled in *The Free Southern Theatre by the Free Southern Theatre* (New York: Bobbs-Merrill, 1969).

    The FST was established in Jackson, Mississippi, to attract a dispersed rural population. During the summer of 1964 it produced a show to protest the deaths of three young freedom riders. During that first season, the company numbered twenty-five and staged five productions, only two of which were written by blacks: *Purlie Victorious* by Ossie Davis and *Don't You Want to Be Free* by Langston Hughes. Completing the repertory were *In White America*, an adaptation of *Antigone* by Ann Flagg, and *Mother Carrar's Rifles* by Brecht, all of which were foreign to the realities of the South but related to the social and political climate of the sixties. Two original productions, *Bogalusa* and *Jonesburg Story*, were specifically created for local groups.

28. Culturally, New Orleans held a unique position. It is traditionally closer to Africa, and certain practices like voodoo were still alive. The French and Spanish history of the area made it able to oppose Anglo-Saxon domination. Moreover, the former culture of the Creole caste was perpetuated by such activities as Carnival and elite literary endeavors. The FST faced a heterogeneous and stratified public. The complexity of the sociocultural climate led the group to rethink its objectives, one of which was to erase internal conflicts and enhance the sense of a common destiny.

29. Typed brochure, Dover, Schomburg Collection, New York Public Library.

30. The most violent campaign was led by Paul Fino and by R. Sargent Shriver, director of the antipoverty program.

31. Assessing BART several years later, Cruse attributed its failure to a misunderstanding of two requirements: a critical perspective and artistic creativity. The first is possible only if enough distance is kept from ideology; the second is preserved only if the artist avoids being absorbed by tasks external to his vocation. The only politics the artist-intellectual should embrace is a politics of culture. Cruse, *Crisis*, p. 543.

32. A more detailed analysis can be found in Geneviève Fabre, "The Free Southern Theatre: 1963-1979," *Amerikastudien* 25 (1979): 270-279.

33. In this book I do not discuss the activity of FST in the South after 1966 or Jones/Baraka's experiments after BART when he organized the Spirit House Movers in Newark. The history of the new black theatre contains so many attempts to promote theatre in different communities that it is impossible to cover all such initiatives here. The two examples of the FST and BART illustrate both the different paths taken by the directors and organizers and the similar problems they encountered.

34. I have discussed this more fully in an earlier work, *En Marge* (Paris: Maspero, 1976). I insist here simply on the influence this revolutionary climate had on the life, the cultural politics, and, more important, the theatre of black Americans.

35. On the importance of names and naming in black culture, see Ralph Ellison, "Hidden Name and Complex Fate," in *Shadow and Act* (New York: Random House, 1972 ed.), pp. 144-146.

36. LeRoi Jones, "State/Meant" in *Home: Social Essays* (New York: Morrow, 1966), p. 252.

37. *Home*, p. 210.

38. Ibid., p. 212.

39. Ibid., pp. 70, 92.

40. Ibid., p. 213.

41. Ibid., pp. 105-115.

42. Jones is quoted by Larry Neal in Addison Gayle, ed., *The Black*

Aesthetic, (New York: Doubleday, 1971) p. 261.

43. "Black art was first the restoration of life and the restoration of hope," Jones said in an interview in the *New York Times*, November 16, 1969.

44. *Home*, p. 85.

45. "The black artist is a creator. The Creator. He must become the creative force of the universe." *Raise Race Rays Raze* (New York: Random House, 1971).

46. These manifestos and articles have been collected in anthologies: Gayle, *Black Aesthetic*; C. W. E. Bigsby, ed., *The Black American Writer* (Baltimore: Penguin, 1971); Woodie King and E. Anthony, eds., *Black Poets and Prophets* (New York: New American Library, 1972); and Abraham Chapman, ed., *New Black Voices* (New York: New American Library, 1972).

47. In Gayle, *Black Aesthetic*, pp. 256–271. Neal coedited with LeRoi Jones *Black Fire* (New York: Morrow, 1968).

48. Jones, *Home*, p. 112.

49. "On Black Theatre" in Gayle, *Black Aesthetic*, pp. 294–311. Riley particularly blames the actors.

50. Gayle, *Black Aesthetic*, pp. 275–287.

51. Ibid., p. 309.

52. Jones, *Home*, p. 110.

53. *Raise Race Rays Raze*, p. 126.

54. Quoted by Neal in Gayle, *Black Aesthetic*, p. 258.

55. "Black Theatre—Go Home," in Gayle, *Black Aesthetic*, p. 290.

2. The Militant Theatre

1. See the introductory notes to the sections of James V. Hatch and Ted Shine, eds., *Black Theatre, USA: 1847–1974* (New York: The Free Press, 1974). Hereafter cited as Hatch and Shine.

2. James Hatch, "Theodore Ward: Black American Playwright," *Freedomways* 15 (First Quarter 1975): 37–41.

3. Theatre at the beginning of the century provided other models. *Caleb, The Degenerate* (1903) presented one of the first prototypes of the "bad nigger," a character who also appears in *Bad Man* by Randolph Edmunds (1941). The hero in *Caleb*, who is both good and evil, kills his father and mother. Conversely, the hero in *Bad Man* sacrifices his life to save his brothers and sisters from being lynched. In *Appearances*, Garland Anderson treats the difficult subject of a black youth falsely accused of rape, with a typical Broadway ending. Randolph Edmonds' plays (*Six Plays for a Negro Theatre*, 1934) oppose a fatalistic conception of Afro-American destiny. Sentimental nonetheless, they often become melodramatic. Hall Johnson's ballad-opera *Run, Little Chillun* (1933) combined realism, melodrama, and exoticism. In many plays, however, the protagonist has only two possible ways to thwart fate or to escape an

adversary: murder, or seeking the aid of supernatural powers. In the fine play *Plumes* by Georgia Douglass Johnson a black youth kills the seducer of his girlfriend; in *Louisiana* (1933) Agustus Smith rescues the heroine by using both Voodoo and Christianity. Most of these plays use elements popularized by white dramatists. They fall back upon familiar stereotypes, particularly the superstitiousness of blacks, although these characteristics are mostly attributed to minor figures.

4.   In Hatch and Shine, pp. 588–617.

5.   In King and Milner, pp. 439–473.

6.   In Darwin Turner, ed., *Black Drama in America* (Greenwich: Fawcett Publications, 1971), pp. 380–463. Hereafter cited as Turner, *BDA*.

7.   In William Reardon and Thomas D. Pawley, eds., *The Black Teacher and the Dramatic Arts* (Westport, Conn.: Negro Universities Press, 1970), pp. 301–396.

8.   Turner, *BDA*, pp. 297–325. See also *Dry August* by Charles Sebree (1949)—from which the Broadway musical *Mrs. Patterson* (1954) was derived—in which a talented and ambitious girl discovers the duplicity and corruption of her friends.

9.   Hansberry's later play *The Drinking Gourd* (in Hatch and Shine, pp. 713–736), written for television, takes up the subject of *The Escape* a century later. The play reveals how economic imperatives overcome moral and humanitarian considerations and how religion has served the interests of capitalism. The argument, however, is weakened by the tribute paid to whites who seek to better the condition of blacks.

10.   The same problem was raised by the success of the television showing of Alex Haley's *Roots* in 1977. *Roots* presented the Afro-American struggle as a "saga of an American family." With the same deliberate ambiguity that some viewers found in Hansberry's play in 1959 when both the undeniable ethnicity of Afro-Americans and the triumph of integration were proclaimed, the family of Kunta Kinte became representative of immigrant families that make up America. Yet one knows that Afro-Americans were not like other immigrants. *Roots* tried to show both the uniqueness of the black experience, due essentially to slavery, and the exemplary nature of this experience. Thus every American should be able to identify with this worthy American family which overcame obstacles and whose descendants are so well integrated today.

11.   Turner, *BDA*, pp. 465–533.

12.   *Wine in the Wilderness* by Alice Childress (in Hatch and Shine, pp. 737–755) also uses satire, but to a more serious end. It strikes out at racism, bigotry, and myths about whites and blacks, all the while seeming to imply optimistically that the era of prejudice is over and that race relations will improve.

13.   New York: Dell, 1964.

14.   "To Survive the Reign of the Beast," *New York Times*, November 16,

1969.

15. New York: Apollo Editions, 1964. Further citations appear in the text.

16. Heine's story, *Aus den Memoiren des Herren Von Schnabellewopski* (1834) inspired the Wagner opera of 1841.

17. *Home*, p. 230.

18. Of the several analyses of *Dutchman*, note Hugh Nelson, "LeRoi Jones' *Dutchman*: A Brief Ride on a Doomed Ship," *Educational Theatre Journal* 20 (March 1968): 53–59.

19. In Hatch and Shine, pp. 813–825. Further citations appear in the text.

20. "Crossing the Lines," *Saturday Review* 68 (January 9, 1965): 46.

21. See *Literary Times*, May-June, 1967, p. 19.

22. In Turner, *BDA*, pp. 535–556.

23. Mel Watkins, "A Talk with LeRoi Jones," *New York Times Book Review*, June 27, 1971, p. 26. Jones disclaims the play's too ambiguous ending, a move that recalls the questions found in his poem "Look for You Yesterday, Here You Come Today," in *Preface to a Twenty Volume Suicide Note* (New York: Totem Press, 1969), pp. 15–18.

24. Theodore Hudson, *From LeRoi Jones to Amiri Baraka* (Durham: Duke University Press, 1973), p. 159.

25. Evergreen Play Script, no. 10 (New York: Grove Press, 1966).

26. In *Four Black Revolutionary Plays* (New York: Bobbs-Merrill, 1969). Further citations appear in the text. Hereafter this volume is cited as *FBRP*.

27. See, for example, E. U. Essein-Udom, *Black Nationalism* (New York: Dell, 1964), p. 145; and *Muhammed Speaks*, July 15, 1960, p. 25.

28. Jihad, the Muslim Holy War, is also the name Jones gave to his press in Newark.

29. In *FBRP*, pp. 1–15. In reconstructing the stages of a symbolic action, in Jones' theatre, the logical order of discourse is more important than the chronology of composition (this play was written before *A Black Mass*).

30. In *FBRP*, pp. 65–87. Further citations appear in the text.

31. A play by Val Ferdinand, *Blk Love Song* (1969), in Hatch and Shine, pp. 865–874, echoes and extends the ending of *Madheart*.

32. In *FBRP*, pp. 41–63. Further citations appear in the text.

33. Lucien Goldmann, *Structures mentales et création culturelle* (Paris: Christien Bourgois, Collection 10/18, 1970), p. 290.

34. Chicago: Third World Press, 1970. Further citations appear in the text.

35. Instead of answering questions, Rochester will now ask them: "Why don't you drive me?" His threats amount to no more than emotional blackmail: To "We're supposed to be friends," he replies, "Your stone friend, huh? If we so tight, why are you the one with all the money and I work for you?" Rochester no longer accepts the joys of slavery: "thirty-five years of service, of good work and cheerfulness all shot and gone at once." And he invents another role for Benny as he does for himself: "You ain't my brother. Ha, you must be Mack. That cat that people talk to in gas sta-

tions and train stations, maybe they're carrying the baggage" (p. 19).

36. *FBRP*, p. 89.

37. After dismissing the ambiguity of another play, *We Righteous Bombers*, Jones stated that theatre should speak its message like a poster. Four other plays by Jones belong to this cycle of agitprop theatre: *Home on the Range*, *The Drama Review* 12 (Summer 1968): 10–11 (hereafter this issue is cited as *TDR*); *Police*, *TDR*, pp. 11–16; *Arm Yrself or Harm Yrself*, written for street performances and published by Jihad in 1967; and *Junkies Are Full Of . . .*, in King and Milner, pp. 11–24. These plays are analyzed in my contribution to an as yet untitled collective work on agitprop theatre to be published in 1983 by Presses de la Cité, Lausanne.

38. *The Death of Malcolm X*, in Ed Bullins, ed., *New Plays from the Black Theatre* (New York: Bantam, 1969), pp. 21–39. Hereafter this volume is cited as Bullins, *NPBT*.

39. Newark: Jihad, 1969.

40. The quotations are from Nietzsche's *The Birth of Tragedy*. Nietzsche shows that music and myth are inseparable and endowed with powerful magic. His analysis of the dionysiac spirit can be applied with some qualification to plays from black theatre, but his conclusions about the nature of artistic pleasure are not relevant here. Black theatre that expresses "the aptitude of a people for the dionysiac spirit" has had to defend itself against the charge of justifying the sorrow from which music and the tragic myth were born. Black theatre challenges traditional notions of tragedy and calls into question both artistic pleasure and catharsis.

41. In King and Milner, pp. 25–32. Further citations appear in the text.

42. New York: Random House, 1972.

43. *Raise Race Rays Raze*, p. 125.

44. In *Home*, pp. 210–215.

45. "Have your actors shoot the mayor if necessary right in the mayor's actual chamber. Let him feel the malice of the past . . . We will change the drawing rooms into places where real things can be said about a real world, or into smoky rooms where the destiny of Washington can be plotted." "What the Arts Need Now," *Negro Digest*, August 1967, pp. 5–6.

46. In *Ebony*, February 1971, p. 131. Jones repeated the basic functions of black revolutionary theatre: to educate and to demystify.

47. Antonin Artaud, *The Theatre and Its Double*, trans. Mary Caroline Roberts (New York: Grove Press, 1958), p. 9.

48. Ibid., p. 28.

49. Ibid., pp. 31–32.

50. "The Myth of a Negro Literature," in *Home*, pp. 105–115.

51. See Ernst Cassirer's analysis of language and myth as quoted by Suzanne K. Langer, *Reference on Art* (New York: Dover, 1946), pp. 56–7.

52. Artaud, pp. 83, 86.
53. "Black Art," in *Black Magic: Poetry 1961–1967* (Indianapolis: Bobbs-Merrill, 1969), p. 116.
54. In Alice Childress, ed., *Black Scenes* (New York: Doubleday, 1971), pp. 19–27.
55. In King and Milner, pp. 243–251.
56. In King and Milner, pp. 33–76. Further citations to *Junebug* appear in the text.
57. In King and Milner, pp. 229–242.
58. In William Couch, ed., *New Black Playwrights* (New York: Avon, 1970), pp. 27–46. Hereafter, this anthology will be cited as Couch, *NBP*.
59. In Couch, *NBP*, pp. 47–82.
60. In Ted Shine, *Contributions* (New York: Dramatists Play Service, 1970), pp. 5–26.
61. In *TDR*, pp. 50–52.
62. In *TDR*, pp. 41–42.
63. In *TDR*, pp. 47–50.
64. In King and Milner, pp. 389–397.
65. In Bullins, *NPBT*, pp. 189–194.
66. Ibid., pp. 175–188.
67. In *TDR*, pp. 141–142.
68. See Bertolt Brecht, *Ecrits sur le théâtre* (Paris: Arche, 1963).
69. New York: Farrar, Straus and Giroux, 1965.
70. San Diego: Black Book Production, 1969.
71. In Bullins, *NPBT*, pp. 119–120.
72. In King and Milner, pp. 407–428.
73. For example, *Shoes* by Ted Shine (in *Contributions*, pp. 27–28) presents a revolt by a group of teenagers who have just been paid and who discuss how to spend their money. Most will give the money to their mothers to help out at home, but two of them rebel against the values of work and sacrifice. One buys a revolver to gain respect from his friends; the other, a pair of expensive shoes.
74. In *TDR*, pp. 126–138.
75. In Ed Bullins, ed., *The New Lafayette Theatre Presents* (New York: Doubleday, 1974), pp. 126–138. Hereafter this anthology will be cited as Bullins, *NLTP*.
76. Another particular example is *Star of the Morning* by Loften Mitchell, which shows the manipulations that victimized Bert Williams and George Walker.
77. In *TDR*, pp. 62–69.
78. In King and Milner, pp. 147–166.
79. Ibid., pp. 475–524.
80. In *Contributions*, pp. 49–66.
81. In King and Milner, pp. 167–227. The same theme is treated by Arna

Bontemps in his novel *Black Thunder* (1935).

82. In Bullins, *NPBT*, pp. 247–304.
83. Ibid., pp. 201–246.
84. San Diego: Black Book Production, 1968.
85. In Bullins, *NPBT*, pp. 97–108; quote on p. 99.
86. In *Four Dynamite Plays* (New York: Morrow, 1972), pp. 40–118.
87. New York: Hill and Wang, 1973.
88. In Bullins, *NPBT*, pp. 21–96.
89. In *Caligula and Three Other Plays*, trans. Stuart Gilbert (New York: Vintage, 1958).
90. A full account of this panel discussion is given in *Black Theatre*, no. 4, pp. 16–25.
91. In Bullins, *NLTP*, pp. 219–301.
92. In *Scripts* 1 (May 1972): 93–98.
93. In *TDR*, pp. 78–83.
94. Ibid., pp. 94–105.
95. In Clayton Riley, ed., *A Black Quartet* (New York: New American Library, 1970), pp. 27–36.
96. Ibid., pp. 115–136.
97. San Francisco: Julian Richardson, 1972.
98. A son kills his mother in Jimmy Garrett's *And We Own the Night*. Another condemns his mother and eliminates her in *Coda* by E. Walker.
99. Gilbert Varet, *Racisme et psychologie* (Paris: Denoel, 1957), p. 12.
100. In *Four Dynamite Plays* (New York: Morrow, 1972), pp. 119–179.
101. *Drama Review*, September 1970, p. 93.
102. *Black World* 21 (April 1972): 54–69.
103. *Black World* 20 (April 1971): 39.
104. In *Four Dynamite Plays*, pp. 1–16.
105. Significantly, the sentence from Trotsky is quoted by Soyinka and used in his analysis . See Wole Soyinka, "Drama and the Revolutionary Ideal," in *In Person: Achebe, Awoonor and Soyinka*, ed. Karen L. Morell (Seattle: University of Washington, Institute for Comparative Foreign Area Studies, 1975), p. 74.
106. *Ombres collectives* (Paris: PUF, 1973), p. 21.
107. Quoted by Duvignaud, ibid. p. 45.
108. Montreal: Nouvelle Optique, 1976.
109. *Wretched of the Earth*, p. 44.
110. These are terms frequently used by Brecht and by critics of his theatre. See notably Roland Barthes on *Mother Courage* in *Essais critiques* (Paris: Le Seuil, 1964), p. 48.
111. A phrase used by Louis Althusser, "Notes sur un théâtre matérialiste," in *Pour Marx* (Paris: Maspero, 1969), pp. 140–141.
112. Ibid., p. 146.
113. Ibid., p. 151

3. The Theatre of Experience

1. *Negro Digest*, April 1968; rpt. in Gayle, *Black Aesthetic*, p. 291.
2. *Village Voice*, November 1973, p. 60.
3. Preface to *The Theme Is Blackness* (New York: Morrow, 1973), p. 12ff. Later chapters trace the path Bullins followed from agitprop to theatre of experience. Hereafter this volume is cited as Bullins, *TTB*.
4. Paul Carter Harrison, *The Drama of Nommo* (New York: Grove Press, 1972).
5. Milner, in Gayle, *Black Aesthetic*, p. 289.
6. Bullins, *TTB*, p. 84. A dramatic discourse is built around this theme of blackness and covers several modes of representation. If some of the plays under consideration explore black experience directly, others pursue the same goal more ambiguously, and still others do both. Thus some works previously analyzed as part of the militant theatre may also be examined as part of the theatre of experience. New plays are presented in this discussion because they come closer to a theatre of experience than to militant theatre. Only in a few cases does the use of one category over another become justified through the need to examine all that can be grouped under the label "theatre of experience."
7. "A Musical Epic," in King and Milner, pp. 349–388.
8. In King and Milner, pp. 349–388.
9. In Childress, *Black Scenes*, p. 24.
10. In King and Milner, pp. 399–405.
11. In *Podium Magazine* (Amsterdam), November 1965.
12. See *The Drama of Nommo*, pp. 150–153. This play was first performed in Amsterdam in 1962.
13. With far less dramatic power, Ed Bullins' *It Has No Choice* (*TTB*, pp. 38–55), picks up the theme of *Dutchman*. The man is unmasked and the woman is condemned to wander between rejection and hysteria.
14. First staged by Woodie King at the Henry Street Settlement, then at the New York Shakespeare Festival at the Public Theatre.
15. Interview in the *New York Times*, May 18, 1975.
16. *No Place to Be Somebody* (New York: Bobbs-Merrill, 1969). Staged at the Public Theatre in 1969.
17. In William Couch, ed., *New Black Playwrights* (New York: Avon, 1970), pp. 93–180. Hereafter this volume is cited as Couch, *NBP*.
18. *The Drama of Nommo*, p. 27.
19. In *Underground: Four Plays by Edgar White* (New York: Morrow, 1970), pp. 1–56.
20. Ibid., p. 35.
21. New York: Dramatists Play Service, 1972.
22. For an examination of this symbolism see Robert L. Tener, "Theatre of Identity: Adrienne Kennedy's Portrait of the Black Woman," *Studies in Black Literature* 6 (Summer 1975); and Kimberly Benston, "*Cities in*

Bezique: Adrienne Kennedy's Expressionistic Vision." *College Language Association Journal* 20 (December 1976).

23. Kennedy had worked with Albee in 1962. The play was presented at the East Side Theatre in 1964. In Clinton Oliver and Stephanie Sills, eds., *Contemporary Black Drama* (New York: Scribners, 1971), pp. 187–206.

24. In Paul Carter Harrison, ed., *Kuntu Drama* (New York: Grove Press, 1974), pp. 170–187. Written in 1963, the play was performed at the Public Theatre in 1969.

25. The direction by Seth Allen in 1969 at La Mama drew heavily upon the technique of Japanese Noh, emphasizing narration, dance, and mime; a communion cup was even passed among the spectators who were asked to come to the altar on stage.

26. Other plays by Kennedy extend the image of the bastard further and use animal references for characters and their bodies. See *A Rat's Mass* (in Couch, *NBP*, pp. 82–92) and *A Beast's Story* (in *Kuntu Drama*, pp. 192–201). The latter play is often presented along with *The Owl* under the general title *Cities in Bezique*, as in the 1969 production. Kennedy is one of the most original dramatists of contemporary theatre.

27. In E. Parone, ed., *Collision Course* (New York: Random House, 1968). pp. 35–40.

28. In *Scripts*, I (November 1971): pp. 51–56.

29. *The Negro Family: The Case for National Action* (Washington, D.C.: U.S. Government Printing Office, March 1965). This report has been analyzed and criticized in Lee Rainwater and William C. Yancey, eds., *The Moynihan Report and the Politics of Controversy* (Cambridge: MIT Press, 1967).

30. After so many rash generalizations about the black family, Herbert Gutman's *The Black Family in Slavery and Freedom, 1750–1925* (New York: Pantheon, 1976) shows the important role the family played in the history and development of black culture. Following the work of black sociologist E. Franklin Frazier, *The Negro Family* (1939), Gutman emphasizes the existence of a complex cultural network in which the family plays a determinant role. Frazier maintained that the socioeconomic conditions forced upon blacks had helped to destroy the family. For Gutman, the black family not only survived but served several functions and was a dynamic element in the cultural life of the community.

31. Ironically, in *Raisin* blacks could only afford housing in the white neighborhood, for costs were prohibitive in black sectors. Houses in the ghetto were too run-down to provide decent lodging. In one sense, the deal Mrs. Younger struck for the house is just as dangerous as the business deal Walter proposed; she merely moves her family from one ghetto to another. The play refuses to go a step further to show the consequences of Mrs. Younger's generous obstinacy or the life of her family condemned to exile.

32. Hansberry, *A Raisin in the Sun*, p. 22.
33. *Behold Cometh the Vandekellans* (New York: Azakiel Press, 1967).
34. In Couch, *NBP*, pp. 247–285.
35. New York: Samuel French, 1970.
36. In King and Milner, pp. 325–347.
37. In *The Free Southern Theatre*, pp. 185–206.
38. In Hatch and Shine, pp. 854–863.
39. *The Marriage* by Donald Greaves, in King and Milner, pp. 253–300, also concerns a couple's misunderstanding and a son's initiation by his adoptive father.
40. New York: Dramatists Play Service, 1972.
41. As in *To Kill A Devil* by R. Furman, in Childress, *Black Scenes*, pp. 14–18.
42. *Negro Digest* 17 (April 1968): 54–73.
43. In *The Langston Hughes Reader* (New York: Knopf, 1958), pp. 239–243.
44. In King and Milner, pp. 301–324.
45. In Budd Schulberg, ed., *From The Ashes: Voices of Watts* (New York: New American Library, 1967).
46. The dozens are discussed in various studies of black culture; see in particular Levine, *Black Culture and Black Consciousness*, pp. 344–358, and Alan Dundes, ed. *Mother Wit from the Laughing Barrel* (Englewood Cliffs, N.J.: Prentice Hall, 1973).
47. John Dollard, "The Dozens: Dialectics of Insult," in Dundes, *Mother Wit*, p. 277–294.
48. See Dundes' introduction to Roger D. Abrahams' article in *Mother Wit*, p. 297.
49. *Negro Digest* 17 (April 1969): 53–68.
50. In Bullins, *NLTP*, pp. 169–219.
51. In King and Milner, pp. 429–438.
52. In Hatch and Shine, pp. 865–875.
53. Keil, *Urban Blues* (Chicago: University of Chicago Press, 1966); Liebow, *Tally's Corner* (Boston: Little, Brown, 1967).
54. Ulf Hannerz argues that two value systems coexist, one in the ghetto, the other in the dominant society. "What Ghetto Males Are Like," in Norman E. Whitten and John F. Szwed, eds., *Afro-American Anthropology* (New York: Free Press, 1970), pp. 317–328.
55. The analysis that follows is drawn from the theoretical framework developed by Greimas in "Sémiotique topologique," *Sémiotique et sciences sociales* (Paris: Le Seuil, 1976), pp. 129–157. It is applied here specifically to the black world.
56. On this subject see Brecht, *Ecrits sur le théâtre:* "The epic theatre makes a point of locating its model-type in a street corner, of returning to a natural theatre, a social enterprise whose motives, means and ends are practical and of this world" (p. 144). See also Irving Goffman, *The*

Presentation of Self in Everyday Life (New York: Doubleday Anchor, 1959).

57. *The Drama of Nommo*, p. 23.

58. See Statie Damianakos, "Culture populaire et groupes marginaux," *Les Temps Modernes* 331 (February 1974): 14–47.

59. Harrison especially attacks *Black Rage* by William H. Grier and Price M. Cobbs (New York: Bantam, 1968). See *The Drama of Nommo*, pp. 119–162.

60. Lee Rainwater, *Soul* (New York: Transaction Books, 1970); Ulf Hannerz, *Soulside* (New York: Columbia University Press, 1969).

61. Jones, *Blues People*, p. 219.

62. Jones, *Home*, p. 174.

63. In Bullins, *NLTP*, pp. 117–132.

64. This play, performed in 1971, has not been published.

65. See J. Horton, "Time and Cool People," in Rainwater, ed., *Soul*, pp. 35–50.

66. "Hustler" and "pimp" are difficult terms to define. The first means any individual who earns his living by dishonest schemes; the second refers to a victimizer of women. Both terms describe ways of living off others by manipulating them.

67. New York: Dramatists Play Service, 1970.

68. Christina Milner, *Black Players: The Secret World of Black Pimps* (Boston: Little, Brown, 1972).

69. Ann Ubersfeld, *Lire le théâtre* (Paris: Editions Sociales, 1977), pp. 119–151.

70. On this process of theatricalization, see E. Burns, *Theatricality: A Study of Convention in the Theatre and in Social Life* (New York: Harper Torchbooks, 1972) and Goffman, *The Presentation of Self in Everyday Life*.

71. *The Drama of Nommo*, pp. 21–22.

72. In Bullins, *TTB*, pp. 98–126.

73. These forms of verbal behavior have been well studied. See, for example, Roger Abrahams, *Deep Down in the Jungle* (Hatboro: Folklore Associates, 1964); Thomas Kochman, "Towards an Ethnography of Black American Speech Behavior," in Whitten and Szwed, eds., *Afro-American Anthropology*, pp. 145–162; M. Rozenberg, "Rapping," *Journal of Popular Culture* 7, no. 3, pp. 518ff.

74. It might be useful to extend this analysis using the framework offered by Freud's study of jokes, but I have deliberately restricted this examination to the most obvious processes. It seemed to me that however rich psychoanalytical explications are, they have often been applied too rigidly to black behavior. They have oversimplified a very complex reality and perpetuated prejudices and stereotypes. Here I attempt to clarify the uniquely Afro-American mechanisms of humor by examining the

historical and cultural context in which they appear.

75. See the interview with Gaines in Bullins, *NLTP*, pp. 69–70.
76. Ibid., p. 72.
77. *Shadow and Act* (New York: Random House, 1964), p. 78.
78. New York: Bantam Books, 1973.
79. "Littérature et signification," in *Essais critiques*, (Paris: Le Seuil, 1964), p. 258.
80. New York: Bantam Books, 1973.
81. New York: Knopf, 1926.
82. "Profile: Ed Bullins," *New Yorker*, June 16, 1973, pp. 40–79.
83. "Up from Politics," *Performance* 1 (April 1962): 52–60.
84. Bullins started the San Francisco Drama Circle with the director Burt Hartman, had an angry collaboration with Martin Pouch at the Freehouse Repertory Theatre, then did a brief stint at the Contemporary Theatre. With Marvin X and Duncan Barber, he tried to organize the Black Arts West center. All of these experiments failed. Black plays suffered in competition with plays written by whites, and black playwrights could find neither producers nor permanent theatres for their works.
85. Bullins, *NPBT*, p. ix.
86. "Black Theatre, Bourgeois Critics," *New York Times,* August 27, 1972.
87. Mill Valley, Calif.: Illuminations Press, 1967.
88. In *Five Plays by Ed Bullins* (New York: Bobbs-Merrill, 1969), pp. 215–246.
89. In *Five Plays*, pp. 249–282.
90. Ibid., pp. 1–98.
91. Ibid., pp. 101–182.
92. In Bullins, *NPBT*, pp. 129–174.
93. New York: Morrow, 1971.
94. See Ubersfeld's analysis of theatre space in *Lire le théâtre*, pp. 150–202.
95. Bullins, *NLTP*, pp. 7–67.
96. Bullins, *TTB*, pp. 144–181.
97. In *Underground*, pp. 172–245.
98. Ibid., pp. 63–119.
99. Ibid., pp. 121–189.
100. *The Crucificado: Two Plays* (New York: Morrow, 1973), pp. 66–146.
101. See Gerhardt Mensching, *Das Groteske im modernen Drama* (Bonn: Reinische Friedrich Wilhelms Universität, 1961); Fritz Gysin, *The Grotesque in American Negro Fiction* (Bern: Franke Verlag, 1975); and Mary Canfield, *Grotesques and Other Reflections* (New York: Harper and Row, 1927).
102. See Roger Bastide, *African Civilizations in the New World*, trans. Peter Green (New York: Harper Torchbooks, 1971), p. 11–12.
103. Ibid., pp. 27, 25–26. See also Whitten and Szwed, *Afro-American Anthropology*.

104. *The Drama of Nommo*, pp. 24, 23.
105. Karl Jaspers, *Vom Ursprung und Ziel der Geschichte* (Zurich: Artemis Verlag, 1949); Bronislaw Malinowski, *The Dynamics of Cultural Change* (New Haven: Yale University Press, 1947); Janheinz Jahn, *Muntu*, trans. Marjorie Grene (New York: Grove Press, 1961).
106. Jahn, *Muntu*, p. 16.
107. Like Jahn, Harrison discusses Neo-African culture as one would talk about Western culture. Jahn defines this culture as the result of subtle transformations of traditional culture after contact with the West. He attempts to construct a theoretical model able to integrate a broad range of cultures beginning with specific observations in different African countries. The terms he provides do not cover empirical reality, but the models created from it. Jahn's point of departure is comparable to those of certain ethnologists, notably Lévi-Strauss, for whom "the idea of a model is instrumental, not ontological; the model is not the object of understanding, but its means." See Jean Pouillon, "L'Oeuvre de Claude Lévi-Strauss," Foreword to Claude Lévi-Strauss, *Race et histoire* (Paris: Médiations, 1968), p. 108.
108. Jahn, *Muntu*, p. 105.
109. *Cahier d'un retour au pays natal* (Paris: Présence Africaine, 1956 ed.), p. 41.
110. Jahn, *Muntu*, p. 138.
111. Jahn calls our attention to two kinds of rhythm: *polyrhythm*, which accents and syncopates a single basic meter in different ways, and *polymetry*, which combines several basic and separate meters. Polymetric structure superimposes several meters, creating a lag between the measures of different beats and between the entry time of each part of the polyphony; this superposition creates a "complex total rhythm" that is repeated regularly. In polymetric structure, "several rhythmic versions of the one meter are combined together." The two structures share the principle of crossed rhythms where the main accents "do not agree, but are overlaid in criss-cross fashion over one another, . . . interlaced cross-rhythmically." *Muntu*, p. 165.
112. *The Drama of Nommo*, p. 46.
113. This is the title of a novel by William Melvin Kelley, who borrows the expression from Thoreau and gives it new meaning in an Afro-American context.
114. Harrison, ed., *Kuntu Drama*, pp. 257–352.
115. See several variations in Langston Hughes and Arna Bontemps, eds., *The Book of Negro Folklore* (New York: Apollo Editions, 1958), pp. 366–367; in Roger Abrahams, *Positively Black* (Englewood Cliffs, N.J.: Prentice Hall, 1970), pp. 44–45; Bruce Jackson, *Get Your Ass in the Water and Swim like Me* (Cambridge: Harvard University Press, 1974), pp. 184–196.

116. On John Henry see Guy B. Johnson, *John Henry: Tracking Down a Negro Legend (Chapel Hill: University of North Carolina Press, 1929); Louis W. Chappell, John Henry: A Folklore Study* (Jena: Frommensche Verlag, 1933); Richard Dorson, "The Career of John Henry," *Western Folklore* 24 (1965): 155–163; Leon R. Harris, "The Steel-Drivin' Man," in Dundes, *Mother Wit*, pp. 561–567; and the bibliography on the bad nigger that precedes the article by H. C. Brearly, "Ba-ad Nigger," in Dundes, *Mother Wit*, p. 579.

117. Here I draw on the character functions and typology suggested by Vladimir Propp, *Morphology of the Folktale* (Austin: University of Texas Press, 1958).

4. Theatre and Culture

1. Fanon, *Wretched of the Earth*, p. 175.
2. O. Ducrot, *Dire ou ne pas dire* (Paris: Hermann, 1972).
3. Jones, *Blues People*, p. 219.
4. See William Francis Allen et al, *Slave Songs of the United States* (New York: A. Simpson, 1867).
5. The devil plays an ambiguous role in black culture. He is an enemy but also a creature to be identified with. By his penchant for games and teasing, he plays a subversive role in creation: the king of thunderstorms and a cunning trickster. Following his example, the black man delights in sowing terror and discord in the white world.
6. Natalie Curtis Burlin, "Negro Music at Birth," *Musical Quarterly* 5 (1919): 88.
7. Clifton Furness, "Communal Music among Arabians and Negroes," *Musical Quarterly* 16 (1930): 49–50.
8. *The Drama of Nommo*, p. 86.
9. Ethnologists have questioned to what extent possession is a theatrical phenomenon. According to some, it is not the possessed person who acts, but the possessing spirit. For others, this manifestation is provoked, controlled, and codified. It is a question of domination rather than possession. See Michel Leiris, *La Possession et ses aspects théâtraux chez les Ethiopiens de Gondar* (Paris: Plon, 1958).
10. Raymond Ogoo, "African Theatre and Afro-American Drama (Masters Thesis, Université de Paris III, 1974). The *djego* is a rite of initiation into the society of women. Only the first part involves the initiates and excludes men; the rest is a real *spectacle*: one part is danced and depicts the killing of a panther (*djego* means panther), the "destruction of evil," by a mother who avenges the death of her children. This act becomes a catharsis: it relieves anxiety. The act must take place before everyone and involve the audience whose presence, like the dance itself, theatricalizes the mother's actions.

   The *egun* is a ceremony for men. The rite is composed of two sequences: one limited to initiates and held in a secret place, the other performed for the entire community. The task of the egun, who embodies the ancestors, strongly resembles that of an actor. He must modulate his voice to imitate a diety. The ancestor spirit comes up from the forest and gives advice or reprimands. He is offered gifts and accepts or rejects them before he disappears. Theatricality lies not only in important scenic devices (dance, music, costumes, and masks) but also in the dialogue between actor-priest and actor-deity. The egun reappears for a second time and dances in the circle formed by the community, which has joined the initiates. The deity thus gives his warnings or reproaches, and the dialogue enlarges to encompass the entire assembly.

11. Franck Fouché, *Vaudou et théâtre* (Montreal, Nouvelle Optique, 1976), p. 22.

12. Roland Barthes, *Mythologies* (Paris: Le Seuil, 1957), p. 202; Limougoun, *Mythes et littérature en Afrique* (Paris: Gallimard, 1972).

13. Joseph Adedeji, "Traditional Yoruba Theatre," *African Art, Arts d'Afrique* 3 (October 1969): 60.

14. Mircea Eliade, *Aspects du mythe* (Paris: Gallimard/Idées, 1963).

15. See Harrison's description in *The Drama of Nommo*, pp. 208–210. Among the rituals of the New Lafayette Theatre were also "Ritual to Help Black People Survive the Struggles to Come" (1969); "To Raise the Dead and Foretell the Future" (1970); "The Devil Catchers" (1971); "The Psychic Pretenders" (1972). These were didactic shows that depicted the triumph of the black soul over obstacles and adversity.

16. Mimeographed text, theatre files, Schomburg Collection, New York Public Library.

17. "The National Black Theatre," *Essence*, March 1971. p. 50.

18. Lynne Fanley Emery, *Black Dance in the United States from 1619 to 1970* (Palo Alto: National Press Books, 1972); Marshall and Jean Stearns, *Jazz Dance: The Story of American Vernacular Dance* (New York: Macmillan, 1968); Harold Courlander, *The Drum and the Hoe* (Berkeley: University of California Press, 1960), and the descriptions of dances that appear in slave narratives collected by the WPA. Jahn also devotes one chapter in *Muntu* to the meaning of black dance.

19. Before Independence, black Americans would gather in Manhattan at the present site of Washington Square to celebrate Carnival according to their tribe or country of origin. In New Orleans, these gatherings were held in Congo Square until the middle of the nineteenth century.

20. Jahn, *Muntu*, p. 84.

21. *Poèms* (Paris: Seuil, 1964), p. 24.

22. Walter Benjamin, *Essais sur Bertholt Brecht* (Paris: Maspero, 1969), p. 36.

23. Marie-Claire Pasquier, *Le Théâtre américain d'aujourd'hui* (Paris: Presses Universitaires de France, 1978).

24. Ubersfeld, *Lire le théâtre*, pp. 18–20.
25. *Eléments pour une sociologie du spectacle* (Paris: Christien Bourgois, Collection 10/18, 1973), p. 346.
26. Marc Jimenez, *Adorno: Art, idéologie et théorie de l'art* (Paris: Christien Bourgois, Collection 10/18, 1973), p. 239.
27. Barthes, *Mythologies*, p. 270.
28. Althusser, "Notes sur un théâtre matérialiste," in *Pour Marx*, p. 149.

Conclusion: Myths and Ambiguities of Theatre Practice

1. Anne Ubersfeld, *Lire le théâtre*, p. 302.
2. Theodor Adorno, *Aesthetische Theorie* (Frankfurt: Suhrkamp, 1970), trans. Bernard Bellot and Marc Jimenez (Paris: Klincksieck, 1974); Herbert Marcuse, *Kultur und Gesellschaft* (Frankfurt: Suhrkamp, 1965).
3. This same process of neutralization is found in psychoanalytic interpretations of art, which tend to deny the existence of any project of ethnic and revolutionary theatre, and to bring artistic creation back to the subjective and individual level. The use of imagination is seen as an escape from reality; the rebel artist is defined as a maladjusted individual. The phenomenon of artistic creation is explained by the same mechanisms that describe psychic states: repression, sublimation, compensation. Created out of repression, art becomes the realization of desire.
4. *Sémiologie et sciences sociales*, pp. 178–179. The role that theatre plays for a certain bourgeois class has been studied in a different context by J. Baudrillard in *La Société de consommation, ses mythes, ses structures* (Paris: S.C.P.P., 1970).

Index